SALTWATER AQUARIUM MODELS

Recipes for Creating Beautiful Aquariums That Thrive

JOHN TULLOCK

BICENTENNIAL
1807
WILEY
2007
BICENTENNIAL

Wiley Publishing, Inc.

For general information on our other products and services or to obtain technical support please contact our Customer Care Department within the U.S. at (800) 762-2974, outside the U.S. at (317) 572-3993 or fax (317) 572-4002.

Wiley also publishes its books in a variety of electronic formats. Some content that appears in print may not be available in electronic books. For more information about Wiley products, please visit our web site at www.wiley.com.

Library of Congress Cataloging-in-Publication data is available from the publisher upon request.

ISBN-13: 978-0-470-04424-7
ISBN-10: 0-470-04424-1

Printed in the United States of America

10   9   8   7   6   5   4   3   2

Book design by Elizabeth Brooks
Cover design by José Almaguer
Book production by Wiley Publishing, Inc. Composition Services

TABLE OF CONTENTS

Part II
Saltwater Aquarium Mechanics

CHAPTER 6

CHAPTER 7

Part III
Saltwater Aquarium
Model Designs

CHAPTER 8

CHAPTER 9
Biotope Tanks 127

CHAPTER 10
Small Tanks 175

Part IV
The Appendixes

THE ALLURE OF SALTWATER AQUARIUMS

My personal interest in saltwater aquariums goes back about thirty years. I had been fascinated with saltwater invertebrates since childhood, thanks to family trips to the beach. By the time I reached graduate school, I was on track to become a freshwater biologist. Then in 1975 I took a field course in invertebrates, and for the first time I had the opportunity to observe a tropical coral reef. Needless to say, I was hooked on saltwater. Since then, I have returned many times to the site of that first experience, the now-defunct marine laboratory on Pigeon Key, Florida. As both hobbyist and dealer, I have had the opportunity to work with hundreds of tanks and thousands of fish, and to interact with dozens of wonderful people who have shared their enthusiasm and expertise. Despite all this, I have a lot more to learn, and each time I contemplate saltwater aquarium keeping, I recognize a different angle, a new possibility. I sincerely hope this book sparks your interest in saltwater aquariums the way that trip to Florida sparked mine so long ago.

Just consider how much research has demonstrated the many benefits of owning an aquarium.

- One study found that patients whose dentists had aquariums in their waiting rooms were less anxious about their impending treatments than patients with only magazines to read while waiting.
- Watching the movements of fish helps infants learn to focus on objects and strengthens their eye muscles, another study claims.
- Still another investigation found that patients are more likely to follow the doctor's orders later if they have the opportunity for a little fish watching in the waiting room.
- People also say that owning an aquarium gives them a sense of control in an often chaotic world.
- Almost everyone agrees that fish watching lowers stress.

Hobby versus Passion

The overwhelming majority of aquarium owners simply find themselves attracted to the natural beauty of the underwater scene. The aquarium in this context becomes a living work of art, complementing the interior décor of the home. It makes a statement about the owner's lifestyle, forges a connection to nature that is often absent from urban life, and, sometimes, boasts of success. Residences these days may be graced by installations of a size and level of sophistication that in years past were only found in museums and public aquariums. One company that specializes in custom designs recently introduced a "basic" system at around $15,000. I once visited the office of a business in Connecticut that was spending $20,000 a month just to *maintain* several very large aquariums.

Because not all of us are positioned to invest thousands for professional installation and maintenance of an aquarium, the majority of tank owners are do-it-yourselfers. If you are one of these people, or are thinking about becoming one, then this book is for you. Following my recommendations will improve your chances of having a successful aquarium that will enhance the appearance of your home and provide years of relaxation and entertainment, without the necessity of becoming too deeply immersed in the chemistry of seawater or the biology of coral reef fish.

In fact, the vast majority of saltwater aquarium owners are not "hobbyists." They are not pursuing a passion, eager to understand every aspect of the operation of their aquarium, the needs of its inhabitants, and the options for enhancing the experience. Their interest in owning an aquarium stems from the simple desire to weave the color, movement, and "naturalness" of a tropical coral reef into the fabric of their everyday lives.

On the other hand, saltwater aquarium hobbyists devote a remarkable amount of effort to the pursuit of their passion.

- They read aquarium magazines, buy books about aquariums, and make the rounds of the local fish shops regularly.
- They often hold strong opinions about a certain aquarium methodology.
- Many specialize in one or a few types of fish or invertebrates. A few even try to discover how to breed saltwater fish and rear the offspring.
- Several hundred may attend one of the major annual saltwater hobby conventions.

But hobbyists like these account for only a tiny minority of all the saltwater aquarium tanks sitting out there in America's cozy family rooms.

What You Can Find in This Book

When I owned a retail aquarium store, most of my customers weren't hobbyists, and one of the things I did to improve my customers' chances of success was to offer them free classes. One Tuesday evening each month, I'd give a presentation on some aspect of water chemistry, or a particular family of fishes, or the pros and cons of different types of filters. After these sessions, we poured free coffee and talked about fish. People often told me they appreciated the information, but could I please just tell them what fish they should keep? It took quite a while for me to realize that the majority of casual aquarists were not really interested in becoming what I thought of as a hobbyist. They were not "fish nuts" like me; they saw an aquarium not as a preoccupation for their weekends, but rather more as art, something to enhance the look and feel of their personal space. And they wanted it "plug-and-play." Never mind all the water chemistry, just tell me what to do and how often to do it. As I helped more and more people design aquariums that looked good and were easy to maintain, I learned what works and what doesn't. Much of that experience has been incorporated here.

Chapter 1, "Caring for an Aquarium," explains the basic skills for setting up and maintaining a home aquarium. I cover all the important bases without becoming bogged down in too much biology and chemistry. Chapter 2, "Bringing out the Best in Saltwater Aquariums," explains the essential elements of good aquarium design, and chapter 3, "Making Your Aquarium Look Real," presents practical techniques for creating a natural-appearing scene within the aquarium's limited space. Chapter 4, "Understanding Invertebrates," acquaints you with the fundamentals of invertebrate biology. Invertebrates provide perhaps the most fascinating dimension to saltwater aquarium-keeping. Chapter 5, "Nuts and Bolts," will interest anyone thinking of a built-in aquarium. Suggestions for designing for ease of maintenance will also interest those planning free-standing installations. And everyone should pay attention to the information about safety found in chapter 5, "Nuts and Bolts."

I devote two chapters to model designs for saltwater aquariums of all sizes; chapter 10, "Small Tanks," is devoted to model designs for smaller aquariums. Each model design focuses on a simple theme. Those in chapter 7, "Basic Setup Procedures," emphasize form and color, while the other model designs are based on particular biotopes (see the section, "How Saltwater Differs from Freshwater," for more on biotopes).

As you will see from reading later chapters, saltwater fish and invertebrates exhibit a far wider range of feeding strategies, social needs, and adaptability to aquarium life than freshwater species do. I have attempted to catalog this information for the most popular and widely available species in order to help you choose tank mates appropriate to each other. Is your heart set on a particular fish? You should be able to select compatible species by using the cross references I provide in the back of the book. Do you intend to set up a spectacular tank with living corals? You will need to provide abundant light, as shown in the table on page 57.

Seaweeds, which are algae, take the place of plants in the saltwater tank. Like freshwater plants, seaweeds have specific needs if they are to thrive in the aquarium. I have included a section on the diverse and beautiful seaweeds aquarists might want to grow.

While I direct most of my advice and suggestions to the casual aquarium owner, seasoned hobbyists will find, I hope, ideas for new horizons to explore. No doubt, you will improve upon my model designs with insights of your own.

How Saltwater Differs from Freshwater

Most of the model designs are based on particular biotopes. A biotope is a small geographic area, such as a lagoon, with characteristic kinds of life. Saltwater organisms, though amazingly adaptable, thrive best in conditions similar to those found in their native biotope. The vastness and complexity of the coral reef ensures that many possible biotopes will exist wherever reefs occur. Coral reefs do not develop at random, however. The peculiar needs of the tiny animals that comprise the living coral restrict coral reefs to certain areas of the sea. Because of the narrow range of conditions required for abundant growth of coral, in some ways reefs everywhere share many similarities. This contrasts with freshwater habitats, which vary dramatically from place to place.

Not only coral reefs, but all marine habitats occur in seawater of the same composition. Thus, saltwater aquariums all share the same set of water parameters. Again, this contrasts with the wide differences in freshwater chemistry from one habitat to another. For example, an acidic South American pond might have a pH of 5.0 and a hardness near zero, while Lake Tanganyika has a pH of about 9.0 and extremely high hardness. The fish from each of these habitats are unlikely to survive for long if kept, say, under the other habitat's conditions in the aquarium. In the case of marine habitats, the water surrounding the coral reefs of Australia has about the same pH and salinity as the water surrounding Key West, Florida. The saltwater aquarist has less to worry about than his or her freshwater counterpart, in terms of water chemistry. See chapter 1, "Caring for an Aquarium," for more details on saltwater chemistry.

Creating a Plan

I would like once and for all to dispel the notion of a "hierarchical" approach to aquarium-keeping. The conventional wisdom goes either of two ways:

1. Rank beginners must start with freshwater and graduate to saltwater.
2. A saltwater novice must begin with fish only and graduate to an invertebrate aquarium.

Anyone with the ability to understand the basic chemistry and biology needed to successfully maintain a saltwater tank should set up whatever aquarium they choose. Provided, that is, they take the time to research and create a *plan*. Time and again, I have heard customers lament about problems they could have avoided by working from a plan rather than choosing inhabitants for their saltwater aquariums on impulse. The danger in impulse buying stems from the vast diversity and extraordinary degree of specialization among the denizens of coral reefs. For example, the threadfin butterflyfish, *Chaetodon auriga*, learns to eat chopped shrimp from the fingers of its owner; the ornate butterflyfish, *C. ornatissimus*, will starve rather than accept a substitute for its natural diet of living coral polyps. Obviously, the former adapts to aquarium life and the latter does not. Creating an aquarium plan, in which you list all the fish and invertebrates you intend to incorporate, encourages you to do some research before you buy and thereby avoid disappointment. For a large selection of aquarium sizes and styles, I have saved you the trouble by providing ready-made plans. You should be able to maintain any of these tanks successfully by following the steps I suggest. Arm yourself with the basic chemistry and biology presented, with a minimum of technical terms, in chapters 1 and 4.

On the other hand, oceanic environments in general, and coral reef environments in particular, harbor a far greater diversity of living organisms than freshwater environments do. Freshwater aquarists seldom maintain invertebrate tanks, for example, but a major portion of the saltwater aquarium hobby consists of aquarists who maintain "minireef" tanks in which invertebrates play the starring role. Hundreds of varieties of invertebrates find their way into the aquarium trade, and new ones appear all the time. Easily 500 species of coral reef fish can potentially be available to a hobbyist on any given day. All this diversity means that the saltwater aquarist must have a keen understanding of the biology of each organism inhabiting his or her tank. You will find more about invertebrate biology in chapter 4, "Understanding Invertebrates." Fish biology, as it pertains to captive care, is covered in each of the model designs.

An aquarium based on a coral reef can provide a truly breathtaking glimpse into a world most people have never witnessed. Maintaining a small suite of aquarium water parameters within their correct ranges requires scarcely more knowledge of chemistry than that required for maintaining a swimming pool. Providing for the needs of the aquarium's inhabitants demands only that you understand their natural roles and offer them something similar. Learning more about the denizens of the reef and applying that knowledge to their care only adds to the experience of watching their colorful forms and graceful movements from the comfort of your favorite chair.

Part I

SALTWATER AQUARIUM BASICS

CHAPTER 1

CARING FOR AN AQUARIUM

B efore you even decide for certain that you want a saltwater aquarium in your living room, you need a clear understanding of the time, effort, and expense involved in maintaining it properly. Although this book emphasizes design over technique, once the design is executed, maintenance becomes all-important.

Coral reefs shelter their diverse inhabitants in one of the most stable environments on Earth. In fact, environmental stability may well explain a substantial portion of that diversity. When you can count on tomorrow being pretty much like today for thousands of years at a stretch, adaptations necessary for coping with, or preparing for, environmental change can be redirected into specialization of lifestyle. In turn, most coral reef organisms have, as a result of that specialization, sacrificed adaptability to change.

To provide the stability necessary for your organisms to thrive in your saltwater aquarium, you need to:

- Regularly monitor and maintain proper water conditions
- Feed the fish
- Keep records
- Perform water changes
- Be alert to potential problems

That said, caring for an aquarium need not be a terrible chore, and anyone can learn how an aquarium works. Even if you consider yourself a rank amateur, you should have a good grasp of the basics by the end of this chapter.

Sources of Saltwater Specimens

Saltwater aquarium enthusiasts have a plethora of choices for purchasing both supplies and livestock, from local specialty dealers to big-box pet retail chains to mail-order suppliers. Finding the right combination of these for your aquarium needs will facilitate the creation of the tank you want at a cost you can afford.

Choosing a Dealer

Look for a store with a large saltwater dry goods section and a varied inventory of healthy marine fishes and invertebrates living in well-maintained holding tanks. A dirty, unkempt, poorly lighted store should be an immediate signal to look elsewhere. If you live in or near a reasonably large city, look for a store that sells only saltwater aquariums. It is likely to have a better selection, more knowledgeable personnel, and better prices than a store where saltwater is a sideline.

Never buy fish on your first visit to any store. First, investigate the range of offerings, quality, and prices in your region before making any decisions, especially if there are several competitors. Make at least two visits a week or more apart. The idea is to find out how the store operates on a continuous basis. Be critical but fair in your evaluations. We all have our good days and bad ones. Ask questions. Do not expect everyone to be an infallible expert, but you should hear correct answers at least to basic questions about water quality, the particular needs (feeding behavior, for example) of any fish in the shop, and steps to prevent or cure common problems. One good sign to watch for: when someone does not know the answer to your question, they take the time to look it up in a book. Good shops always have several well-used reference books behind the counter.

Dealers *are* in business to make money, but a sales pitch should not be the sole communication you have with them. Professional dealers know that the key to their business success is for their customers to be successful hobbyists. It is in the dealer's best interest, for example, to steer you away from fishes that would be inappropriate for your tank because of size or compatibility problems. Remember, though, that most dealers will sell you anything you want if you insist.

The next step is to evaluate the specimens themselves, and there are several factors that you should consider.

Purchasing Fish Based on Collecting Practices

Care in purchasing may be the most important aspect of managing your aquarium. Here are some suggestions for making wise decisions in this regard.

Collecting from Wild Populations

Bear in mind that most saltwater fish have been collected from wild populations. The time between being collected and arriving at your local shop typically ranges from two to three weeks. During this time, the fish may or may not have been maintained under optimum conditions. Unfortunately, it is seldom possible for you to know much about this chain of custody.

Against the practice of wild collecting, two primary arguments are raised:

- Overfishing
- Generalized damage to the reef itself

In favor of wild collecting, the response concerns the importance of this source of income to local fishermen lacking other options for feeding their families. Establishing hatcheries in the source country, rather than collecting from its waters, maintains the income stream while reducing the toll on the reef. Fishing for food already removes substantial numbers of reef fishes, though not usually the same species as those collected for the aquarium. Stresses induced by turbidity from shore development, increased water temperature due to global warming, and the influx of human-created pollutants contribute far more to the decline of reef health than does aquarium collecting. Nevertheless, most saltwater enthusiasts would prefer that their aquarium not contribute to the decline of the coral reefs it is intended to depict!

For thirty years or more, the problem of using poisons to collect reef fish has been a subject of controversy within both the aquarium industry and the conservation community. Despite a huge investment of expertise and millions of dollars, a satisfactory resolution of the issue has yet to emerge. Anyone who owns a saltwater aquarium must be aware that at some point they may purchase a fish that was collected by poisoning. No certain method exists to determine, after the fact, if chemical exposure has taken place. Little agreement seems to have been reached regarding the effects of chemical collecting on the survivability of fish subsequent to being collected. Trying to account for the effects of holding and handling methods, shipping circumstances, and the capabilities of aquarists themselves on survival presents significant challenges.

COLLECTING FROM GOOD SOURCES

One way to avoid unhealthy fish is to choose species that routinely come from good sources. Several popular aquarium fishes come largely or exclusively from Hawaii, for example. Fish-collecting in that state is well regulated. Shipping to the mainland is relatively inexpensive and does not involve red tape, since it is interstate commerce. Therefore, travel time is minimized. Good Hawaiian fishes include the yellow tang (*Zebrasoma flavescens*), Potter's angelfish (*Centropyge potteri*), Vanderbilt's chromis (*Chromis vanderbilti*), and several desirable butterflyfishes, such as the raccoon (*Chaetodon lunula*), threadfin (*C. auriga*) and longnosed (*Forcipiger flavissimus*).

The tropical west Atlantic and Caribbean regions also supply many good aquarium fishes, such as the French angelfish (*Pomacanthus paru*), the royal gramma (*Gramma loreto*) and the yellowhead jawfish (*Opisthognathus aurifrons*). I have noted remarkably few problems with Florida or Caribbean specimens over the years. Shipping time from Florida, of course, is minimal to most locations in the country, with specimens sometimes arriving the same day.

If you want to be completely sure of chemical-free fish, avoid purchasing fish from areas known for a chemical collecting problem. This can be tricky. Many popular aquarium species may come from any of several source countries. Only the importer knows where a particular batch originated. On the other hand, even in the Philippines, where chemical use has historically been widespread, some collectors use only nets to harvest specimens.

Catching Fish, Killing Coral

Coral reefs can be directly affected by collecting activities associated with the aquarium trade. In some regions of the world, divers use poisons to make fish easier to catch. The chemicals can kill coral polyps, which take a long time to regrow. Like so many other places on the planet, coral reefs face even greater dangers from pollution and global warming. Unlike freshwater aquarium fish, the majority of saltwater fish are taken from their natural habitats rather than produced in hatcheries. Aquarists must recognize that they have a responsibility to avoid contributing to the degradation of coral reefs by their purchasing decisions.

For more than twenty years I have involved myself in efforts to keep saltwater aquarium-keeping a sustainable hobby and industry. Home saltwater aquariums can do an enormous amount of good by bringing ordinary folks up close and personal with some of the sea's most remarkable denizens. A broader awareness of the fragile beauty embodied by coral reefs can only increase the desire to protect them for future generations. Biology imposes constraints upon the potential for captive propagation of many saltwater fishes. This has seldom been the case with freshwater species. Less than 10 percent of saltwater fish and a still smaller fraction of invertebrates come from captive propagation. Despite many efforts to learn how to spawn and rear them, some of the most desirable (from the aquarist's point of view) saltwater species will come from wild stocks for a long time to come. That being the case, we should choose wisely and avoid species that have little or no chance of adapting to captivity. The obligately coral-feeding butterflyfishes, such as *C. ornatissimus* mentioned above, provide a perfect example. On the other hand, home aquarists should encourage the efforts to breed saltwater fish and invertebrates commercially by seeking out captive-propagated specimens whenever possible. I am proud to serve on the scientific advisory board of Reef Protection International (www.reefprotect.org). This organization has produced *the Reef Fish Guide* listing both recommended species and those that hobbyists should think twice about. You can download a copy from the Web site, and I will be referring to this guide in the chapters that follow.

Your saltwater aquarium dealer will likely become a major source of advice regarding your aquarium. No one has more control over the health of the fish you will place in your aquarium than the retail dealer. Saltwater fish endure a difficult journey before eventually arriving in your town. How the dealer selects fish and how he treats them while in his possession can make all the difference to your success. Fish can experience delayed mortality, meaning that their circumstances today can produce effects that may not manifest themselves for weeks, long after you've brought the fish home. In 1995, I founded the American Marinelife Dealers Association (www.amda reef.com) to enlist like-minded saltwater aquarium dealers in combating negative environmental impacts resulting from the aquarium trade. Check the Web site for an AMDA dealer in your area, and when you visit, be sure to tell them I sent you.

Captive-propagated fish are among the best possible choices for the saltwater aquarium. Many species of anemonefishes are available from hatcheries, along with several kinds of gobies and dottybacks. Dealers usually advertise that they have captive-propagated stock, but always inquire. Captive-bred specimens may be smaller than wild caught counterparts but will of course grow to the size typical for their species. In all cases, captive-bred fish acclimate better to aquarium conditions and have fewer problems than do similar specimens harvested from the wild. Captive propagation takes some of the pressure off natural populations.

Widespread development of hatcheries for the production of both fish and invertebrates may provide the key to solving some of the thorniest problems related to the collecting of wild specimens for aquariums.

Selecting Healthy Fish

Here are some characteristics of healthy fish:

- Their colors are bright.
- They search actively for food.
- Their fins are held erect.

Follow these tips to avoid taking home unhealthy fish:

- Watch out for rapid movement of the gill covers ("panting" or "gasping"). This could indicate that the fish is infested with parasites.

- Beware of ragged fins and the presence of lesions, open wounds, or similar abnormalities. Fish can lose a bit of fin tissue or a scale or two without serious consequences, but any damage should appear to be healing.

- No bloodiness or cottony fungal growth should be apparent.

- Unless the behavior is characteristic for the species, a fish that hides excessively is in some kind of distress.

- Look for signs of poor nourishment, such as a hollow belly or a thinning of the musculature behind the head.

- When viewed head on, the fish should be convex in outline, not concave.

WARNING The usual advice is to look for obvious signs of disease when shopping for saltwater fish. This is a good suggestion, but only a very foolish, or very busy, dealer will leave a sick fish in the display tanks. The problems you may encounter will be of a more subtle nature. How was the fish collected? What has happened to it since that time? How has the dealer cared for the fish after its arrival? Neither you nor the dealer will have reliable information on any but the third question. Quarantine, either by the dealer or by you, offers the best option for avoiding trouble once the fish enters your display aquarium. Another recommendation often given is to ask to see the fish eat before you purchase it. Of course, a prospective fish should be willing to eat, but this is no guarantee of its health. A mishandled fish can experience delayed mortality even though it may feed normally. Quarantine will help to assure any latent problems develop away from the main tank.

Ideally, the dealer will quarantine all new arrivals for at least a week before releasing them; two weeks would be better. If this is not the routine at the store you select, the dealer should at least be willing to hold a fish for you if you agree to buy the fish after the holding period is up. Saltwater fish have a harrowing journey from the reef to the dealer. They require a period of rest and adjustment before yet another move. A few days, or just until the fish has had its first meal, is not enough time for recovery. If the dealer cannot, or will not, provide this kind of quarantine period, you should make plans well in advance to quarantine all specimens at home yourself. I suggest a minimum quarantine of two weeks.

Making Rational Purchasing Decisions

Why, I am often asked, are saltwater fish so expensive? Fish and invertebrates are commodities to the aquarium shop. Every dealer has to make a living. But can a fish really be worth $300?

Many factors affect the retail price of saltwater aquarium fish. These include the species, source, size of the store, geographic location of the store, nature of the store's competition, and operating costs. My only advice is this: do not shop for price alone. Common sense must play a role in your evaluation of the "worth" of a particular specimen. For example, if an individual animal is being offered at a price that is "too good to be true," I urge extreme caution. A cheap fish is no bargain if it only lives a week or two after you take it home. Once you find a dealer that consistently provides you with good-quality fish, your best bet is to support that dealer with your business, even if a particular specimen is a few dollars less across town.

Here are some guidelines:

- Check out the dealer's reputation with experienced aquarists. You can find them at your local club or in online chat rooms.
- Ask the dealer about the collecting and shipping of his or her livestock. A good dealer should be willing to share this information.
- If your dealer has a separate, behind-the-scenes holding facility, ask for a tour. Seeing how the tanks are maintained out of the customer's view should reveal a lot.
- Ask yourself if the shop appears to be prospering. A struggling enterprise is more likely than a thriving one to cut corners on livestock sourcing and care.

Trans-Shipping

Trans-shipping is a cost-saving method. An exporter in, say, Indonesia, ships an entire air cargo container of fish to a trans-shipper in Los Angeles. The trans-shipper meets the plane with a sheaf of orders from retail dealers throughout the country. At the airport terminal the trans-shipper opens the cargo container and sorts out the plastic bags of fish and invertebrates into boxes, each corresponding to a dealer's order. When the sorting is done, the boxes are sealed, labeled, and handed back to the airline. Eventually, the boxes arrive at the dealer's airport. The fish may have been in the plastic bag for as long as seventy-two hours. Trans-shipped specimens may not recover completely for several weeks, and may suffer delayed mortality. But they are cheap.

Ordering Fish by Mail

A good mail-order supplier can be better than many local shops. Otherwise, how would the supplier have managed to stay in business when customers must pay freight costs and have no opportunity to see the fish that they are buying? Shop owners often complain about mail-order livestock suppliers, but the fact is that the customers would not buy live specimens by mail order if they were not frustrated with their local dealer. I can recommend this avenue to anyone for whom the local merchants fall short, but with a cautionary note. You might save a lot of money by ordering. You might find rare and unusual livestock. On the other hand, fish can arrive in poor condition, even dead. Getting a replacement or refund may be problematic.

Don't buy fish on impulse. Aquarium shops sell fish that grow much too large for the home aquarium. They sell fish that cannot be enticed to eat in captivity. They sell fish that will devour everything else in your tank. They sell fish that may bite or sting you. So, always do some research on any fish or invertebrate you consider purchasing. This can save a lot of headaches in the long-run.

The best way to zero in on good dealers, local or otherwise, is by talking to their other customers. Get to know the other aquarists in your local shop. Join an aquarium club, or chat online. When you travel, visit shops and compare them to the ones in your hometown. Finally, remember that the ultimate responsibility for your aquarium lies with you. If you purchase foolishly, suffering the consequences later is your fault, not the dealer's.

The Chemistry You Need

I warned you already that you would have to understand some basic chemistry in order to understand your saltwater aquarium. If you desire more in-depth information, it is readily available in books or online.

"Most people realize the sea covers two-thirds of the planet, but few take the time to understand even a gallon of it," says Miles O'Malley, the protagonist of Jim Lynch's novel, *The Highest Tide*. We may know the sea is salty, but the basic composition of seawater remains a mystery to most people. When you take on the responsibility of a saltwater aquarium, the properties of seawater become highly relevant.

The range of optimum water conditions for a saltwater aquarium is much narrower than for a freshwater tank. In order to keep conditions in the aquarium within that narrow range, the aquarist must engage in a regular process of what I like to call "test and tweak." You periodically perform some key chemical tests. If water conditions are found to be out of line, you tweak them back into place. Often, the tweak involves a partial water change; at other times the addition of a supplement may be necessary. Making a judgment about what to do with a saltwater tank requires a somewhat broader background than that required for freshwater aquarium-keeping.

Salinity

The planet is composed of chemical elements, all of which can be found at some level in seawater. When dissolved in water, an element assumes a chemical form known as an ion. Ions bear either a positive or a negative electrical charge and can participate in reactions with other ions. These facts bear heavily on the interactions between seawater and the life forms swimming in it. *Salinity* is the total amount of dissolved ions in seawater. Seawater contains eleven major ions at a concentration of one part per million (ppm) or more, comprising 99.9 percent of the dissolved components. They are: chloride, sulfate, bicarbonate, bromide, borate, fluoride, sodium, magnesium, calcium, potassium, and strontium. The major ions are said to be conserved, meaning that the total amount of these ions can vary locally, but their relative proportions remain constant.

Besides the major components, two other groups of ions contribute to salinity. Minor ions are those that are present at a level less than 1 ppm, but greater than 1 part per billion (ppb). Trace ions are those that are present in concentrations lower than 1 ppb. An important distinction between the major ions and the minor and trace ions is that major ions are largely unaffected by local conditions, but the concentrations of minor and trace ions may be altered substantially by chemical and/or biological processes. Changing the concentrations of certain ions has definite biological effects. Adding iodide can result in accelerated growth of certain organisms, for example. Adding phosphate often results in an algae bloom.

Copper provides an example of a trace ion with significant concentration-dependent effects. At 0.2 ppm, copper produces little noticeable effect on fish. On the other hand, any amount of copper detectable with a hobbyist test kit is lethal to echinoderms (starfish and their kin). Copper is an essential element for many life forms; the requirement, however, is extraordinarily minute. The presence or absence of other trace ions, such as vanadium, may be of no consequence, as they play no important biological role, at least so far as we know.

Because of their known concentration-dependent effects, minor and trace ions must be tracked by the aquarium keeper under certain circumstances. See the sections "Phosphate" and "Copper" discussed below for more information on these trace ions.

The salinity can be different in different locations, but the gross chemical composition of seawater is constant everywhere in the sea. Around coral reefs, salinities of 35–36 parts per thousand (ppt) prevail. This means the seawater bathing the reef contains 35–36 grams of dissolved salts per kilogram of water. Since weighing out a kilo of seawater, evaporating it, and reweighing the remaining salts is impractical, salinity is seldom measured directly. Salinity is determined by various methods, with hydrometers, refractometers, and conductivity meters being the major ones.

HYDROMETERS

Hydrometers may be of two types. A floating hydrometer consists of a weighted glass tube that floats higher or lower in water samples of different salinities. A scale on the tube allows a direct reading of the specific gravity. A dip-and-read hydrometer, the most common type in the aquarium trade, consists of a sample cup in which an indicator points to the specific gravity on a scale engraved into the cup. Specific gravity is the ratio of the weight of the sample to that of an equal volume of pure water. Thus, the specific gravity of pure water is 1.0000. Dissolved substances add weight, resulting in a specific gravity greater than 1.0000. After determining the specific gravity, the salinity can be estimated from a set of conversion tables if the temperature is also known.

First, measure the specific gravity of your aquarium and write down the observed reading. Next, find the temperature column in Table 1 that is closest to the temperature of your tank.

Table 1: Conversion of Specific Gravity to Density by Temperature Correction

Observed hydrometer reading	Temperature					
	68	70	72	73	75	77
1.0170	10	12	15	17	20	22
1.0180	10	12	15	17	20	23
1.0190	10	12	15	18	20	23
1.0200	10	13	15	18	20	23
1.0210	10	13	15	18	21	23
1.0220	11	13	15	18	21	23
1.0230	11	13	16	18	21	24
1.0240	11	13	16	18	21	24
1.0250	11	13	16	18	21	24
1.0260	11	13	16	19	22	24
1.0270	11	14	16	19	22	24
1.0280	11	14	16	19	22	25
1.0290	11	14	16	19	22	25

From the temperature column in Table 1, note the conversion factor. Add this to the specific gravity reading. In the table, two leading zeroes are omitted from the conversion factors. Thus, for specific gravity reading of 1.0260 at 75°F, the density is 1.0282. (1.0260 + 0.0022). Now look up the density in Table 2 and determine the corresponding salinity.

Table 2: Conversion of Density to Salinity

Density	Salinity
1.0180	25
1.0185	25
1.0190	26
1.0195	27
1.0200	27
1.0205	28
1.0210	29
1.0215	29
1.0220	30
1.0225	30
1.0230	31
1.0235	32
1.0240	32
1.0245	33
1.0250	34
1.0255	34
1.0260	35
1.0265	36
1.0270	36
1.0275	37
1.0280	38
1.0285	38
1.0290	39
1.0295	40
1.0300	40

REFRACTOMETERS

A refractometer estimates the salinity of a water sample by measuring its refractive index. You place a drop of water in the sample chamber and read the salinity directly from the scale by looking through the instrument. As with specific gravity, the refractive index varies with temperature. An individual refractometer is designed to operate at a certain temperature. Make sure the one you choose is designed for water at 75°F.

DIGITAL CONDUCTIVITY METERS

A digital conductivity meter has a probe that is placed in the water. Salinity is displayed electronically. All of the calculations take place in the meter's microprocessor. Though more expensive than either a refractometer or hydrometer, a meter provides the simplest way to get an accurate reading.

Strive to keep the aquarium at a constant salinity near that of natural seawater. This often entails adding water to compensate for evaporation. Use distilled or tap water for this purpose, not seawater. Adding seawater will cause a gradual increase in salinity that will ultimately reach harmful levels. I suggest checking and adjusting salinity weekly. When carrying out a partial water change, make sure the salinity of the replacement water matches that of the aquarium.

pH Measurement

The degree of acidity or alkalinity of a solution is expressed as pH. It affects everything from the respiration of fish to skeleton construction in corals. Natural seawater has a pH of 8.3. The pH of pure water is 7.0. Acidic solutions are lower than 7.0 on the pH scale, while anything above 7.0 is alkaline. Aquarium pH is easily measured in much the same way as it is for a swimming pool or hot tub, with either a chemical kit, a dip-and-read test strip, or a digital meter. Digital pH meters can be costly. They also need repeated calibration to give accurate readings. The pH probe requires a lot of care to avoid frequent replacement, which can represent half the cost of the instrument. Meters do provide great accuracy, however. On the other end of the spectrum, dip-and-read tests are simple and cheap but may not offer enough precision; a tenth of a pH unit is needed. For a home aquarium, the best choice is a pH test that involves placing a water sample in a vial and adding a chemical that changes color in response to the pH. The color of the sample is compared with a printed chart to determine the corresponding pH.

The pH of any saltwater aquarium can vary due to a number of factors, including the time of day. Photosynthesis by algae is responsible for the daily fluctuation. When light is available, algae remove carbon dioxide from the water. This tends to drive up the pH. During darkness, photosynthesis ceases and carbon dioxide accumulates, lowering the pH. In an improperly maintained aquarium, this fluctuation can be so dramatic as to cause a wholesale loss of fish overnight. Most of the carbon dioxide in aquarium water comes from respiration by fish and invertebrates. Overcrowding will lead to carbon dioxide buildup that cannot be effectively countered.

Carbon dioxide exits the aquarium not only by photosynthetic conversion, but also by chemical conversion and diffusion into the atmosphere. Vigorous water movement facilitates diffusion to the atmosphere. Chemical conversion depends upon a complex relationship in which various ions participate, taking the carbon dioxide out of the solution through the formation of insoluble carbonates. Because of these interwoven processes, aquarists should monitor alkalinity as well as pH.

Alkalinity Measurement

Alkalinity refers to the ability of seawater to maintain a constant pH as acid is added. The higher the alkalinity, the greater the amount of acid needed to change the pH. The alkalinity of seawater is about 7 milliequivalents

Alkalinity Conversion Factors

Alkalinity is expressed in milliequivalents per liter (Meq/L). Other terms you may encounter are:

Carbonate hardness expressed in parts per million (ppm) 50 ppm = 1 Meq/L

Alkalai reserve expressed in grains per gallon (gr/gal) 2.92 gr/gal = 1 Meq/L

German hardness (KH) expressed in degrees (dKH) 2.8 dKH = 1 Meq/L

Depending upon the brand of test kit you purchase, you may need to convert your readings to alkalinity, using the conversion factors above.

per liter (Meq/L). Saltwater aquariums should maintain this level of alkalinity, or be slightly higher. The most useful alkalinity test for home aquariums involves mixing the water sample with a small amount of pH indicator, then adding a standard acid solution until the pH changes abruptly, evidenced by the color change of the indicator. Each drop of acid corresponds to a unit of alkalinity. Alkalinity is expressed in different ways, so you may need conversion factors to derive milliequivalents per liter from the kit you select.

Calcium

For invertebrates that manufacture integuments of calcium carbonate, the amount of calcium dissolved in the water is crucial to their survival. Calcium is one of the major ions of seawater and occurs at about 400 ppm. If you choose a design featuring corals or giant clams, among other invertebrates, you should monitor the calcium concentration and take steps to adjust it appropriately.

The test for calcium is similar to the alkalinity test. Reagent is added drop by drop to a water sample that has been mixed with an indicator solution. A color change indicates the endpoint of the test, with the number of drops corresponding to the calcium concentration in parts per million.

Studies have shown that calcium is depleted from saltwater aquariums by corals and other organisms, and thus requires regular replenishment. Typically, calcium is added in a concentrated form after the amount needed has been determined by testing. This can be accomplished in several ways.

Limewater, a solution of calcium hydroxide, is a popular calcium supplement. Prepared from dry calcium oxide, it can be dosed in large amounts without adverse effects. Slightly more than one teaspoon of the dry powder makes a gallon of finished product. Limewater, sometimes known by the German term under which it was first introduced, *Kalkwasser*, has a short shelf life because it absorbs carbon dioxide from the atmosphere. This results in the formation of calcium carbonate, which precipitates out, rendering the calcium once more unavailable. Aquarists have therefore sought other methods for replacing calcium.

The *calcium reactor* is merely a piece of pipe in which calcium carbonate in solid form is allowed to react with distilled water. Water passing through the pipe leaches calcium from the solid material, producing a rich supplement of calcium ions for the aquarium.

Reef aquariums featuring many specimens that require calcium may respond best to constant small doses of calcium supplements. Some designs call for a pump and timer to add supplements automatically. Others simply add the supplement to replace evaporated water, either constantly with a drip system or when the water level drops below a certain point, as determined by a float switch. Smaller tanks can be managed effectively without elaborate systems such as these, but large systems should have automated equipment installed.

Dissolved Oxygen

Dissolved oxygen is measured in milligrams per liter (mg/L) and should always be at 100 percent saturation in the saltwater aquarium. (This means that the water holds all the oxygen it theoretically can.) The amount of oxygen necessary to achieve saturation varies with salinity and temperature. For a salinity of 35 ppt at 75°F, 100 percent saturation corresponds to 6.9 mg/L. While the concentrations of both oxygen and carbon dioxide are discussed below in the section on gas exchange, neither parameter is often measured. Carbon dioxide concentration can be calculated from other parameters. Oxygen concentration can only be determined practically with a digital meter, as wet chemical tests are quite cumbersome. Most aquarists do not invest in an oxygen meter, and instead rely on high flow rates to ensure oxygen saturation.

Phosphate

Phosphate, the ionic form of dissolved phosphorus, plays a role in the biology of all organisms. In the aquarium, however, we are primarily concerned with the effect of abnormal phosphate levels on the growth of algae. Phosphate is usually present in great excess in the aquarium, compared to its concentration in the ocean. The phosphate ion (PO_4^{3-}), known as orthophosphate, is the form measured by aquarium test kits. Particulate organic phosphate (POP) is partially degraded organic matter with a high phosphorus content. POP is also present in the aquarium and can serve as a reservoir because it releases orthophosphate as it decomposes. Synthetic seawater mix, tap water, activated carbon, water conditioners, and food may all be sources of phosphate.

Phosphate Test Kits

A phosphate test kit is likely to be one of the most expensive kits you purchase. Make certain that the one you choose uses the ascorbic acid method. This analytical procedure is the only one that works well in seawater. Some commercially available phosphate tests are intended for use in freshwater only and use an alternate procedure. Such tests will give erroneous results in seawater.

When you buy the test, also purchase a supply of disposable plastic vials. Use a fresh vial for each test. When the same test vial is used again and again, phosphate residues from water samples can build up, resulting in spurious test results.

Phosphate is not considered harmful to marine organisms at the concentrations likely to be achieved in the aquarium under normal circumstances, but it does appear that it acts as a fertilizer for undesirable algae growth. In the ocean, the scarcity of dissolved phosphorus in a form that can be utilized by living organisms tends to be a factor limiting algae growth. Herbivores crop algae from the reef almost continuously, too. In the aquarium, where phosphate is abundant and herbivores may be few in number, too much algae may grow. Excess algae may pose a threat to sessile invertebrates because it can smother them, or even poison them by exuding toxic substances. Limiting phosphate seems to be an effective way to avoid this unsightly problem. Ideally, there should never be any phosphate in a coral reef aquarium that is measurable with a test kit that is accurate to 0.05 mg/L. If a test shows any measurable level of phosphate, start looking for ways to reduce the phosphate concentration.

Iodide

Aquarium literature contains numerous references to the benefits of iodide supplementation. Iodide (I⁻) is found in seawater at a concentration of 0.06 mg/L. It is removed by protein skimming and by activated carbon filtration, techniques that will be discussed later in the book. It is essential to many invertebrates and fishes. For example, certain soft corals that exhibit rhythmic pulsing movements may fall motionless if they lack this ion. Test kits for iodide are available in aquarium shops, along with additives for replenishing it. Exercise caution not to overdose.

Copper

The importance of copper to saltwater aquarium-keeping derives from its use as a therapeutic agent in treating the most common parasitic infestations of marine fish. I will have more to say about copper in chapter 6, "Troubleshooting."

Nitrogen Compounds

Tests for ammonia, nitrite, and nitrate enable the aquarist to monitor the crucial process of biological filtration. Ammonia or nitrite in the water is a sign of trouble. Nitrate accumulation can be used as a rough indicator of the overall biological state of the aquarium. The concentration and form of nitrogen present in aquarium water changes in response to a complex cycle of biological activity. Proper operation of this important chemical cycle is fundamental to the success of your aquarium.

Physical and Chemical Cycles

The most important physical and chemical cycles operating within the saltwater aquarium are biological filtration, gas exchange, and the day/night cycle. Without biological filtration, an aquarium requires water changes so frequently as to be impractical. Life in an aquarium cannot exist without the exchange of oxygen and carbon dioxide at the surface. Photosynthetic organisms require both light and darkness for their survival, and the alternation of light and dark regulates the metabolism of both fish and invertebrates. Good aquarium design and regular maintenance take care of all these requirements.

Water Quality Parameters

The chemistry of the surrounding seawater varies little from one coral reef to the next. Therefore, only one set of parameters is needed for all saltwater aquariums that display reef fishes and invertebrates. Some authors recommend maintaining the temperature at a slightly higher range than recommended here. Otherwise, broad agreement exists regarding the numbers presented here.

Temperature: 72–78°F

Salinity: 35 parts per thousand (ppt), 36 ppt for Red Sea

Specific Gravity (at 75°F): 1.0260

pH: 8.0–8.5, optimum 8.3

Alkalinity: 7 Meq/L

Dissolved Oxygen: 6.9 mg/L (= 100 percent saturation)

Calcium: 380–420 ppm

Iodide: 0.06 ppm

Phosphate: undetectable

Nitrate: see page 36 for a discussion of nitrate concentration and what it may mean

Nitrite: undetectable

Ammonia: undetectable

Biological Filtration

Fish excrete their wastes directly into the water. Under natural conditions, fish population density, considering the total volume of water surrounding a coral reef, is much lower than that of even the largest aquarium. Dilution, therefore, immediately counters fish waste pollution in the ocean. Additionally, in a short time natural processes degrade the wastes into simple compounds that can be taken up by algae or utilized in some other ecological process. When we establish an aquarium's artificial ecosystem, we must harness these same natural processes to promote the survival of our fish and invertebrate display. The totality of these processes as they occur in an aquarium is biological filtration. Biological filtration is the detoxification of wastes by beneficial bacteria known as nitrifiers or nitrifying bacteria. Coating every available surface that lies in contact with oxygenated water, these organisms chemically convert ammonia (the primary component of fish waste) into nitrate (a relatively harmless compound taken up by photosynthesizers). Biological filtration, or biofiltration, readily develops in the aquarium. All that is required is an ammonia source (fish) and the right kinds of bacteria. The latter are automatically transferred along with fish or any other item taken from the reef or from a previously established saltwater aquarium (the dealer's inventory system, for example). Within a month, nitrifying bacteria will colonize the aquarium system sufficiently to process a moderate amount of waste. The gradual development of biofiltration capacity prompts the widely offered recommendation always to stock the aquarium slowly, over a period of several months. Within six months to a year, the population of beneficial nitrifying bacteria will have matured completely, and biofiltration will be adequate to permit fish to be stocked at full capacity indefinitely.

Though biofiltration is a totally natural process, most aquariums are outfitted with some kind of filtration system. Designed to maximize biofiltration capacity, aquarium filtration equipment may employ a variety of techniques to increase the surface area available for colonization by nitrifiers. The bacteria refuse to carry out the desired chemical transformations when they float freely; they need to be stuck to a solid surface. Thus we have rotating "bio-wheel" devices, "wet/dry" systems, and "fluidized bed" technology. All these filtration methods provide extremely efficient biofiltration, converting all the ammonia generated within the tank to nitrate in a short period of time. Aquarium system design sometimes focuses on biofiltration to the exclusion of other important factors because the aquarist is often seen as trying to squeeze the maximum number of fish into the minimum number of gallons. Although you could buy a highly efficient filter system and have the tank teeming with fish, you would be inviting disaster, nearly guaranteeing it, because you would exceed what I like to call the true carrying capacity of the system.

CARRYING CAPACITY

We can debate all day about carrying capacity; that is, how many fish of what size a particular aquarium can support. If by *support* we simply mean "adequately detoxifying the ammonia waste produced," we can bump up the number of fish to high population densities indeed. Consider how many fish might be packed into a dealer's inventory system, for a case in point. Ten saltwater fish in a fifty-gallon tank would not be considered unusual. For the home aquarium display, biofiltration is not the whole story. We must think about the long-term success of an aquarium whose residents will be there for the rest of their lives. Fish and other organisms need what I like to call ecological space. A given species may need swimming room, a minimum number of companions of its own species, or a certain amount of water movement to really thrive. The ability of the aquarium to provide for these needs as well as for basic waste removal is a measure of the true carrying capacity. Taking into account not only waste removal, but also the need for ample oxygen, swimming room, and benign social interactions, ecological space must be allotted in the process of designing the aquarium. Care must be taken not to exceed the true carrying capacity of the system.

WATER CHANGES

Regardless of its design, every aquarium needs regular partial water changes. I suggest removing 10 percent of the water weekly and replacing it with freshly prepared synthetic seawater. Depending upon your schedule, you might elect to change 20 percent every two weeks or 40 percent monthly, but the aquarium will look better and its inhabitants will appear more vibrant with more frequent, smaller changes. Partial water changes not only dilute nitrate that accumulates as a result of biological filtration, but also removes other forms of pollution that can harm fish and invertebrates.

Gas Exchange

Gas exchange is crucial. The water must continuously contain sufficient oxygen and must be continuously rid of carbon dioxide. While photosynthetic organisms, algae, and some invertebrates absorb carbon dioxide during daylight periods, at night this may not be enough to prevent the accumulation of CO_2. Carbon dioxide dissolves in water to produce carbonic acid, which drives down the pH and can inhibit critical respiratory processes in the fish. In sufficient concentration, CO_2 is lethal. Merely agitating the water at the surface facilitates most, if not all, needed gas exchange. All saltwater filtration systems require water movement, and this usually creates plenty of surface action. Problems sometimes do occur when accumulated debris clogs the filter and causes it to slow down, and the resulting change in flow rate goes unnoticed. Many aquarists add immersible water pumps, known as powerheads, to increase both surface agitation and movement deeper in the water.

Gas exchange may be inhibited, regardless of the degree of water movement, when too little surface area exists for the volume of water in the tank. A tall, narrow tank has considerably less surface area per gallon than a shallow, broad one. Consider the following comparison between two commercially available sizes of tanks:

A fifty-gallon breeder tank (36 x 18 x 18 inches) has 4.5 square feet of surface, or a ratio of 0.09 square feet per gallon. A seventy-seven-gallon show tank (48 x 12 x 24) has only 4.0 square feet of surface, or 0.05 square feet per gallon. That is roughly half as much surface for 1.5 times as much water volume. To maintain the oxygen content of the water in the larger tank, plenty of water movement is required.

Gas exchange must be taken into account in developing an aquarium design. A tall tank may be dramatic in appearance, but it needs to be correspondingly broad (most aquarium shop owners would say deep) to provide adequate surface area.

Oxygen enters the aquarium and carbon dioxide escapes it via the water surface, but water must circulate within

> ## Filter Numbers
>
> Filter throughput for a saltwater aquarium should be at least five times the total tank capacity per hour. For example, a 100-gallon tank needs 500 gallons per hour of turnover or more. Pumps capable of delivering such flow rates necessarily create water currents.

the tank so that oxygen remains constantly available to the inhabitants. Similarly, carbon dioxide must not accumulate. Photosynthesis can account for significant oxygen production and carbon dioxide removal during the daylight hours. At night, photosynthesis ceases, and organisms that were formerly adding oxygen and removing carbon dioxide are now doing the opposite. In the dark, surface exchange must be relied upon. Even if the filter turnover rate meets the 500 gallons per hour standard suggested above, you may need to provide additional water movement via powerheads in order to facilitate adequate gas exchange.

With a pH test kit, you can determine if you have enough water movement. Without sufficient exchange, carbon dioxide accumulates in your aquarium, reducing the pH. Remove a gallon of water to a bucket and aerate it vigorously overnight. The next morning, test the pH of both the tank and the bucket. If the pH of the bucket is 0.2 or more pH units higher than that of the tank, you need more water movement.

Lighting

You must decide if your saltwater aquarium is to house any organisms that depend upon photosynthesis for their survival. This includes seaweeds and a host of invertebrate animals that harbor photosynthetic symbiotic partners. Make the critical decisions about lighting early in the design process. Aquarium lighting should show off the underwater scene to its best advantage and, if necessary, provide energy for photosynthesis. If the design relies solely on plastic reproductions or coral skeletons, then a single fluorescent lamp positioned over the tank may be enough. Even in an all-plastic ecosystem, more light always makes the tank appear inviting and fosters the growth of filamentous algae upon which many fish feed. Sometimes, unconventional lighting (by which I mean anything in addition to, or other than, the standard fluorescent strip across the top of the tank) can be used to produce striking effects. For example, a spotlight shining in can direct the eye toward a particular underwater feature, in much the same way that stage lighting directs the attention of the audience.

In the tropics, corals of all types reach their greatest abundance and diversity in clear, shallow waters, such as the shallows off the Florida Keys. Under such conditions, sunlight penetrates well. Even under the most favorable circumstances, however, the amount of available light underwater is only a fraction of that shining on the surface. Reflection, absorption with increasing depth, and turbidity all limit light availability in the reef environment. Even so, enough light for photosynthesis can reach the bottom to support dense growth because sunlight is quite intense. Few home aquariums rely on sunlight as the main light source and must make do with artificial lighting. Choosing an artificial-lighting system for a particular aquarium design requires knowledge of the available types of lighting equipment and their respective capabilities. In order to make comparisons, we must first define the terms used to describe light sources and light intensity.

The amount of light energy emanating from a source is measured in units known as lumens. The light intensity, or irradiance, over a given area is measured in *lux*, or lumens per square meter. Over a cornfield in Iowa in the middle of summer, the midday sun may provide irradiance of 100,000 lux or more. You'd be lucky to find an aquarium lighting system that can deliver 10 percent of this amount to the tank underneath it.

Several factors conspire to limit the efficiency of aquarium lighting. For example, the reflector housing the lamps cannot be 100-percent perfect, and therefore not all light emitted will reach the water surface. Reflection from the water surface itself reduces light penetration, too. Further, as the tank becomes taller, the amount of light reaching the bottom decreases dramatically due to the inverse square law of optics. Light intensity decreases in proportion to the square of the distance between the source and the object illuminated. In practical terms this means that the same light fixture over a tank twelve inches in height delivers only one-fourth as much light to the bottom if the height of the tank is increased to twenty-four inches. Double the distance, and illumination decreases fourfold. Further, the greater height of the water column means more absorption by water itself. This again reduces the effective light intensity.

The implications for aquarium lighting design are straightforward:

- For aquariums up to about twelve inches in height, two fluorescent lamps of the maximum length that can be accommodated across the length of the tank should be used.

- For deeper tanks up to four feet long, use four fluorescent lamps of the maximum possible length.

- For larger tanks, use one to several metal halide lamps to provide extremely bright light.

Although I suggest here choosing lamps by length, in actual practice it is the wattage that matters; the higher the wattage, the brighter the lamp. For example, a lamp four feet long consumes 40 watts of electricity and produces about 3000 lumens. Data on the lumen output of various types of lamps can be found on lighting manufacturer's Web sites. Appendix C, "Tank Specifications," provides lumen requirements for all the standard types of aquarium tanks.

For saltwater applications, several types of special lighting exist. For example, as one descends to greater depths, sunlight becomes selectively attenuated, with mostly blue wavelengths reaching the organisms. Many aquarists use actinic lighting to mimic these conditions. Where appropriate, I have included special lighting recommendations for some of the model designs given later.

Natural lighting varies as the sun first climbs and then descends across the sky. Cloud cover, reflection due to water movement at the surface, and turbidity, not to mention water depth, all affect the amount of light actually reaching marine organisms. If you obtain captive-propagated coral specimens, you may be able to learn the lighting conditions under which they were grown. Seldom do you have this information from a collected specimen. Therefore, some experimentation may be needed to optimally light any given item you obtain. As a rule of thumb, provide illumination that averages around 5000 lux over the course of a day. Thus, a forty-gallon long-style tank has 0.4 square meters and requires about 2000 lumens to achieve an irradiance of 5000 lux. You can check lumen output data for various lamps on the manufacturers' Web site. Use the average lumen value, if it is given. Reduce this number by 30 percent to allow for losses due to reflector inefficiency, reflection from the water surface, etc. Then total up the number of individual lamps you require to achieve the proper level of irradiance.

The length of the day is an important factor in regulating the growth of many species, and coral reef denizens are no exception. Reef fish and invertebrates usually do best with twelve hours of light daily. Use a timer to control the lighting system and provide a consistent day-night cycle. Large installations with complex lighting systems can mimic not only dawn-to-dusk fluctuations but also incorporate night illumination corresponding to the phases of the moon. While it is certainly not necessary to go to such lengths to have a successful reef tank, the lunar cycle definitely influences the reproductive cycle of many corals in their natural habitat.

Lighting a Living Reef Tank

You cannot grow corals and their relatives, or giant clams, or seaweeds without sufficient light, but unless the water conditions are also correct, you will end up growing only filamentous algae, even if you have the best lighting system on the market. Besides light, seaweeds and invertebrates need pollution-free seawater with the correct chemical and physical parameters. If you aspire to owning a living reef tank, you should be aware that invertebrates are less tolerant than fish.

Foods and Feeding

Choosing foods appropriate for your aquarium should pose little difficulty if you keep a few basic points in mind. Saltwater fish tend to be specialists when it comes to food. Quite a few vegetarians exist, for example. Some of them feed on many types of algae, others need a specific kind. Carnivores can usually be satisfied with a varied diet, but some feed only on specific classes of food, such as crustaceans. Many predatory saltwater fish need the movement of living prey to stimulate their feeding response, and only learn to eat nonliving foods as a result of the aquarist's efforts. I have already mentioned that species with strongly specialized feeding requirements, such as coral-eating butterflyfishes, should be avoided altogether. I provide feeding recommendations at various points throughout the book, usually when a given type of fish is first discussed.

Feeding Invertebrates

Fish grab food and swallow it. Feeding them is straightforward. Invertebrates, on the other hand, provide some special challenges. Invertebrates exhibit a variety of feeding methods, from hunting to straining the surrounding water for particulate food items. As a result, they require captive diets tailored to those methods. Some soft corals, for example, rely entirely on the photosynthesis carried out by their symbiotic algae, and thus need no food at all provided lighting is sufficiently intense. The majority of corals also has symbiotic algae but nevertheless consume small particles of food when it is available. Some invertebrates feed almost continuously, others only at certain times of the day. Let's consider each feeding strategy you are likely to encounter.

FILTER FEEDERS

Filter feeders strain the surrounding water for particles of food. Usually, a particular animal specializes in particles of a certain size and has a feeding apparatus designed accordingly. Fanworms provide a good example. The worm's fan of feathery radioles entraps food particles and secretes mucus in which the food becomes embedded, preventing it from simply washing back into the sea. Along the midrib of each radiole, tiny hairs beat back and forth, creating a current that directs the mucus-coated food to the mouth, located at the center of the fan. Fanworms specialize in dust-sized particles and usually subsist quite well in a mature tank without specialized feeding. They respond well to small amounts of fish or shrimp juice, and they appear to capture brine shrimp nauplii, also.

Other types of filter-feeding invertebrates include sponges, which remove extremely small particles, such as bacterial cells, from the water. In fact, most sessile encrusting invertebrates are filter feeders. Virtually all corals and other coelenterates are capable of feeding this way to supplement photosynthesis. The nonphotosynthetic corals require feeding with brine shrimp and other products several times a day. Some species may feed only at night, others feed continuously. You can usually tell if a specimen is actively feeding, because its tentacles, radioles, or other apparatus is visible.

SCAVENGERS

Quite a few common invertebrates can be included in this group. Hermit crabs, shrimps, and brittlestars all scour the aquarium and seldom need to be deliberately fed. They perform a valuable service by cleaning up food missed by the other inhabitants of the tank.

Tiny Foods for Invertebrates

Besides live brine shrimp, there are many options for filter feeders. Various foods are sold for the purpose. You can also add the juice that collects when you chop seafood for feeding to the fish. Seafood can be puréed in a blender and strained through a fine net. The particles that pass through the net can be used as invertebrate food. With any of these nonliving foods care must be taken not to add an excessive amount, or you risk overloading the aquarium's capacity for waste removal. For this reason, and to avoid wasting the food, I suggest you use a medicine dropper or plastic syringe to squirt little "puffs" of food in the vicinity of the invertebrate you're feeding. It doesn't take much, maybe a teaspoon at a time. After all, these critters just sit in one place all day, so they have relatively small food requirements compared to an active, mobile creature. Filter feeders have such appeal for minireef enthusiasts that a plethora of commercial products for feeding them have appeared on the market.

GRAZERS

This group includes critters placed into the tank primarily for algae control. Snails and small hermit crabs constitute the "lawn-care" patrol. Sea urchins also feed on algae but are not above munching a piece of shrimp unnoticed by the fish. Larger invertebrates that need a steady diet of algae will eat fresh or dried seaweed or frozen foods containing a high proportion of green matter.

PREDATORS

A few invertebrates are active hunters, and many are capable of subduing a tank mate and killing it when no other food is available. Starfish, for example, normally feed off sessile invertebrates and bivalve mollusks. Predatory starfish can be distinguished from brittle stars because the latter have flexible, snaky arms, while the former are shaped like the stars on the American flag. The larger the starfish, the more likely it hunts for a living. Lobsters and crabs of all types, with the exception of anemone crabs, feed both by scavenging and predation. Large crustaceans of any kind are not to be trusted with small fish or delicate sessile invertebrates. Similarly, large snails are usually predatory, unless they have been sold specifically for algae control. Any of these invertebrates can be kept in an otherwise fish-only aquarium, assuming the fish won't pose a threat to them. They are not good choices for a miniature reef tank.

PHOTOSYNTHESIZERS

As already discussed, many invertebrates manufacture their own food with the help of symbiotic algae. Nearly all of these, with the exception of giant clams and a few types of coral, also feed on brine shrimp, uneaten fish food, and even fish feces that happen to fall on them. In this way, they obtain important nutrients not supplied by their symbiotic algae. As a rule, it is not necessary to feed photosynthetic invertebrates deliberately, as long as food is being added to the tank now and then for other inhabitants. However, no photosynthetic invertebrates do well with inadequate lighting. Most anemones have symbiotic algae, but all of them do best with a weekly feeding of a small bit of fresh shrimp or fish. A piece the size of a bean is adequate for a four-inch-diameter anemone, measured when fully expanded. Increase the size of the food in proportion to the diameter of the oral disk for larger anemones.

SPECIALIZED FEEDERS

Many types of invertebrates have specialized food requirements that cannot be easily met by everyone. If you are considering purchasing an unfamiliar specimen, make sure you understand its feeding requirements before you commit. Some mollusks, for example, require living corals as food. The beautiful harlequin shrimp feeds only on the tube feet of living starfish! With diligence, such specialists can be accommodated, but make sure you are up to the task.

Availability of Foods

Commercial fish foods can consist either of a single ingredient, such as freeze-dried brine shrimp, or a compound of many ingredients, such as most flake foods. The trick to providing a balanced diet for your aquarium is to feed a wide variety of foods, alternating among two or three kinds during the course of a week. If your fish are primarily vegetarian, you will find products made just for them. Supplement these with small amounts of animal protein, frozen brine shrimp, for example. Conversely, if your fish are primarily carnivorous, supplement their diet with small amounts of vegetable matter, such as products containing salt-water algae.

Fish food may be supplied as flakes or as pellets, in freeze-dried form or frozen. Many dealers also stock live foods.

Feeding

Beginning aquarists usually give too much food. This results in an excessive load on the filtration system, since uneaten food simply decays on the bottom of the tank. The notion that fish will eat themselves to death is nonsense, but the pollution in an overfed aquarium can certainly wipe out its inhabitants.

A fish's stomach approximates the size of its eye. Obviously, it will not take a lot of food to fill it up. One rule of thumb is to feed only as much as will be consumed in ten minutes. You can determine the correct amount for your situation by trial and error. When in doubt, feed less. Fish can go for a surprisingly long time, weeks in many cases, without eating, so the likelihood of starving them is quite small in comparison to the likelihood of polluting the tank with uneaten food.

Most people find twice daily feedings work best with their schedule. If your schedule permits, though, feed a community of smaller fish about five times daily with just a tiny pinch of food at each feeding. Feed about an hour after the lights come on in the morning, and again about an hour before darkness falls. You will need to modify this schedule if you have, for example, large predators like groupers and lion fish. For these, the usual feeding regimen is three or four times a week. On the other hand, vegetarians feed almost continuously. These fish do best when there is plenty of algae growing in the tank to supplement the twice daily feedings.

Be careful not to feed vegetarian fish a diet rich in animal protein, even though they may eat such food greedily. The vegetarian digestive system is not designed to cope with such a diet, and problems will develop. Similarly, fish that need plenty of animal protein will not get enough to eat if kept on a diet better suited to vegetarians.

In the natural environment, of course, diets consist mostly of living foods. Some live foods can be cultured at home, provided you have the time and inclination. Ideally, one would feed only live food, but this is usually impractical at home.

Live Foods from the Aquarium Store

Virtually all aquarium dealers stock feeder goldfish. They are sold by the dozen and keep well for a week or so in a small, aerated container. Ten gallons of water accommodates about one dozen. Instead of a glass tank, you can use a plastic trash can outfitted with an airstone. Goldfish do fine in cold water and can be kept outside year round, as long as the water does not freeze. If you only purchase, let's say, a dozen a week, change the water between batches of goldfish. Unfortunately, only large, predatory tropical fish will consume them, so feeder goldfish are not for every aquarist.

You can also buy feeder guppies by the dozen at the aquarium shop. They will be eaten by any fish large enough to swallow them. Since they breed continuously, you can have many different sizes of guppies, from newborn to adult, available at all times to suit the varied sizes of fish in your aquarium. Fifty adult guppies are fine in ten gallons of water, provided it is well aerated and the water is changed between batches of feeders. They can tolerate water temperatures down to about 50°F, and so can be kept in an unheated garage or outbuilding during the winter. In warm weather, they thrive in a small outdoor pond or child's plastic wading pool located away from direct sunlight. To maintain a high population density, the aquarium or pond requires filtration or a weekly change of half the water.

Some shops stock live blackworms. These are small relatives of the earthworm that live in clean, cold water. Shops sell them in portions of a tablespoon or two. Purchase a shallow plastic food-storage container at the grocery store. The ones designed to hold a sandwich are perfect. Place the blackworms in the container and cover them with no more than a quarter inch of tap water. Store in the refrigerator. Remove a few worms every day with a spoon and feed them to your fish. Rinse the worms and change their water each day. Simply pour off as much as you can and replenish with cold water straight from the tap. Repeat a couple of times until the water rinses off clear. Treated this way, the worms will keep a week or two easily. The hard part about keeping blackworms is negotiating with the other members of the household regarding the refrigerator space.

Live adult brine shrimp can be found on the menu at many good aquarium shops, particularly those that stock saltwater fish. They are usually sold in portions amounting to about two teaspoons when the shrimp are drained in a net. Because they don't keep too well without careful attention, it is best to purchase a small quantity and feed them to the tank within a couple of days. Use a net to separate the shrimp from the strong salt solution in which they grow. Rinse under the tap before adding to the aquarium. They will die within about an hour in fresh water. Therefore, make sure to feed only the amount likely to be eaten by your fish within a short time.

With the exception of brine shrimp, the foods just mentioned should not be fed exclusively to your saltwater fish. Their nutritional needs are better met by foods derived from marine sources. Live marine feeder fish are impractical as food unless the aquarium is near the ocean. It is therefore often necessary to train predatory saltwater fish to accept nonliving foods such as frozen fish.

Culturing Live Foods

Live foods for the saltwater aquarium can be cultivated at home. You will need some extra space and equipment, but the added effort will pay off in healthier, more vibrantly colored fish and thriving invertebrates.

BRINE SHRIMP NAUPLII

Larval brine shrimp, known as nauplii (singular, nauplius), have been used for decades as fish food. They are rich in nutrients and can be easily hatched from the resting cysts, often incorrectly referred to as brine shrimp eggs. The ability to breed and subsequently rear saltwater fish in hatcheries depends upon the use of brine shrimp nauplii, once the fry grow large enough to take them. The cysts, nearly indestructible, keep for months, even years, with proper storage. They are collected from evaporation ponds and other highly saline environments, and look like coarsely ground cinnamon. Hatching them is a cinch.

Fill an empty wide-mouth quart jar with water up to the shoulder and add two tablespoons (about an ounce, or thirty grams) of synthetic seawater mix. (Seawater mix is available wherever saltwater aquariums are sold.) Drop in an airstone and connect it to a pump. Aerate the water vigorously. You will want to locate your brine shrimp hatchery where the salt spray will do no harm, as it is impossible to keep it from splattering out of the container. The jar should be in a spot that remains around 75–80°F. Bright, indirect light will improve the yield of the hatch, but keep the jar out of direct sun, or it will get too warm. As soon as the salt mix dissolves, add 1/4 teaspoon of the cysts. They will hatch in twenty-four–fourty-eight hours, depending upon the temperature. The warmer the water, the quicker the hatch. You can see the tiny nauplii swimming jerkily in the water. When you are ready to harvest, turn off the aeration. This will allow the empty cysts to float to the top of the container. Separating the cysts from the shrimp is the main difficulty in using brine shrimp nauplii. If the cysts are added to the aquarium, they will form an unsightly ring just above water level, and they can be harmful if fish ingest them. The nauplii are attracted to light, and you can exploit this trait to collect them. Make a sleeve out of thin cardboard that will encircle the jar, cutting a one inch hole just above the bottom. When you are ready to harvest shrimp, place the sleeve around the jar and shine a flashlight into the hole. The shrimp will gather at this point, from which they can be siphoned out with a length of flexible plastic tubing. Trap the nauplii with a net, and rinse under the tap before adding them to the aquarium. They will be relished by virtually all tropical fish. Like the adults, the nauplii survive only about an hour in fresh water, so feed accordingly. Try to feed your entire hatch within forty-eight hours because the nauplii will lose much of their nutritional value during that time.

BRINE SHRIMP ADULTS

Nauplii can be grown to adulthood if you have the space. Fill a shallow container that holds at least fifty gallons, such as a child's plastic wading pool, with synthetic seawater prepared at the ratio of four ounces of dry seawater mix per gallon. The container should be located in bright light but out of direct sun. Add a pinch of soluble garden fertilizer (such as Miracle-Gro) and a quart of either natural seawater collected from the ocean or water from an established saltwater aquarium. After a couple of weeks, the water in the rearing container will be green with algae growth. Hatch the cysts as just described and add the nauplii to your rearing pond. They will feed on algae and grow to adulthood in about two weeks. You can feed them to your fish at any point. About once a week, add another batch of nauplii. In this way you will be able to grow a continuous supply of adults. When harvesting the adult shrimps, use a net with relatively open mesh, so smaller individuals can escape and grow.

ROTIFERS

Rotifers are nearly microscopic invertebrates that swim by means of specialized structures unique to their phylum. The saltwater rotifer, *Brachionus*, has been extensively used to rear larval saltwater fish. Cultivation of rotifers requires that you also culture the single-celled algae on which they feed and may not be practical to do at home.

PHYTOPLANKTON

Single-celled marine algae, collectively known as phytoplankton, are an important part of the diet of many filter-feeding organisms. If you have the space and equipment, phytoplankton can be cultivated, but most enthusiasts opt for commercial products. Believe it or not, bottled phytoplankton can be stored under refrigeration for several months.

Routine Maintenance

Change part of the water in your saltwater aquarium regularly. I recommend changing 10–15 percent per week, but you can do it biweekly or monthly, so long as you change roughly half the water every month. This simple procedure will do more to enhance the appearance of the tank and the health of the fish and invertebrates than anything else you do as an aquarist.

Changing Water

Aquarium shops sell various types of siphons for removing water from the tank. Purchase one with a long enough hose to reach from the bottom of the tank, over the top edge, and down to the floor. You will also need a couple of plastic five-gallon buckets. Use them only for aquarium maintenance. Don't mix garden fertilizer or paint in a bucket and then later carry water in it. You may inadvertently poison the aquarium.

Before removing water from the tank, make certain to turn off all equipment, especially the heater, which should be unplugged.

Fill the buckets and discard the used water until you have removed the correct amount. Refill the aquarium with previously prepared synthetic seawater.

> **WARNING** If you expose the heater to the air, it will get hot enough to blister you if it should switch on. Subsequent contact with water is likely to cause the heater to crack, which may create a dangerous electrical hazard, and will certainly ruin the heater.

Carefully pour the replacement water into the tank. If the tank is a large one, you may find hoisting heavy buckets to its rim too much of a chore. In this case, purchase a small submersible pump and a suitable length of hose to take care of the work. A five-gallon bucket full of water weighs over forty pounds. Please don't hurt your back trying to lift this much weight in a controlled manner; do it only if you are physically up to the task.

The fish, of course, will freak out over the disturbance, but it is doubtful any will suffer long-term harm. Since you have to remove the light fixture to get at the tank, the darkness will help some in this regard. Once the tank is full again, switch the pumps and heater back on and check for normal operation. I suggest leaving the lights off until the next day to allow the fish to calm down. Don't feed them, either, on water-change day.

For a large built-in aquarium, the plumbing system should be designed to permit draining and filling the tank via the filter sump, as will be discussed in chapter 5, "Nuts and Bolts."

You may want to do some housecleaning as part of your water-change routine. This is a good time to clean algae from the front and sides of the tank, and to siphon out any noticeable accumulations of debris. It is likely that you will stir up fine debris in the course of maintenance. It will be removed once the filter is restarted. This is the ideal time to check and replace filter media, which may become clogged with particulate matter. I save the major work for once a month, but you may want to clean the inside of the glass weekly. Use a plain plastic scouring pad (such as Scotch-Brite) from the supermarket for this purpose if you have a glass tank. Acrylic tanks require the use of a cleaning pad made especially for them. In either case, always be careful not to get a piece of gravel or a grain of sand between the pad and the tank wall, or you will scratch it.

Before replacing the cover, clean it thoroughly on both sides with plain water and the scouring pad you use for algae removal. Water spots, dust, and algae on the cover glass can seriously reduce light penetration. If you maintain corals or other photosynthetic invertebrates, they will need all the light the fixture can provide. Also, wipe off the fluorescent lamp itself. You will be surprised how it picks up household grime due to the electrical charge it bears when in operation. Make a note when the tank is first set up, and on the anniversary date each year replace all the lamps in your fluorescent fixture. Light output decreases as the lamps age, even though you may not notice this visually. If using metal halide lighting, follow the manufacturer's directions regarding an appropriate lamp replacement schedule.

Now and then you will need to replace worn parts such as the impeller in your filter pump. Plan to do this, too, while the equipment is shut down for a water change.

Once you complete the water change and other routine maintenance, you will be amazed at how the tank sparkles. The benefits of a short time spent on maintenance will be clearly apparent.

Water Tests

One important aspect of maintaining your saltwater aquarium is keeping water conditions within rather narrow limits. It's easier to do than it sounds. Make regular tests, then make adjustments. For example, evaporation causes a gradual increase in salinity. This happens because only water leaves the tank, and the same quantity of salt thus becomes concentrated in a diminishing volume of water. Your job is to keep the change to a minimum, which you accomplish through maintenance. Checking the salinity weekly and adding fresh water to compensate for the loss is the appropriate response to evaporation. Similarly, for other important parameters, such as pH, alkalinity, and nitrate, test the water regularly and make appropriate adjustments when conditions begin to deviate from their target values. I like to say, "test and tweak."

Neglecting maintenance to the point that you can only bring the water conditions back in line by doing a massive water change virtually guarantees problems. This, nevertheless, is a common mistake. Regular testing and small corrections are the way to go. Buy good test kits, use them on a regular basis, and keep a written record of the results. Keeping a record lets you compare your results with previous tests, in order to refine your technique. You may learn, for example, that your aquarium evaporates about ten ounces of water every week, consistently. Knowing that, you can just add ten ounces of fresh water every Friday and dispense with testing until the next water change.

If the tank has been set up properly and maintenance carried out on schedule—and if you don't overstock or fail to feed the fish with restraint—it is unlikely that ammonia or nitrite, the two major pollutants that pose an immediate threat to fish health, will accumulate. If you do regular water changes, excess nitrate accumulation is unlikely, also.

With that in mind, it still pays to be prepared to take quick action in case the fish show signs of distress. It is always worthwhile to have a basic water chemistry lab available for troubleshooting purposes. For that I suggest purchasing test kits for the following:

- Ammonia
- Nitrite
- Nitrate

Aquarium water should never have any detectable ammonia or nitrite. The presence of either one indicates that biofiltration is not proceeding as it should. Immediate action should be taken to reduce the concentration of either of these compounds should you discover them. Change enough water to substantially reduce the level. Keep testing on a daily basis, changing water as needed, until the system returns to normal. Stop feeding during this time. The fish will not starve, and more food will only exacerbate the problem.

NITRATE

Nitrate is another matter. If you check nitrate just before doing a water change, you will note that it increases by about the same amount every month. Immediately after the water change, it will be reduced in proportion to the amount changed, that is, a 50-percent water change will reduce nitrate by 50 percent. By the next water change, more nitrate will have accumulated. The difference between the nitrate level immediately after a water change and the level immediately before next month's (or next week's) change represents the normal amount of nitrate production for your particular situation. A deviation from that norm means that something has upset the equilibrium established between ammonia production, biological filtration, and nitrate removal. Several factors can produce this deviation. Adding a fish produces a noticeable change, for example. Similarly, rotting food or a dead snail decomposing behind a rock adds ammonia, and this will eventually result in nitrate accumulation. Thus, it is important to keep a record of each nitrate test. Should an anomaly appear, try to identify an obvious explanation, e.g., new fish were added. Otherwise, you need to track down the culprit.

Ask yourself the following questions:

Did I carry out the test correctly? (It is always worth doing a confirming test before looking for other explanations.)

Have water changes been skipped?

Have fish been added?

Have I fed more than I normally do?

Is everyone present and accounted for? (Small fish or invertebrates sometimes die unnoticed.)

Have I added anything out of the ordinary? (Medications, especially, may disrupt bacterial activity and thus change the nitrogen equilibrium.)

Nitrate may be removed by natural processes, such as conversion to nitrogen gas by specialized bacteria. This process, *denitrification*, takes place in the absence of oxygen. Live rock (see page 64) harbors denitrifying bacteria beneath its surface, where oxygen cannot readily diffuse. Your partial water changes may constitute the primary way nitrate leaves the aquarium, particularly if it is a fish-only tank. Measuring nitrate accumulation allows you to spot anomalies that may be a sign of trouble.

The amount of nitrate produced per unit of time remains constant as long as conditions do not change. Conversely, changes in aquarium conditions will be reflected in changes in the nitrate concentration of the water. Each partial water change lowers the total amount of nitrate in the aquarium, creating a new point from which accumulation begins again. Note that the trend in nitrate concentration will always be upward unless 100 percent of the water was changed each month. At some point—I suggest every six months—you will need to do an extralarge water change to return the tank to a reasonable base line position with regard to nitrate. When fish are added a new, higher base line for nitrate is established, owing to the additional waste output. Adding more live rock, which increases the rate of denitrification, results in the removal of nitrate from the water. This changes the base line in the opposite direction. Invisible nitrate, therefore, can be an indicator of the overall biological activity in your aquarium. Thus, it is worth carrying out this one test on a regular basis.

How to Tweak Nitrogen Compounds

Finding ammonia or nitrite during a routine test is always cause for concern. Determine the source of the problem immediately.

Common possibilities are:

- The aquarium contains too many fish.
- Uneaten food or a dead animal is decaying in the aquarium.
- An antibiotic has been added to the aquarium, killing the nitrifying bacteria.
- There is a shortage of oxygen.

Responses to these problems are:

- Remove some fish.
- Find whatever is decaying and siphon it out.
- Remove the antibiotic with activated carbon filtration or by doing a large water change.
- Repair the pump or add additional powerheads to increase the water movement.
- Lower the temperature by installing a chiller.

The Nitrate Base Line

The best way to keep tabs on the balance between food going in and bacterial activity is by measuring nitrate accumulation weekly. Any increase in nitrate from the base line level indicates changes in the utilization of food. As fish grow, their food requirements increase. This results in a change in the nitrate budget of the whole system. Similarly, adding or removing specimens alter the slope of the accumulation line. As you add or remove specimens, regular nitrate measurements must be taken to determine the new base line. A stable system will show stable nitrate accumulation, and any sudden deviation should be taken as a warning sign. A system in nitrogen equilibrium has a nitrate base line of zero, because denitrification exactly balances nitrate production.

Not all nitrate tests are created equal. Some test total nitrate and some test nitrate nitrogen. Without going into the details, suffice it to say that you must always record the same parameter if your test results are to be of any value for comparison purposes. Don't switch brands of test kits, unless you are sure that the new kit is measuring the same thing your old one did. (Different brands that test the same parameter may give different results with the same water sample, but the difference will be slight.) If you simply cannot find, for example, a total nitrate test and are forced to rely on one for nitrate nitrogen, multiply the result by 4.4. Similarly, to convert total nitrate to nitrate nitrogen, divide by 4.4.

pH

If the pH is low because too much carbon dioxide accumulates in the water, increased water movement may be all that is needed to alleviate the problem. Keeping the aquarium at the correct pH can also be accomplished by adding a buffering agent to increase and stabilize the pH. A host of products are offered in aquarium shops for this purpose. Products that help both to buffer pH and to maintain alkalinity may be the most useful. Seawater mix brands vary in the degree to which they maintain the correct pH when mixed. Always check each new batch of seawater before using it. If you find consistent problems, try a different brand. The use of aragonite sand as part of the substrate can also aid in pH stabilization. As the sand slowly dissolves, ions are released, helping to maintain alkalinity and calcium levels. When the alkalinity of the aquarium is at natural seawater level or above, the pH tends to remain within a suitably narrow range. Test pH weekly and use one of the buffering additives if you need it. Make sure to follow the directions on the package.

CALCIUM AND ALKALINITY

You need to monitor and adjust the calcium concentration of the aquarium if you have a minireef. Corals, soft corals, clams, snails, scallops, shrimps, crabs, starfish, sea urchins, and even some algae all need calcium for their skeletons. Several techniques exist for keeping the calcium content of the aquarium close to that of natural seawater, 400 mg/L. A simple approach is to add limewater. Limewater is a saturated solution of lime in water. It is prepared by adding dry calcium oxide to distilled water, allowing the mixture to settle, and decanting. Use about two teaspoons of lime per gallon of water. Some undissolved powder should always remain at the bottom of the container. Calcium oxide is sold in supermarkets for making lime pickles, or you can purchase it at an aquarium shop. Use limewater to replace all evaporated water. Limewater is alkaline. Take care that additions do not drive the pH above 8.6 for more than a few hours at a time. An hour after adding a dose, check the pH. You can quickly determine how much to add on a routine basis after a few weeks of testing and keeping records. After that, just add the correct amount on a regular basis, and only check the calcium concentration once a month. Make up only enough limewater for a week's supply. Over time, atmospheric carbon dioxide will cause much of the lime to precipitate out of solution as insoluble calcium carbonate.

In aquariums with a thick substrate layer of aragonite sand, the pH will be very low in the anoxic regions deep in the substrate. The low pH causes aragonite to dissolve and return both calcium and carbonate ions to the water. Depending upon the makeup of the community of organisms in the aquarium, pH/alkalinity/calcium balance may be maintained through this process alone, and no limewater or other additives will be required. Other aquariums may need additional help in the form of limewater additions, as described above, or through enhancement of the aragonite dissolution process by means of a calcium reactor. This is simply a device that allows acidified distilled water to be passed over a layer of aragonite, which results in the enrichment of the water with calcium and carbonate ions. This water is then added to the aquarium to replenish evaporation. This technique avoids the drawbacks inherent in the use of limewater, but requires more work. You can purchase a calcium reactor, or make one yourself. It is basically a plastic pipe with screen at one end to keep the aragonite from falling out. Water is added at the top of the reactor, flows through the aragonite, and is collected below. Using distilled water to which a small amount of vinegar (about a tablespoon per gallon) has been added is most effective in dissolving the aragonite.

As acids are produced by the biological activity in the aquarium, alkalinity decreases. Restoring the alkalinity to normal levels is part of routine maintenance. Using a chemical additive such as limewater, adding aragonite sand to the substrate, or adding calcified water from a calcium reactor will all increase the alkalinity. The relationship between alkalinity and calcium concentration is reciprocal. Increase one, and the other decreases. In the early days in the life of your aquarium, you may have to experiment with repeated testing to determine the best way to keep pH, alkalinity, and calcium all within their proper ranges. Of greatest importance to the inhabitants of the aquarium is the pH, influencing as it does not only the respiration of fish, but the deposition of calcium carbonate by invertebrates. If the pH is correct, the specimens can get along with less than the natural amount of dissolved calcium. Therefore, focus on maintaining the correct pH. The higher the alkalinity, the easier this will be. If you do not use limewater or some other means of calcium supplementation because you have no invertebrates, there are plenty of commercial additives for maintaining the alkalinity.

Record Keeping

Because each aquarium is unique, there is no good substitute for a complete, conscientiously maintained record book. Buy a calendar, notebook, or three-ring binder and make notes regarding water changes, lamp replacement, and other routine maintenance. You can also jot down your observations on the behavior or growth of the fish and other inhabitants. Not only will having such a record help you remember things like when to change the filter pads, but also with time the notebook will become a history of the tank that you will enjoy looking back upon. If you find yourself wondering how old that clownfish is, you can check your records and find the date you placed it in the tank. This, for me, is part of the fun, and is also a good way to spot trends.

I like to use a loose-leaf binder to hold both aquarium records and documents like equipment manuals or instructions for test kits. I drop the binder in a large plastic bag and store it under the aquarium. The bag keeps out water damage, and the binder is there whenever I need it. Keeping everything organized and handy makes it easier to stay on top of maintenance and testing. If you have to scour the house for your notes and equipment, you are less likely to do what's required at the proper time.

Record the following information about your aquarium in the record book:

- Date

- Test(s) performed and results

- Anything added and amount

- Temperature

- Specific gravity and calculated salinity

- Amount of water changed

- Species and size of fish or invertebrates added

- Incidents of death or disease, treatments, and results

- Any comments or observations you think pertinent

Your aquarium record can be as detailed as you like. The more information you retain, the better. For example, why not use a digital camera to record the appearance of the aquarium at various times. You might want to have step-by-step pictures showing the aquarium in various stages of construction. Each time you add a new fish or invertebrate you create another photo opportunity. Don't overlook using the camera to record problems. You can even e-mail a picture of a sick fish to someone helping you with diagnosis.

Digital technology makes possible continuous monitoring and recording of some important aquarium parameters, not to mention automated control of lighting and other equipment. Temperature, salinity, and pH are relatively easy and inexpensive to monitor in this way. Some tests, such as those for ammonia and nitrite, are difficult to automate, but having other routine tests automated saves time for carrying out manual testing. Aquarium monitoring and control devices usually interface with a PC to permit display of information in various forms, such as a graph of pH versus time. You can find sources for such equipment on the Internet or in hobby magazines.

Equipment Maintenance

Everything wears out, of course, but you can prolong the life of your aquarium equipment by properly maintaining it. Doing equipment maintenance at the same time as your monthly water change makes sense.

1. Turn off the tank lights and unplug the fixture. If you use metal halide lighting, the lamps will need to cool down before you can move the fixture, or you risk damaging them. Besides, a dark tank makes the

whole operation less stressful for the fish. Check the light fixture for any signs of salt accumulation or corrosion. Remove any that you find with a cloth dampened in fresh water. If corrosion is developing, try to determine why, and take steps to prevent further damage. Aquarium lighting is designed to resist corrosion and to protect electrical connections from saltwater, so corrosion is a sign of improper installation or a break in the water barrier. Any damage you discover to the electrical parts of the lighting system should be repaired immediately by a skilled person. Such damage may pose an electrical or fire hazard. Problems such as this are rare with good-quality lighting equipment.

2. With a damp cloth, carefully clean dust and salt spray from the lamps themselves, as any accumulation will reduce the light output. You may need to remove the lamps from the fixture in order to do this effectively, depending upon the fixture design. Many fixtures also have a plastic sheet that protects the lamps. The side of the plastic nearest the water surface invariably becomes spotted from droplets of seawater. Again, carefully clean the plastic with a damp cloth, ensuring that the maximum light output reaches the aquarium.

3. Shut down the filter pump and protein skimmer.

4. Wipe clean the outer surfaces of all the plumbing fittings and hoses. You'll be surprised at how much dust they can accumulate. Also clean dust from any portion of the pump intended to ventilate the pump housing. Dust clogging the vents reduces the cooling effect, and makes the pump wear out faster. Pump designs differ from brand to brand. Follow the manufacturer's directions for cleaning and maintenance of the pump. If it's time to replace the impeller, do so now.

5. Disassemble the protein skimmer and clean it in the sink, in accordance with the manufacturer's recommendations. Usually, the skimmer collection cup and the tube through which foam rises toward the cup accumulate scum on their inner surfaces that interferes with efficient skimming. After a good cleaning to remove the scum, you'll find that foam "climbs" up the tube more readily, and you may need to adjust the skimmer to prevent overflow. Only a process of trial and error will permit you to set a schedule for skimmer maintenance, since every tank is different. Your skimmer may get thoroughly dirty in a week's time, while mine may take two weeks to lose efficiency because of accumulated gook. Try to develop a schedule that results in a relatively constant amount of foam being collected per unit of time. If you keep track of the volume each time you empty the collection cup, you will note that a sparkling clean skimmer produces mostly thick, dark green foam, while a yucky skimmer collects a lot of diluted foam and water. You want to strive for a happy medium between these two extremes during the course of a month. Because skimmer designs vary, and because the amount of organic matter in the water also varies from one aquarium to another, it is impossible to give exact guidelines for properly adjusting the skimmer. You'll get the hang of it after a month or two. Skimmers that use air diffusers may need these replaced every month or so, as they will become clogged with mineral deposits. Similarly, air-supply lines can develop mineral deposits where air and water come into contact. These deposits will eventually close off the line. They can be easily removed by soaking in a weak solution of vinegar and water, scraping with a toothpick, and rinsing in fresh water before reconnecting.

6. Always remember to unplug the heater before removing any water from the tank. Submersible heaters are usually trouble free, but it doesn't hurt to check for any damage as a regular part of your maintenance routine.

The "Hurricane Effect"

Every now and then a hurricane or typhoon strikes near a reef. Wind-driven wave surges break off tons of coral fragments. The hurricane also stirs up debris, making the water turbid. Despite the apparent devastation, a hurricane actually benefits the reef ecosystem by flushing out accumulated sediments and pruning the coral. Coral fragments that happen to land in a suitable spot often resume growth as if nothing happened, creating a potential site for a new patch reef to develop.

You probably won't want to be breaking off coral fragments in the process, but creating a "hurricane" in your saltwater aquarium now and then is not a bad idea. Sediment tends to accumulate on any horizontal surface in the aquarium, just like dust gathers on your furniture. Periodically removing it not only helps keep the aquarium looking tidy, but also exposes the area under the sediment to light, providing algae and sessile invertebrates a clean spot on which to grow.

Start by gently manipulating the top inch or two of the substrate layer with your fingers. This will stir up a lot of debris. If there are algae mats growing on the surface of the substrate, break them up with your fingers. Much of the sediment and algae will settle on the rocks and corals, but don't worry about that at this point.

Disconnect one of your powerheads. Holding it in your hand underwater, direct the outflow from the powerhead toward your live rock while someone else plugs the cord back in. Play the water jet over the surfaces of the rocks and corals, blasting debris into suspension where it can be picked up by the filter system. While the "hurricane" rages, you can also temporarily run a canister filter to "polish" the water by trapping most of the suspended sediment inside the filter. Try to sweep as much sediment as possible toward the front of the tank. With only a little practice, you will learn to operate the powerhead like a leaf blower to move piles of debris. When this step is completed to your satisfaction, turn off all pumps and allow suspended debris to settle out. Wait an hour or more. Overnight is fine. Then, use a length of hose to siphon as much of the sediment as possible off the bottom of the tank. Collect it in a bucket and discard. Top off the aquarium with freshly prepared seawater. Voilà! Hurricane complete, minireef freshly scrubbed. Doing this once or twice a year works wonders for keeping the aquarium looking healthy and sparkling.

Using a Maintenance Service

While I assume the owner of the aquarium will be the one taking care of it, the possibility does of course exist for a hands-off approach. An aquarium maintenance service makes a lot of sense if you lack the time required to give the aquarium the weekly attention it needs. Nevertheless, feeding and checking key conditions on a daily basis, especially for a reef tank, can occupy more than a few minutes. On a weekly basis, an hour or so is required to carry out testing and record keeping, and part of the water should be removed and replaced with previously prepared synthetic seawater. Seaweeds, and even some invertebrates, may require pruning, algae may grow in places where you don't want it, and equipment will need servicing. Depending upon the size of the tank, maintenance may thus involve more time than you can spare. Because conditions in even the best-designed system tend to deteriorate quickly without regular maintenance, if you don't have the time for upkeep, you will need to hire someone to carry out these chores to avoid disaster.

If you decide to go this route, choose the service with care. Make sure responsibilities, yours and theirs, are clearly understood. Confirm that the price quoted covers both labor and materials, such as synthetic seawater, that will be replaced in the course of normal care. If supplies cost extra, you should have the option of shopping for them yourself, rather than purchasing only from the maintenance company. Everything should be spelled out in a written agreement. The cost for professional maintenance can be considerable, and most companies charge a monthly minimum. However, proper care is the key to long-term enjoyment from any aquarium, but especially so in the case of saltwater. Failing to appreciate this fully has resulted in many a would-be aquarium owner's disappointment.

SUMMARY

You don't need a scientific background, or a lot of experience, to have a successful saltwater aquarium with thriving fish and invertebrates. All you need to do is use common sense and stick with my basic rules. In summary, they are as follows:

- Set up the largest aquarium that your resources can accommodate.

- Know the optimal conditions for saltwater chemistry, and maintain those conditions in your tank.

- Choose a lighting system adequate for corals and other photosynthetic organisms, if you choose to include them in your tank. There is no substitute for light. Otherwise, use plastic reproductions.

- Understand the critical process of biofiltration.

- Add fish gradually. Start with no more than 10 percent of the total number you eventually will keep in the tank. This allows biofiltration to keep pace with the fish population.

- Add hardy fish first. Save delicate species for later, when the tank is more stable.

- Always choose fish and invertebrates with care. Even if you follow a recipe from this book precisely, bringing home a sick fish will create problems.

- Understand why nitrate is an indicator of the overall condition of the aquarium.

- Feed a varied diet in small amounts.

- Carry out partial water changes on a regular schedule without fail.

- Keep a notebook of observations, such as water test results, to refer to when making changes or diagnosing a problem.

Most importantly, sit quietly near the tank for a short while each day and watch what's going on. Not only will you learn a lot about the coral reef environment, your stress level will decrease, you'll learn to relax, and, hopefully, you will live longer. Not a bad trade-off, in my view.

CHAPTER 2

BRINGING OUT THE BEST IN SALTWATER AQUARIUMS

S etting up a successful coral reef aquarium involves more than just placing a bunch of fish and inverte-brates in a glass box. Although as we saw in the previous chapter 1, "Caring for an Aquarium," the coral reef environment is physically and chemically similar across the planet, the lifestyles of the reef's inhabitants are extraordinarily varied. On the reef, competition for food, living space, mates, and even sun-light is fierce. Fishes, invertebrates, and even seaweeds have evolved a remarkable suite of strategies for win-ning the struggle for survival. They do not abandon these strategies when removed to a captive reef. It behooves the aquarist, therefore, to learn how to make wise selections that result in a compatible community.

Guidelines for Design

Creating an aquarium involves bringing together diverse elements, both living and nonliving, and integrating them into a functioning system. An aquarium is not a true ecosystem, of course, but does tend to exhibit many of the characteristics of natural ecosystems. A simplistic example is the formation of an aquarium food web. Even in the absence of added food, an aquarium contains producers, consumers, and degraders, whose lives depend, at least to some extent, upon each other. Algae growing on a rock harbors small crustaceans that are eaten by a fish, which in turn excretes waste that is broken down by other organisms, ultimately pro-ducing nitrate that fertilizes another round of algae growth.

Years ago, aquarium literature often made mention of the ideal, balanced aquarium, in which this cycle of production, consumption, degradation, and reuptake proceeded indefinitely in the absence of external influ-ences such as feeding or water changes. Few, if any, aquarists achieved this ideal, not because it is impossible to accomplish, but rather because it takes a huge volume of water and a great many plants to support a small population of fish. Setting up a one-hundred–gallon aquarium to house a few one-inch fish seemed like wasted effort.

In fact, modern filtration systems are designed and deployed with one primary goal: to increase the number of fish that can be housed in a given volume of water. The aquarium remains balanced only so long as the filter system properly functions. The implication of this simple principle is obvious: Effort must be expended on a continuous basis to keep the aquarium functioning properly. It will not "take care of itself." If we make the mistake of beginning with a collection of species having widely divergent needs, we compound the problem because providing for one of them may simultaneously work against the interests of another. The aquarium, in effect, is constantly teetering on the brink of disaster. Eventually, a tipping point is reached, and the impending disaster becomes reality. Too often, this is the experience of the home aquarist. Therefore, the first priority for good aquarium design is to emulate conditions that favor a natural balance:

- A relatively large volume of water
- Control of waterborne pollutants
- A relatively small number of fish

Beginners often find the huge variety of saltwater aquarium fishes, invertebrates, and seaweeds, each with its peculiarities and special needs, extremely daunting. The possibilities seem endless. Indeed, they almost are. If we were to try to list all possible combinations of just twenty kinds of fishes and invertebrates, for example, we would end up with more than a million billion aquarium designs.

Fortunately, ways can be found to sort out all of this diversity. By applying a simple set of guidelines, the process of designing a successful aquarium can be greatly simplified. Here are the guidelines I have developed over the years:

- **Focus on a single biotope.** A biotope is a small geographic area, such as a lagoon, with characteristic kinds of life. Reef biotopes can be characterized by a variety of factors. They can vary with respect to the water depth, substrate, current, and so forth. Aquariums featuring fish and plants from only one biotope are far more likely to remain free of problems than those cobbled together with species from a diversity of biotopes.

- **Focus on one or a few fish species.** Hundreds of species of saltwater fishes are collected or raised for the aquarium. No individual aquarist is likely to see them all, much less have the opportunity to keep them in a tank at home. Smaller tanks are likely to fare better with only one species, while a large tank devoted to only one species is truly stunning. For most aquarium displays, though, the ideal community of inhabitants comfortably occupies the middle ground between monotonous and chaotic. Regardless of how many species you wish to exhibit, allow at least 20 gallons of water for each individual fish.

Selecting Invertebrates and Fishes

The options may seem endless when it comes to all the saltwater fishes and invertebrates you have to choose from to stock your tank. However, by making the following considerations you can make selections that work well for your tank.

Types of Fishes

The commercial trade in coral reef fish provides us with comparatively few large groups into which virtually all species can be sorted. Looking at potential aquarium inhabitants in terms of which group they belong to makes more sense than trying to treat each variety as unique. Thus, we can identify five basic types of marine aquarium fish:

1. Large, aggressive predators
2. Peaceful community fish
3. Bottom-dwelling scavengers
4. Algae and plant eaters
5. Oddballs

Large, aggressive predators and oddballs usually do best if provided with a tank to themselves. Representatives of the other three groups can be combined in one tank to create a community that reflects a natural biotope.

TAKING SIZE INTO ACCOUNT

Some fish are just naturally better aquarium fish than others. A good aquarium fish should remain relatively small at maturity. Space and money constraints limit aquarium size. The size of the tank defines the upper limit on fish size within it, obviously. Custom-built aquarium systems, of course, can be any size your budget permits, but most people reading this book will be considering systems holding 150 gallons or less. That translates into a six-foot-long tank, the largest most stores have in stock. Unless you intend to exhibit only one or two fish, four inches is about as large as any individual specimen should grow to be. Many possibilities exist in this size range, although as a rule saltwater fish grow large.

That said, we won't rule out larger fish species in the model designs presented later. We'll simply use only one fish as the focal point, or recommend a community of two or three species suitable for a really large home tank.

ASSESSING ADAPTABILITY

A good aquarium fish should also adapt readily to captive circumstances. This would seem obvious. Yet, plenty of fishes are doomed to an early death simply because their ecological requirements are difficult or impractical to satisfy in a home aquarium. Some species will only take live food. We have already mentioned butterflyfishes that feed exclusively on coral polyps as an example. Some fishes just do not ship well. They arrive at the dealer in poor condition and never manage to recover. While I have not ruled out the use of wild-caught fish in the model designs presented later, I encourage you to begin with selections from the many tried-and-true varieties that are available from hatcheries.

CONSIDERING COLORATION AND BEHAVIOR

A good aquarium fish should either exhibit brilliant coloration or possess some interesting behavioral quirk to justify the effort required of the aquarist. Some marine fishes sport beautiful colors as juveniles, then grow into drab, gray adults. On the other hand, the various species of lionfish are mostly brown and white in color, but their elaborate finnage and graceful movements endear them to aquarium keepers. Behavior involving specific relationships can form the basis for a fascinating small aquarium. Nowhere else on Earth does symbiosis flower as it does on the coral reef.

Symbiosis literally means "living together." Two different species (and sometimes more) are characteristically found together. The exact relationship may take many forms. Perhaps the most widely recognized example is that of the clownfish living among the tentacles of a host anemone. Of greatest importance to the life of the reef is the symbiosis between corals and photosynthetic algae. Known collectively as zooxanthellae, the algae live within the tissues of certain corals and participate in all manner of important metabolic functions. Keeping the zooxanthellae happy is the prime goal of any minireef aquarium design.

Types of Invertebrates

Invertebrates, although they appear in great profusion in the aquarium trade, can, like fish, be sorted into relatively few groups. These are:

1. Photosynthetic invertebrates (except clownfish host anemones)
2. Clownfish host anemones
3. Utilitarian invertebrates
4. Other nonphotosynthetic invertebrates

Each group has a role to play in the minireef tank, while fish-only aquariums are usually limited to the last two groups.

Seaweeds

Seaweeds can add the perfect touch to a saltwater aquarium. I broadly define *seaweed* as any desirable algae visible to the naked eye. My definition therefore includes encrusting, calcified varieties known as coralline algae, as well as green, leafy types that resemble terrestrial plants. Depending upon the availability of light, seaweeds figure in the ecology even of fish-only aquariums.

CAPTIVE PROPAGATION

Far more varieties of invertebrates and seaweeds come from captive propagation than is the case with fish. Seaweeds have been cultivated for centuries. Techniques for their commercial production have been adapted for the aquarium varieties. Many species of invertebrates can simply be cut into pieces, and each one will regenerate a completely new specimen. Analogous to the production of horticultural varieties, "fragging" invertebrates has become something of a cottage industry among dedicated reef enthusiasts. Even organisms with more elaborate life cycles, such as giant clams, are hatchery produced.

One of the most useful saltwater aquascaping materials, live rock, is farmed by depositing quarry rock at sea, and coming back in a year or so to bring it up again. Live rock harvesting is prohibited in some places and allowed in others, providing the market with both farmed and "natural" types.

I urge aquarists everywhere to seek out captive-propagated fish, invertebrates, seaweeds, and live rock, and to look for collected specimens that have been harvested sustainably.

Quarantine Tanks

By far the best way to ensure that your saltwater aquarium display remains as free of problems as possible is to quarantine all new fish in a separate tank for a week or two after you bring them home. Any problems that develop can thus be treated without affecting the main display tank. The quarantine tank need not be an elaborate system, and needs only to be large enough for the maximum size and number of fish that you anticipate purchasing at any one time. Thirty to fifty gallons is about right for most saltwater aquarists. You will need a separate tank with sufficient light if you plan to quarantine invertebrates as well as fish. Twenty gallons will probably be enough for the largest invertebrate specimen you might obtain. In both tanks, provide hiding places for new arrivals. You can use short sections of plastic drainpipe for this purpose. Maintain conditions in the quarantine tank to match those of the main tank to minimize stress when you transfer specimens. If you have a large display aquarium holding a valuable collection of fishes and/or corals, a quarantine tank should be considered an essential part of your total aquarium system.

Acclimating New Arrivals

New fish require a gradual process of introduction into their new aquarium. Aquarists call this acclimating the fish to the new tank. You should acclimate all new arrivals to your quarantine tank as described below. Moving them to the display aquarium later does not call for another acclimation routine, provided conditions match in the two tanks.

First, make sure your quarantine tank is in good shape before you plop in any newcomers. Do a partial water change a couple of days before you expect to bring a fish home. Placing an already stressed (from the move) fish into poor water conditions practically guarantees problems.

The dealer will place the fish in a plastic bag filled about halfway. Most dealers fill the bags with oxygen, add a second bag to help guard against a puncture and then place the bag in darkness as soon as possible. All this trouble helps reduce fish stress, but will be moot if you do not take precautions, also. Please don't make the fish store your first stop on an extended shopping excursion; head straight home with your new acquisition. Don't stop at the supermarket on the way. If you leave the bag sitting in a hot or frigid car, you are asking for trouble. You might even parboil the fish in the bag.

As soon as you arrive home, turn off the aquarium lights. Darkness helps to calm the new fish. Float the unopened bag in the quarantine tank for thirty minutes. Then gently open the bag and roll down the top like a sock. Next, transfer about a cup of water from the tank to the bag. Continue dipping water from tank to bag every ten minutes until the bag sinks, allowing the fish to swim out. Some aquarists do not allow the bag to sink. They scrupulously avoid introducing any of the water from the bag into their aquarium. Instead, they remove the bag and dump it through a net, straining out the fish, which is then plopped into the tank. The stress imposed on the fish by this treatment probably outweighs any benefit. You also run the risk of the fish becoming entangled in the net.

Should the fish exhibit obvious signs of distress during acclimation, go ahead and remove it from the bag and place it immediately in the tank. Leave the lights off until the next morning. It may take a few days for the fish to start eating. Some species hide for a while at first. By the end of a week, though, your new fish should be searching for food. Offer live food, if possible, or whatever the dealer says the fish has been eating previously, at the first sign of interest. Once the fish starts eating, stick to the same schedule as you follow for the display tank, which depends upon the type of fish.

During the quarantine period, check daily for signs of disease. See "Selecting Healthy Fish" on page 13, as well as the information on identifying and controlling disease problems in chapter 6.

Developing a Stocking Plan

Just as you must plan the physical layout of the aquarium, you must also develop a plan for stocking it. You cannot put in everything at once because this will quickly overload the filtration system and cause problems. Knowing what to add and when structures your stocking plan.

Once the aquarium is partially filled with seawater and the filtration system is running, dead substrate material (if used) is added first. Add live sand (if used) in a layer on top of the substrate. Either dead or live rock next may be placed on top of the sand, stacked in a realistic-looking arrangement. At this point, you must begin operating the lighting system to encourage seaweeds and filamentous algae to grow. After about two weeks, you can add utilitarian invertebrates such as small hermit crabs, algae-eating snails, sea urchins, brittle stars, and burrowing sea cucumbers, depending upon compatibility with the eventual fish population, of course. A week or so after that, add mobile invertebrates such as small starfish, shrimps, and crabs, unless they need a fish or an anemone as a symbiotic partner. Symbiotic partners, with the exception of anemonefish and their respective anemones, should be added simultaneously, near the end of the stocking period.

When the shrimps and other mobile invertebrates have settled in, seaweeds can be added. Allow them to grow for at least two weeks before you add more animals. You may find they grow enough to require a bit of pruning, even in this short time frame. Even though seaweeds may eventually be eaten by fish, their presence early in the stocking phase of the aquarium helps to condition the water.

Now the tank is starting to take on the appearance of a natural reef biotope, and you can begin adding photosynthetic invertebrates if they are to be a part of the display. Try to place them where they won't touch each other, and be sure to allow room for growth. Make sure they are located where they will receive plenty of light.

By now the aquarium should be showing signs of maturity such as the presence of numerous, nearly microscopic invertebrates in the substrate and on the rocks. These tiny crustaceans are feeding on microorganisms too small for you to see, but which nevertheless are vital to the aquarium ecosystem. They may, in turn, become food for invertebrates and fish.

Once the aquarium has reached this stage, there should be enough natural food present to feed nonphotosynthetic, filter-feeding invertebrates such as fanworms. Corals and anemones also benefit from the presence of natural foods. If you plan on cultivating an host anemone, now is the time to add it.

Fish should be added to the aquarium at the end of the stocking period. Pay attention to the information on aggressiveness given in the descriptions of fishes. As a rule of thumb, add docile fishes first, giving them an opportunity to stake out a territory, before adding more aggressive species. Bold species, such as surgeonfish and dwarf angelfish, should be added last. Anemonefishes can be added as soon as their host is settled and thriving. If you plan to keep anemonefishes without a host, add them any time.

> WARNING Don't add new fish more frequently than every two weeks. Altogether, it takes about a year for a new saltwater aquarium to be stocked completely. Don't try to rush it, and observe the tank carefully for problems shortly after each new addition. Most problems occur within the first two weeks that a critter is in the tank.

SUMMARY

Creating a successful saltwater aquarium involves two major efforts:

1) Establishing and maintaining proper conditions of water chemistry, lighting, gas exchange, and biological filtration.

2) Choosing a community of fish and/or invertebrates appropriate not only to the capacity of the tank but also to each other's normal behavior and temperament.

In this chapter, I have provided the essential information needed to guide your planning in these two areas. In the following chapter we will turn our attention to combining the essential elements so as to achieve a natural looking and aesthetically appealing aquarium.

CHAPTER 3

MAKING YOUR AQUARIUM LOOK REAL

I endeavor to design aquariums that reflect nature. One basic approach I employ is to combine fish, invertebrates, and other materials that come from the same geographic regions, although I sometimes combine elements from different areas of the world that share similar biotopes. Incorporating elements from the same geographic region or biotope type is the first step in making the artificial aquarium habitat look like a genuine coral reef. Arranging invertebrates and/or nonliving elements with care completes the illusion.

Freshwater aquariums vary quite a bit in terms of temperature, pH, water hardness, and so forth, while coral reef aquariums all require the same water chemistry and temperature. Except for its capacity, however, one freshwater filtration system is pretty much like another. This is hardly the case with saltwater systems, though all designs share the goal of creating a satisfactory substitute for the coral reef environment.

Many modern saltwater aquariums are much more than mere displays of fishes. They are true miniature reefs, usually abbreviated "minireef." To be sure, a minireef offers more challenges than an aquarium featuring only fishes. You have more kinds of critters and their respective needs to cope with. Water quality maintenance often involves more tests and more adjustments. On the other hand, some aspects of a minireef work in the aquarist's favor. The more diverse biological community that develops in the minireef actually helps to maintain stable water conditions by natural means. To a great extent, a mature minireef takes care of itself. In the case of the fish-only aquarium, the filtration system and the aquarist carry the primary responsibility for water quality maintenance. For this reason, the emphasis is on the minireef in the model designs I suggest.

The success of all the types of minireef designs described later results from facilitating the natural chemical, physical, and biological cycles that develop in the aquarium. These processes are mediated by microorganisms and tiny invertebrates, in the same way that soil bacteria and earthworms create suitable conditions for the plants in a garden. The organisms fulfill their important functions in the artificial ecosystem with the same efficiency they exhibit in the sea. In minireef aquariums, the largely unseen organisms forming the base of the ecosystem actually create water conditions suitable for themselves and other reef dwellers. The minireef may display a stunning collection of fish and invertebrates, but the invisible microscopic life actually plays the lead role.

Space Limitations of Tanks

The most significant constraint on your design will be imposed by the tank. The front glass is the window into the microcosm you create within. This effect is greatly enhanced with a built-in tank, which is often surrounded by molding or trim work that gives the impression of a framed picture. If the tank is free-standing, develop your design by thinking only about the view from the front, as if it were a picture. Consider also how this picture will be framed by the support furniture. The cabinet or stand should not be a distraction. Stick with simple lines and colors that blend with the surroundings.

Remember that even the most naturally designed aquarium requires a life-support system. You must sacrifice some portion of the available space to accommodate equipment. For a natural look, you want that equipment to be as inconspicuous as possible. Therefore, give some thought to the arrangement of the equipment while the aquarium is in the planning stage. I suggest creating a scale drawing using graph paper to help visualize how the tank will look with equipment in place.

One lesson I have gained in years of aquarium keeping is to avoid trying to do too much within a single tank. Strip down your design to its essentials. It is always surprising how an aquarium that appears quite large when empty becomes confining when you begin to add decorations.

Tank Proportions and Habitat Types

Unless you plan on ordering a custom-built tank, you will have to make do with one of the stock sizes. In my experience, people usually purchase a tank based on their budget. I would suggest you consider both the size and proportions of any tank in terms of how your intended habitat will fit.

Appendix C lists typical aquarium sizes from 20 to 300 gallons. A quick inspection of this table reveals that manufacturers maintain certain proportions from one tank to the next. In aquarium lingo, *depth* is the distance front to back, while the dimension corresponding to water depth is referred to as *height*. Thus, a 20-gallon tank is two feet in length, a 30-gallon is three feet, a 40-gallon is four feet, and all three are the same height and depth. It is worth mentioning that tank capacities are nominal. The actual volume of water in the completed tank will be somewhat less.

Manufacturers produce tanks in different proportions with the same nominal capacity. Thus, you will see a 20-gallon *long*-style (base dimension 30 x 12 inches) only twelve inches in height, and a 29-gallon *high*-style with similar base dimensions but a depth of twenty inches. As a rule, long-style tanks are long and narrow and high-style tanks are exaggerated in height. The long-style lends itself to shallow water minireef designs, while high tanks work well for deep water or open-ocean designs. Some tank sizes shown are impractical for a minireef, usually because they are difficult to illuminate adequately.

Lighting

Lighting plays a critical role in aquarium design, as indeed it does in many other design situations, such as home interiors. Several aspects of aquarium lighting require attention:

- Aesthetic value: Light is obviously needed to allow people to see into the aquarium. Since it is rare to be able to illuminate with natural daylight, artificial lighting is installed above the tank. Lighting can be of two types: fluorescent or metal halide. Manufacturers produce both types, and some also make combination units. Fluorescent lighting predominates in most equipment packages because the initial cost of metal halide lighting is considerable.

- Coral growth: Lighting must be sufficiently intense for the needs of corals and other photosynthetic invertebrates living in the aquarium. For larger aquariums, metal halide lighting is absolutely required to provide enough light for proper coral growth. A single lamp provides enough light to illuminate four square feet of water down to a depth of eighteen inches.

- Engineering: Not only must aquarium lighting provide sufficient intensity and good color rendition, it has to fit the tank. Lighting equipment generates heat, and this must be dealt with to avoid overheating. Protecting the lighting equipment from water must also be accomplished, both to avoid electrical hazards and to prevent damage from corrosion and water spots. All of this, not to mention cost, must be taken into account when engineering an aquarium lighting system.

Lighting Systems

FLUORESCENT LIGHTING

Fluorescent lamps come in many types that vary in terms of their intensity, color, and the amount of electricity they consume. The most important of these factors from a purely aesthetic point of view is the color. Ever notice how people appear unhealthy under industrial fluorescent lighting? This is because the lamps typically used in such applications are the "cool white" type. This lamp imparts a yellowish green cast to everything, although it is supposedly the best for illuminating a work area. If you have ever taken a color snapshot (using film, not a digital camera) with only this type of lighting and no flash, you can see the green coloration.

Each type of fluorescent lamp has its own color rendition. Various lighting manufacturers produce 5000–5500°K fluorescent lamps under different brand names. If your aquarium shop does not stock them, check with a lighting company in your area. You can also check out the following Web site to find out the lumen output of typical 40-watt fluorescent lamps: http://palimpsest.stanford.edu/byorg/abbey/an/an16/an16-4/an16-406.html.

Fluorescent lamps come in stock sizes. The longer the lamp, the greater the light output and the amount of electricity consumed. Thus, 40-watt lamps are four feet long, 20-watt lamps are two feet, and so forth. If you are going to use a fixture that sets on top of the tank, and this is the most common design, you will be limited to the lumen output of a certain lamp size, for example, two feet for a twenty-gallon tank. You can always purchase an additional fixture, or one that accommodates two lamps. Once the tank reaches four feet in length, the lighting options are greater. For example, you can purchase an inexpensive fluorescent fixture, or "shop light," at a DIY store and hang it above the tank. Two of them will fit nicely side by side, giving you a total of 160 watts of lighting, enough for many photosynthetic species. You will need to allow for some headroom when working on the aquarium, as well as protect the units from water damage. Hanging them with a pulley system that allows the height to be adjusted works well.

Hanging lights over the tank may not appeal to you, and the finished look is certainly industrial. If the tank is built-in, of course, you can hide the lighting on the other side of the wall. For most of us, none of these will be an option, and we will use an enclosed "hood" or "canopy" that provides both a top for the tank and a housing for lighting equipment. Wood or laminate canopies that match the aquarium cabinet create a finished look to free-standing tanks that is hard to beat. You can purchase a canopy with up to four fluorescent lamps or with metal halide lamps.

The heat-producing transformer, or ballast, needed for fluorescent lighting may be dealt with in one of two ways. In the most common design, the ballast is located in the power cord and sits underneath the aquarium or on the floor, out of the way. Protect the floor finish with a cork pad if you place it there, as the ballast may get too hot to touch. For multiple fluorescent lamps, the ballast is often located within the lighting hood itself. This is because the needed wiring gets complicated, and you would have a fat bundle of cable running from the ballast up to the lamps. To prevent overheating, the manufacturer may install a small fan, such as the one in your computer, to ventilate the hood. A multilamp fluorescent hood may offer you the best balance between cost and lighting efficiency for tanks up to four feet long.

METAL HALIDE LIGHTING

My personal preference for aquarium lighting is metal halide. It provides the very bright light needed for a larger aquarium installation and is hard to beat for light output, color rendering, and durability. The lamps usually last about three times as long as comparable fluorescent lamps, which lose intensity with age. On the downside, metal halide costs considerably more, both for the initial installation and for replacement lamps. Further, the lamps get hot in operation and can be extremely dangerous if broken. Proper design, though, deals with these issues adequately. There are two options: hang the fixtures at intervals above the aquarium (sort of like the lighting above the bar in many restaurants), or use an enclosed hood similar to that described for fluorescent lighting. Hoods containing metal halide lamps absolutely require ventilation via one or multiple fans, and the lamps must be shielded from any contact with water by a clear, heat-resistant plastic panel or tempered glass. All these features contribute to the greater cost. If you are planning a tank much larger than fifty-five gallons, however, metal halide will give the most satisfactory results. A four-foot tank needs two lamps (about 150 watts each) and a six-footer requires three.

Manufacturers of metal halide equipment for aquarium use generally supply them with 5000–5500°K or higher lamps. Besides providing appealing natural coloration, metal halide lighting produces "glitter lines" as it passes through the constantly moving water surface, a decidedly realistic touch. Fluorescent lighting, being diffuse rather than a point-source of light, does not produce glitter lines.

Inverse Square Law

One reason larger aquariums need more light is the inverse square law. Simply stated, light becomes less intense the further you are from the source. This is common sense, of course, but the inverse square law tells us how much the intensity decreases: double the distance and intensity drops to a quarter of its previous level. The effects in an aquarium can be visualized from the table below, a table of light levels at various points below a fluorescent fixture.

The following table demonstrates how light intensity diminishes in relation to various distances from a light source. The researchers took measurements with a light meter underneath a shop light fluorescent fixture with two 40-watt cool-white lamps.

Lighting Table

Height	Foot-candles				
6 in	100	320	520	320	100
12 in	140	250	300	250	140
18 in	130	180	200	180	130
24 in	110	140	150	140	110
	12 in	6 in	Center	6 in	12 in

Horizontal Distance from Center

Data from Barbara Joe Hoshizaki, and Robbin C. Moran, *The Fern Grower's Manual.* (Portland, OR: Timber Press, 2001), 31.

You can see that a considerable drop in intensity occurs as one moves down and away from the center of the light source. To maintain even illumination over the entire aquarium usually requires multiple lamps, either fluorescent, metal halide, or a combination.

Safety and Maintenance

Every precaution must be taken to avoid creating an electrical hazard. We all know water and electricity don't mix! I'll have more to say in general about electrical safety and aquariums in the next chapter. For lighting equipment, specifically, look for units that are made of water repellent materials, that is, plastic, laminates, or properly finished wood. If the design incorporates a protective panel between the water and the lamps, check to see how easy it will be to remove this panel for cleaning. Water spots can significantly reduce the amount of light reaching the plants. No electrical connections should be exposed. When no protective panel is used, the end caps for mounting fluorescent lamps should be waterproof. Metal halide systems should always have a protective panel. The best advice regarding safety is to choose equipment made specifically for aquarium use.

Other than keeping dirt and water spots from blocking the light, maintenance of lighting equipment is minimal. Replace fluorescent lamps annually. Follow the manufacturer's recommendations on metal halide lamp replacement. Periodically inspect for damage that might admit water, and take corrective action.

Backgrounds

I confess an aversion to see-through aquariums. Looking past the fish and plants to view the room or persons on the other side just destroys for me the whole illusion of a natural scene. Nevertheless, I have included a couple of see-through designs in the book. Most tanks will need a background of some kind, both to block the view of the room or wall on the other side and to hide wires and hoses running up from the cabinet. Numerous options exist for backgrounds.

Solid Colors

My first preference for an aquarium background is paint. Simply use masking tape to protect the areas you don't want painted, and spray or brush on an exterior-type paint. Although it scratches easily, it is in the back and should not receive too much contact. Scratches therefore are not likely be a problem. Go ahead and paint the ends if you like, especially if the tank is a built-in, and the outside of the ends won't be seen, anyway.

I prefer paint for several reasons. First, it comes in any color you want and can be mixed to match anything you like. Second, it is cheap. Any leftovers can be saved to do touch ups or to paint another aquarium. Exterior paint stands up to the inevitable water spills. It can also be easily removed with a razor blade if you want to change it. Just remember not to try painting a tank unless it is empty. Paint solvents can be fatal to fish if they find their way into the water.

Aquarium shops sell background materials that come in rolls like wallpaper. Any of them can be taped to the back of the aquarium. Use freezer tape or package-sealing tape for this, as other kinds will eventually come loose in the humid environment around an aquarium. Make sure to use a continuous strip of tape along the entire length of the tank at top and bottom and along both sides. If you don't, foreign matter, dust, and even insects and cobwebs will get lodged between the glass and the background. Nothing more detracts from the appearance of the tank.

The color choice for a solid background is, of course, up to you. I strongly recommend restraint here. Flat black is my favorite choice, because it creates an air of mystery. Something lies beyond the aquarium scene that cannot be seen in the murky water. Black also works with any color of fish, plant, or decorative object. Shades of blue are my second choice. Light blue for an open-water scene, navy to suggest great depth. Stay away from white, or the aquarium will look like a box of water, which is precisely the opposite of the effect you are seeking. Please do not use bright foil or patterned materials. You don't want the background to be a distraction from what's going on in the aquarium.

Photography

Aquarium dealers sell backgrounds that are photographs of underwater scenes. These can be effective and attractive backgrounds, provided that the objects in the photo are 1) their normal size, and 2) appropriate to the rest of the aquarium. For example, you do not want a photo of a submarine in the background. This just looks silly. On the other hand, if the photo contains elements that can be repeated in the tank, corals, for example, you can create the impression of a scene stretching infinitely away from the viewer. Some large custom installations feature a photo background shot from nature and then duplicated with real objects in the aquarium. These are sometimes illuminated from behind the tank, creating a striking effect. Such museum-quality designs are, of course, expensive.

Dry Installations

One of the most effective backgrounds, though requiring considerable time and expense to create, is the diorama. Basically, this is a shallow wooden box placed behind the tank, visible through the back glass. It is illuminated, and contains an appropriate scene, recreated without water. This technique permits the use of materials, such as dried starfish, that might decompose if submerged. A diorama can also accommodate large, heavy chunks of coral rock or coral skeletons that might damage the aquarium tank if used within it. On the downside, the display must remain dust free, or the illusion is destroyed, and so requires regular cleaning. The diorama also needs illumination separate from the tank.

Including Terrestrial Components

Mangroves occur on nearly all tropical shores, often growing into the water and supporting themselves on prop roots. Thickets of mangrove roots provide shelter for many kinds of fishes and invertebrates, often including species found on a nearby reef. Mangrove roots also possess their own characteristic encrusting organisms. Sea grasses such as *Thalassia*, or turtle grass, grow in shallow silted areas and create another kind of habitat from which the saltwater enthusiast can draw inspiration.

Mangroves are easy to grow from their cigarlike floating seeds. You will be able to keep a single mangrove in the same aquarium for only a few years because they grow to be small trees. You can also use mature mangrove prop roots, with their characteristic arching shape, to suggest this habitat, or combine them with small living mangroves for the green foliage. Many saltwater dealers carry mangrove seeds or can order them for you.

Turtle grass requires very bright illumination and a deep layer of silty sand in which to grow, and thus poses special challenges in the home aquarium. It is therefore seldom imported by dealers, although it's easy for collectors to obtain. If you attempt the living seagrass model design on page 178, your dealer can probably order turtle grass for you. An easy alternative exists in the form of plastic reproductions of the freshwater plant, *Vallisneria*, which closely resembles turtle grass.

Aquascaping

The art of underwater interior design has been dubbed *aquascaping*. Just as naturalistic landscaping involves combining the living and nonliving elements of a garden in ways that reflect natural relationships, naturalistic aquascaping seeks the same goal underwater. Although aquariums are built on a much smaller scale than most gardens, you will discover that similar design principles apply to both.

Substrates

Substrate refers to the material covering the bottom of the aquarium. It may be purely decorative or may serve as part of the filtration system. Several materials lend themselves to these different applications:

- **Crushed coral gravel** with grains averaging about 1/8 inch in diameter up to about 1/4 inch in diameter is the most commonly used substrate. Coral gravel comes bagged, and is priced by weight. As a rough guide, twenty pounds covers a square foot of aquarium bottom to a depth of about two inches. Thus, a 24 x 12–inch tank requires forty pounds of gravel.

Buying in Bulk

For installations calling for large amounts of sand or gravel, you can save a lot of money by purchasing in bulk. Sand sold for sandblasting works great and is usually sold in fifty- to one-hundred-pound bags. For still larger quantities, these materials can be as cheap as five dollars a ton, even if you purchase only a couple of hundred pounds. Industrial materials need a thorough washing before being used for the aquarium. That chore is up to you, of course.

- **Natural sand** comes in many colors, ranging from charcoal to eggshell, and is also available. Often, these sands are dredged from a particular area, such as Fiji. Sand, with grains generally smaller than 1/8 inch, can be used instead of, or in addition to, gravel. You will need a little more sand than gravel to cover the same surface at the same depth, about twenty-five pounds per square foot. Avoid fine-grained beach sands, which tend to compact too densely.

> WARNING Please do me a favor and avoid that brightly colored dyed gravel. Some dyes can leach out and harm fish. They all tend to detract from the natural look of the aquarium and to compete with the bright colors of the tank's inhabitants. Colored glass, while completely inert, creates the same jarring detraction from the aquarium's natural beauty.

Decorative Materials

- **Coral rock,** which is fossilized coral reef, is quarried by the ton in, for example, the Florida Keys. Chunks up to about the size of a basketball can be used to simulate a reef when live rock is not used.

- **Plastic corals** and other reef denizens that look remarkably like the real thing have been successfully created by aquarium manufacturers. By all means use them if you wish, alone or in combination with natural materials. Plastic coral reproductions may be the best choice if you do not want to invest in the additional lighting and care that living corals require.

Placement

In all cases of aquascaping, bear in mind how the different materials are found in the sea. The largest pieces will dominate everything else when confined to an aquarium tank, so exercise the greatest care in choosing them, and the greatest amount of restraint in their number. For smaller tanks, limit yourself to three to five larger pieces of rock or dead coral. One large piece usually looks better than several smaller ones. It is often convenient, though certainly not necessary, to place the larger items near the rear of the tank, where they do double duty by hiding unsightly equipment. Large objects should be placed firmly on the tank bottom to avoid the possibility of them toppling. Secure them in place with dabs of silicone aquarium sealant, if necessary. When used, silicone must be allowed to dry and cure for several days before continuing. Move the tank into its permanent position at this point, if it is not already in place. Next, add most of the washed substrate, making sure it fills the crevices between the larger rocks. Sand, when used as a component of the substrate rather than as the sole substrate, should be added last, allowing it to sift naturally into crevices and holes. All this activity will probably leave you with cloudy water. You can start running the filter system at this point. The tank should clear up after a few days, and you can make adjustments to your design. If fine debris settles on top of the rocks, use a turkey baster to direct a jet of water at the debris, resuspending it to be picked up by the filter. You may need to do this several times to remove all the debris. Keep a close check on the filter, and replace or clean the medium when it becomes dirty. Doing all of this first, before you add fish or invertebrates, avoids stressing them needlessly.

On the wild reef, corals adapt their structure to local conditions of water movement, substrate, and light availability. On the turbulent outer reef, the open branching forms of small-polyp corals predominate. In quiet lagoons, large-polyp corals tend to outnumber the branched ones. On muddy bottoms, corals may be shaped like inverted cones, with points down in the mud. On hard substrates, individual coral colonies are firmly attached. On sandy bottoms dwell corals that are able to move around to position themselves for catching prey. It's worth paying attention to these proclivities in placing corals in your minireef. Appropriate placement gives the aquarium a natural appearance, and gives the coral the best chances for adapting successfully to captivity.

Place branching corals, such as *Pocillopora* and *Acropora*, near the top of the reef structure. Here, they will receive maximum illumination. Provide plenty of water movement by means of auxiliary powerheads directed near, not at, the coral. Corals can be secured to the rock in a variety of ways, depending upon how large the coral is and how precariously you want it perched on the rock. Cements for gluing rocks and corals together that set underwater are sold in aquarium shops and online. Glue joints may need to be reinforced. One way to do this is to drill a hole in both rock and coral with a masonry bit and insert a length of rigid plastic pipe tightly into each hole before applying the cement. For small pieces, use a plastic cocktail toothpick instead of the plastic pipe. Don't worry about having the coral or live rock out of the water. Hold them securely in a towel dampened with seawater, and drill away. They are so soft that the bit will cut quickly. You may want to practice on some pieces of dead coral and coral rock to get the feel before trying this on a valuable specimen.

Large-polyp corals that are shaped like an inverted cone, such as *Euphyllia* and *Trachyphyllia*, should ideally be placed on the sand where they can sink in as they normally do. Sometimes these corals grow attached by the tip of the cone to a rock. You can simulate this positioning by drilling and scraping out a small concavity for the coral to sit in. Corals positioned like this may attach themselves and grow onto the rock.

Corals that are able to move about on their own, such as *Heliofungia*, need to be placed on an unobstructed area of soft sand or fine, shelly gravel under brilliant illumination. If placed on top of a reef structure, they invariably try to relocate themselves and topple to the floor of the tank. Usually, they are damaged by the fall and seldom recover. The need for proper placement and a fairly large area in which to roam may explain why these corals are considered difficult to maintain in a minireef.

Borrowing from Japanese Gardeners

People seldom fail to notice the similarities between aquarium design and garden design. Good gardeners make good aquarists, and vice versa. The primary difference lies with scale. Gardeners generally have more than four square feet to work with, whereas a fifty-five–gallon aquarium provides only this much space. Among gardeners, the Japanese have mastered the art of making an impressive garden in a minimum of space. The *tsuboniwa*, or courtyard garden, the *bonseki*, or dish garden, and *bonsai*, or pruned dwarf trees, each draws upon basic principles of design to create the illusion of spaciousness. Four basic principles, developed over hundreds of years, exemplify this technique. Aquarists can apply the same rules. They are:

- Inspiration from nature
- Wildness versus control

- Personal expression
- Idealization

Let's consider how each of these works in designing an aquarium.

Inspiration from Nature

Throughout this book, I emphasize the value of taking inspiration from natural habitats to create aquarium habitats. This, however, should not limit us *solely* to combinations of fishes and corals from the same geographic region. Creating a harmonious aquarium community lies in selecting fishes and other organisms for the ecological roles they play. For example, the Indo-Pacific species of *Pseudochromis* can substitute for the Atlantic-Caribbean royal gramma. These fishes inhabit similar environments and fulfill similar ecological roles. Dozens of other examples can be found.

Wildness versus Control

A simplistic example of wildness versus control is the separation of predators and prey. Although the lionfish may feed on blue damselfish on the reef, we avoid combining them in the aquarium. Similarly, some invertebrates, such as soft corals, need regular pruning and thinning. We don't usually allow them to grow rampantly. Another, more subtle kind of control has to do with manipulating the viewer's perception of space. By the controlled placement of natural objects, fooling the eye into thinking a space is larger or smaller than it is in reality becomes possible. This technique, forced perspective, proves invaluable time and again.

For example, to make the aquarium look deeper, place an especially interesting, tall soft coral with bright coloration near the front glass, slightly to one side of center. A good choice might be *Gorgonia ventalina*, the common Caribbean sea fan. Use a spreading soft coral, such as *Pachyclavularia*, the green star polyp, to create a monotonous layer of color along the rear wall of the tank. In between, place a large piece of branching coral skeleton to obscure the middle ground. This arrangement distorts perspective and fools the eye into thinking that the space is larger than it is. The trick is to keep the view toward the back less well defined than the one in front. The eye will be drawn first to the more interesting object. When the forward object is taller than those in the rear, we tend to perceive the distance between them as greater than it actually is. This arrangement reverses the usual aquascaping advice to keep tall things toward the back.

Conversely, if your intention is to allow the viewer an imagined glimpse into an enclosed space, place a few specimens of the boldly colored *Tubastrea*, the orange polyp stony coral, toward the back of the tank. Frame the view with several tall, bushy gorgonians, such as *Eunicea*, the knobby sea rod, placed in each corner. The eye will again be drawn to the bright colors in back, and in effect bring them forward. In combination with the frame at the front, the arrangement gives the impression of a window into a secluded corner of the reef.

Personal Expression

Allow yourself to experiment with aquascaping until you achieve the look you want. An artistic design maximizes the stress-reducing value of the aquarium. You may evoke calmness or excitement with your choices. For example, fish that constantly dart around, such as tangs, and a strongly directional current create an upbeat mood. Enhance the effect by using bright lighting, a pale-colored substrate, and a pale blue background.

On the other hand, you may find this look too busy. You will aquascape for a calming effect. Use a dark substrate, a plain black background, minimal current, and shallow-water invertebrates such as mushroom corals and zoanthids. Choose a fish more laid-back in its behavior, a dwarf lionfish, perhaps. This design will appear more relaxed.

Idealization

One of the many pleasures of aquarium keeping is the feeling of accomplishment when the design comes together just right. As with the Japanese gardener, the aquarist strives not to imitate nature precisely, but actually to enhance it. We achieve this by incorporating pleasing elements (calmness, brightness) and avoiding unpleasant ones (predation, decay). Aquarists often admit to me the value they place on feeling a sense of control over the microcosm they have built. Like calmness, a sense of control is highly desired amid the stress and hurry of our daily lives.

Designing with Life

The minireef aquarium opens up vast opportunities for aquascaping with living organisms. Two fundamental building blocks for a minireef are live rock and live sand. These are often the first living things placed in the tank. Later, when the aquarium has matured somewhat, the aquarist can begin the exciting project of creating a miniature coral reef using living sessile invertebrates.

Live Rock

An essential component of the minireef aquarium, live rock consists of dead coral skeletons or fossil coral limestone with encrusting live plants and animals attached. The nature of live rock can vary due to the kind of rock, the collecting locality, the depth from which the rock is taken, the numbers and kinds of organisms present at the time of collection, and the method of storage and transport between the collector and the aquarist.

Live rock is harvested from shallow inshore areas. Collecting of natural live rock is prohibited in some places. Farming of live rock provides much of the supply. Live rock is cultivated in the Florida Keys, for example. Rock farming involves dumping quarry rock at sea and retrieving it a year or two later, when encrusting organisms have colonized it.

Regardless of the source, of utmost importance is the treatment that the rock receives between collection and retail sale. You will generally be unable to obtain this information with certainty and must rely on your dealer to stock good-quality live rock and to care for it properly. Collectors do not ship live rock in water. Live rock is packed in wet newspaper and shipped in insulated cartons. Despite these precautions, there always is a significant amount of die-off of the encrusting organisms. The degree to which the organisms that were originally present on the rock arrive intact in your aquarium depends upon how long the rock has been out of water on its journey. When the rock is once again placed under water, decay sets in. This creates a lot of ammonia pollution and generates large amounts of debris. This process, which usually takes about three weeks, is called curing. Curing must take place in a container separate from the display aquarium. Otherwise, the pollution and debris would seriously harm the fish and invertebrates.

Some dealers hold live rock long enough to allow the curing process to proceed to completion. Others do not, and leave it up to you to do the curing at home. You do this in your quarantine tank (see page 49). Since live rock is the first addition you will make to the minireef, using the quarantine tank at this stage won't interfere with the need for it when fish arrive.

After purchasing the rock, inspect it and remove any obviously dead large organisms. Rinse it in a bucket of seawater to dislodge loose material and place the rock in the quarantine tank. There should be about two gallons of water per pound of live rock. The rock remains in the quarantine tank for two weeks, or longer if necessary, to allow beneficial bacteria to restore the rock to health by breaking down dead organisms and replacing the original biomass of encrusting organisms with their own microscopic cells. During curing, certain organisms will be able to reestablish themselves on the rock. This results from a process of artificial selection: small invertebrates and microorganisms able to survive and reproduce during the curing process flourish. After curing, these beneficial organisms are transferred with the rock to the display aquarium. There, they form the basis of the captive ecosystem. When the curing process is complete, the rock has a fresh ocean smell and is free of dead, decaying organisms. Besides a thriving population of beneficial bacteria, the rock will have numerous colonies of pink, mauve, and purple encrusting coralline algae present.

Live rock may develop an assortment of green or red seaweed growth that looks especially good if kept well pruned by herbivorous fish. Few large organisms will be apparent immediately after curing, although the rock harbors spores, holdfasts, and other portions of organisms from which new invertebrates sometimes grow once the rock becomes part of a maturing minireef. Sponges, tubeworms, and other small encrusting organisms often begin to appear after the completed minireef has had the opportunity to develop by itself for several months.

Live Sand

Live sand is analogous to live rock in that it is harvested from the sea and contains a natural population of beneficial small organisms. Simply placing a layer of coarse sand on the bottom of the aquarium and allowing it to develop a population of bacteria, worms, and microcrustaceans appears to be all that is necessary for enhancing the microbial community of the minireef. Use a small amount of live sand as a source of seed organisms to colonize the new sand bed. Some hobbyists prefer to hasten the seeding process by using live sand for all of the substrate. A live sand bed, together with live rock, may facilitate the important process of denitrification, nitrate removal by bacterial activity.

Microinvertebrates

The ocean teems with microscopic and almost microscopic life. *Plankton* is a collective term for any free-swimming or free-floating fish larvae, invertebrates, or algae smaller than a few millimeters in length. If the organism lives attached to a solid surface or crawls on or among the particles of the substrate, we call it a benthic organism. Both plankton and benthic organisms are important components of the ecosystem, providing food for many types of larger creatures, and carrying out the important function of reducing larger debris to smaller and smaller pieces easily decomposed by fungi and bacteria.

Sediment that accumulates in the refugium tank (a separate chamber that provides an opportunity for the reproduction of desirable microinvertebrates unhindered by predation) has been called magic mud. Like live sand and live rock, magic mud harbors abundant microfauna that contributes to aquarium waste management. For this reason, you should not be too scrupulous in trying to remove every spec of debris from your tank. Fine debris causes problems only when it inhibits water flow through some component of the filtration system, or when it is obviously providing a growing medium for slime algae or sulfide-producing bacteria. If you check on your tank every day, you will quickly notice slime algae growth. The odor of sulfide resembles that of rotten eggs, so you are unlikely to miss that, either. The simple remedy for both problems is to siphon out the pile of offending material. Leave the rest of the refugium and the main display tank alone. When you give your minireef the hurricane treatment described earlier, expect an unusually large amount of magic mud to gather in your refugium. Check about a week after the hurricane to see if any piles of it need to be siphoned out.

SUMMARY

By giving careful thought to both the types of materials used and their placement, an aquarist can create an underwater scene that greatly resembles its natural counterpart. Choosing materials derived from the sea, such as coral sand and coral rock, provides an authentic backdrop for fish and invertebrates. Where living corals would be impractical, artificial ones have been developed that are difficult to distinguish from the real thing. The ultimate in authenticity can be achieved using live rock and live sand, in effect literally transferring small bits of the living reef into the aquarium tank. The aquarist can arrange any of these materials, using tricks borrowed from Japanese gardeners, to convey an illusion of space or intimacy, depending upon the requirements of a particular design.

Part II

SALTWATER AQUARIUM MECHANICS

CHAPTER 4

UNDERSTANDING INVERTEBRATES

Minireef aquariums owe much of their appeal to invertebrates. The fish may, in some designs, be secondary players. Even in a fish-only aquarium, a few carefully chosen invertebrates help solidify the illusion of a natural biotope. Invertebrates add color and interest, and in some cases reward the aquarist by reproducing themselves. Many sessile invertebrates grow and spread like garden plants. In time, the aquarium begins to take on a truly natural look that cannot be otherwise achieved.

I find it useful to categorize the hundreds of invertebrate species available to aquarists in two ways, either by their biological classification or by their ecological roles in the aquarium.

Recognizing Relationships

More species of marine invertebrates live on coral reefs than anyplace else in the sea. Classification, or *taxonomy*, helps make sense of this diversity. Based on similarities in the basic body plan, biologists delineate the major groups, or *phyla* (singular, phylum). They base the taxonomy of subgroups within phyla on similarities in anatomical specifics, reproductive behavior, fossil evidence, and a host of other factors. Invertebrate taxonomy is not merely an academic exercise. All these groups and subgroups reflect genetic relationships. The smallest group is the species, a distinct population of animals that does not interbreed with similar populations. Progressively larger groupings become more inclusive, until one reaches the largest group, the kingdom, Animalia, which includes all animal life forms. The levels in between, from smallest to largest are: genus, family, order, class, and phylum. (Subdivisions exist for each of these groups, the result of our ever-increasing understanding of invertebrate diversity.)

At each level up the hierarchy, the degree of relationship between the members of the group decreases. This principle proves helpful to the aquarist by enabling him or her to make predictions about the ecology of an unknown species. If you can recognize its relationship to a known species, you can often predict the lifestyle of an unfamiliar invertebrate species. Lifestyle information is fundamental to providing the invertebrate with an appropriate aquarium environment. As you will learn from the detailed descriptions later in the book, invertebrate lifestyles vary widely. The array of methods for making a living ranges from passive reliance on symbiotic algae to predation.

Fish and all other vertebrate animals, including humans, belong to the same phylum, Chordata, the chordates, comprising about 5 percent of all animals. Invertebrates comprise roughly 95 percent of the animal kingdom. Biologists recognize some thirty invertebrate phyla. With the exception of some minor groups that one might find growing on a piece of live rock, only five invertebrate phyla supply most of the species of interest to saltwater aquarists. These are: corals and their relatives (phylum Cnidaria), segmented worms (phylum Annelida), mollusks (phylum Mollusca), crustaceans (phylum Arthropoda), and echinoderms (phylum Echinodermata).

Aquarium Roles

Taxonomic classification helps to demonstrate the relationships among invertebrates and to identify significant differences from one group to another. For aquarium purposes, we can group invertebrates according to the role they will play in the aquarium community. Looked at this way, the groups are:

- Utilitarian invertebrates
- Anemones
- Other photosynthetic invertebrates
- Filter-feeding invertebrates
- Symbiotic invertebrates
- Predatory invertebrates
- Invertebrate pests

Utilitarian Invertebrates

I have alluded to this group several times previously. I define *utilitarian invertebrate* as any that the aquarist adds, deliberately or by accident, that perform some useful ecological task. Such critters may or may not also be colorful and entertaining to watch. Algae-grazers, including snails, hermit crabs, and small sea urchins, fit the category, as do brittle stars, burrowing sea cucumbers, echiurids, and peanut worms. We can also include sponges, bryozoans, hydrozoans, and many kinds of annelids in that they constantly filter the water, removing food particles. The health and diversity of this portion of the minireef ecosystem reflects the overall robustness of the entire aquarium community.

In the design guidelines presented later, I will not repeatedly mention the addition of utilitarian invertebrates, since every tank needs them. I will point out situations in which certain invertebrates are likely to be eaten by fish. Here is a rundown of commonly available species.

ALGAE GRAZERS

Star shells (*Astraea* sp. and *Lithopoma* sp.) and nerite snails (*Nerita* sp.) are frequently collected from shallow water in Florida and the Caribbean. Turbo snails (*Turbo* sp.) and top snails (*Trochus* sp., *Tectus* sp.) often come from the Pacific. Various species in all of these genera occur throughout the tropics. All feed on attached small algae that they can scrape off. They cannot eat larger types of algae and thus pose no threat to seaweeds cultivated in the tank. Literally millions of these snails are harvested for the aquarium trade each year, and, as Dr. Ron Shimek has pointed out, many die from lack of understanding on the part of the aquarist. *Astraea*, for example, lacks the ability to turn over if it is dislodged, a situation it almost never encounters in its natural habitat. It will simply lie there and starve if you do nothing. All these snails need full-strength seawater and react poorly to changes in salinity. Do not overstock, as many snails will starve in this situation. The usual advice to add one per gallon results in far too many than the tank can support. Finally, do not combine snails with hermit crabs, as the hermits will kill them.

Abalones (*Haliotis* sp.) sometimes are produced by captive cultivation. Good algae consumers, they should be maintained with the same caveats just mentioned for other snails. Another commonly cultivated grazing snail, the queen conch (*Strombus gigas*) reaches a large size and grows rapidly. It feeds only when grazing on sand but does eat algae greedily. Undeniably attractive and interesting, queen conchs do not fit into every aquarium design. Bubble shells include several genera, notably *Bulla* and *Haminoea*, that hide from the light and graze algae at night. *Haminoea* will reproduce in the aquarium.

Small hermit crabs do double duty as both algae grazer and scavengers. They are not above killing a snail for its shell, which the hermit crab uses to protect its own abdomen. Therefore, use either one or the other for algae control. Commonly imported from the tropical Atlantic region, the blue leg hermit (*Clibanarius tricolor*) searches constantly for food. Keep only one per ten or fifteen gallons, as it will also feed on small polyps and other encrusting invertebrates. Found not on the reef but in sandy inshore areas, *C. tricolor* is interchangeable with *Paguristes cadenati*, the scarlet hermit, and *P. digueti*, the red leg hermit. Since all three can potentially be destructive, they are best used for algae control and scavenging in fish-only aquariums.

Also often growing too large for the minireef, sea urchins consume algae, but many also scavenge for animal food. Among the species available, most are better choices for a large, fish-only aquarium rather than a minireef. Useful species include the longspined urchins (*Diadema* sp.), rock urchins (*Echinometra*), tuxedo urchins (*Mespilia* sp., *Microcyphus* sp.), variable urchins (*Lytechinus* sp.), and pencil urchins (*Eucidaris* sp., *Heterocentrotus* sp.). Longspined urchins can inflict a painful jab and should be handled with care. Tuxedo urchins and *variable urchins* camouflage themselves by carrying small bits of material from their surroundings. All need full-strength salinity and sufficient food to survive in the aquarium.

SCAVENGERS

Several varieties of invertebrates qualify as scavengers because they eat detritus and leftover fish foods. Among these are several large hermit crabs that must never be added to a tank with delicate reef animals. Big hermits are, however, a hardy and reasonable choice with some fish. The striped hermit, *Clibanarius vittatus*, from the tropical and subtropical Atlantic, regularly appears in shops.

Among the best minireef scavengers, brittle stars and serpent stars come in many varieties. Easily identified, these echinoderms have a central disc underneath which the mouth is located. Long, snakelike arms, five in number, radiate from the disk. The flexible arms capture all sorts of foods, from detritus to small fishes. Most aquarium imports are harmless. Found all over the world in the tropics, commonly seen genera include *Ophiocoma*, *Ophioderma,* and *Ophiactis*. *Ophiactis* and *Ophiocoma* have spiny arms, while *Ophioderma*'s arms are smooth. The latter may be quite colorful, whereas the other two usually come in drab shades of brown or tan. All hide during the day and feed at night. Add only one or two specimens to your tank, or there may not be enough food to go around. In a starving brittle star, the tips of the arms start to fall apart. At this stage, it may not recover even if more food becomes available.

DETRITUS GATHERERS

I have previously mentioned several minor worm types that perform services by feeding on detritus particles. Certain polychaete annelids also perform this task. Spaghetti worms (family Terebellidae) lie hidden inside a burrow in live rock and have a mass of rubbery tentacles reaching a surprising distance from the entrance. The sticky tentacles efficiently gather debris and convey it to the mouth. Indigestible matter is ejected from the burrow and collects in a pile below the entrance. Often this is the only evidence of the worm's presence. The little piles are easily siphoned out. Red hair worms (family Cirratulidae) resemble spaghetti worms and perform essentially the same function. They differ in that the feeding tentacles are numerous, often red in color, and that they live in sand rather than rocks. They often enter the aquarium via live sand and can become numerous in the substrate.

BURROWERS

With the advent of sand beds in aquariums, many burrowing organisms acquired the interest of aquarists for their role in keeping the sand aerated and mixed. Among these are sea cucumbers, including *Holothuria* and *Actinopyga*. Smaller individuals make good aquarium additions. Ceriths, *Cerithium* sp., are snails that burrow, or more precisely, plow, the upper layers of substrate in search of algae and edible detritus.

Anemones

Few invertebrates inspire so much controversy as sea anemones, in particular the clownfish hosts. Undeniably beautiful, they can be a challenge to keep. Only one, *Entacmaea quadricolor*, can be recommended for home aquariums. It will be discussed in greater detail later in connection with a tank designed with it in mind. Clownfish host anemones are restricted to the Indo-Pacific.

Several anemones from the tropical Atlantic and Caribbean regions adapt well to aquariums that meet their needs. One of my favorites is *Bartholomea annulata*, known as the curlicue anemone. Other good ones include flower anemone, *Phymanthus crucifer*, pink-tipped anemone, *Condylactis gigantea*, and Caribbean carpet anemone, *Stichodactyla helianthus*. Each of these will be covered later. Any can form the basis of a fascinating aquarium.

Other Photosynthetic Invertebrates

This group dominates minireef aquariums and includes the majority of invertebrate species sold for aquariums.

CORALS AND THEIR RELATIVES

Besides the stony corals, various anthozoans adapt with great success to a properly designed and maintained minireef. The groups include:

- False corals (order Corallimorpharia), also known as corallimorphs or mushroom corals
- Sea mats (order Zoantharia), also known as zoanthids or colonial polyps
- Leather corals (order Alcyonacea), including mushroom leather corals and a variety of common names (do not confuse with "mushroom polyps" above)
- Pulse corals (order Alcyonacea), alternatively called waving hand corals, these soft corals often exhibit rhythmic movements
- Organ pipe corals (order Alcyonacea), atypical soft corals with a calcified skeleton; *Tubipora musica* is the only aquarium species
- Gorgonians (order Gorgonacea), also called sea fans and sea whips

Within these broad categories, adaptability to captivity can range from easy to impossible. It is therefore important to understand the differences among them.

First, not all members of these groups are photosynthetic. These are discussed below. Despite the presence of zooxanthellae, many species of anthozoans require planktonic food. Some do so well in captivity they become aggressive, overgrowing neighboring specimens. These, in general, can be kept inbound by pruning, and the pieces can be used to start new colonies or give away.

The stony corals (order Scleractinia) may be subdivided into two groups. Though they are artificial, the groupings are useful in managing their aquarium care.

- Small-polyp stony corals (SPS corals) include many branching types. Species identification cannot usually be achieved without resort to expert advice and microscopic examination. As a rule, SPS corals need good water movement and bright illumination. Attention must be paid to water quality, as insufficient amounts of calcium or too much phosphate spells trouble. Many varieties are capable of rapid growth, and all can probably be successfully produced by captive propagation. Corals compete for space on the reef. They possess the ability to detect encroachment by competitors and to act aggressively to ward off attack. Placing too many specimens of different kinds into the same aquarium can lead to chemical combat, and the demise of some. Resist the temptation to include too many, and your minireef will be more successful.

- Large-polyp stony corals (LPS corals) are often found on the sandy bottom of a lagoon, rather than out on the reef itself. As a rule, they are more tolerant and require more food than their SPS relatives. Many species within this group are imported and make fine aquarium subjects. As with SPS corals, LPS corals can attack nearby potential competitors, resulting in damage or death. Limit the number of species to minimize this problem.

GIANT CLAMS

Until they became commonly available from hatcheries, giant clams were rare in the aquarium trade and expensive. They grow to truly enormous size, and display spectacular coloration. The mantle, exposed through the gaping shell, bears zooxanthellae. Previously thought to subsist entirely from photosynthesis, giant clams in fact need regular feeding to thrive. Phytoplankton products have made it possible for aquarists to obtain amazing results with giant clams. Spawning sometimes occurs in home aquariums, for example. All varieties, which will be discussed separately in the design portion of the book, need bright to very bright light and may therefore not be appropriate for all aquariums.

Filter-Feeding Invertebrates

Include in this category any species that derives all of its nutrition from particulate food it strains from the water. Many bivalves, fan worms, some anthozoans, and even a few crustaceans fit the description. Filter feeders that lack zooxanthellae present special challenges because their food requirements must be met with plankton substitutes added by the aquarist. Designs featuring these animals can be recommended to advanced aquarists only. On the other hand, many anthozoans that bear zooxanthellae obtain additional nutrition through filter-feeding. These are usually easy to keep if provided with sufficient light and small amounts of plankton substitutes.

Symbiotic Invertebrates

Aside from the well-known symbioses between anemones and clownfish, and between corals and zooxanthellae, numerous forms of cooperative living have evolved on the reef. Cleaning, for example, is a form of mutualism practiced by many species of crustaceans and fish. The cleaner removes parasites from the host, usually a larger fish, thereby gaining food while performing a valuable service. Distinctive coloration and behavior patterns identify cleaners, and predators often spare them. This has led to mimicry by false cleaners that gain a measure of protection without performing any service. Some invertebrates merely seek shelter within or upon the body of another animal. Anemone crabs and certain shrimps belong in this category. The anemone crabs are filter feeders, safe from predators among the anemone's tentacles.

Symbioses between invertebrates and fish seem to hold a special interest for all aquarists. The anemone-clownfish symbiosis is undoubtedly the most familiar and popular. Certain gobies share burrows with alpheid shrimps, a relationship that can easily be displayed in the aquarium if appropriate partners can be obtained.

Aquariums showcasing these relationships can often be small, making them ideal for people with limited space or budget. I provide several model designs with this theme, some more difficult than others.

Predatory Invertebrates

Some shrimps and crabs are aggressive enough to pose a threat to other reef inhabitants. In the right setting, however, these creatures can delight the viewer with improbable coloration and interesting behavior. Among the most notorious predators are sea stars, some of which can even catch fish. In an otherwise fish-only aquarium, a large sea star makes a hardy and interesting occupant.

Other Invertebrates

Some invertebrates do not fit the other categories but are nevertheless good aquarium inhabitants. Lacking photosynthetic zooxanthellae, all of them need food. Sometimes, only a specific food will do.

Decorator crabs attach bits of nearby objects to themselves. They are even provided with special bristles to make the job easier. Several kinds are available. Members of another crab family carry a piece of sponge to conceal themselves. The last pair of walking legs is modified for holding the sponge in place.

Colorful small snails may be included in aquarium shipments. With proper identification to determine care requirements, many of them can be accommodated in a minireef or fish-only tank.

Some attractive sea cucumbers imported for aquariums include *Colochirus robustus*, a brilliant yellow filter-feeding form that regularly reproduces in the aquarium. The much larger sea apples, *Pseudocolochirus* sp., while undeniably beautiful, need plenty of planktonic food and may poison the aquarium if they die or are sufficiently distressed.

Several varieties of small, brightly marked shrimps adapt well to aquarium life. The harlequin shrimp, *Hymenocera*, is a fascinating subject for a small tank. It feeds only on sea stars, with which it must be provided. Easier to maintain, camel shrimps, *Rhynchocinetes*, feed at night on small organisms but may damage corals and other polyps. The much larger *Saron* shrimps, too damaging to a minireef tank, may be incorporated into a fish-only system with success. Coral shrimps, *Stenopus* sp., may engage in cleaning behavior but subsist quite well by scavenging and sometimes by preying on other shrimps, worms, or snails. They may be included in aquariums where they won't do damage. Several varieties of small lobsters adapt well to the aquarium, and can be great subjects for a species tank. The bright red reef lobsters, *Enoplometopus*, are the most popular.

Invertebrate Pests

Some invertebrates become serious pests and should be avoided where possible. Pyramid snails, which prey on giant clams, provide a good example. They can be controlled by adding a neon wrasse to the tank. Other types of pests offer more of a challenge.

Harbor Anemones

Aiptasia, variously known as harbor or glass anemones, can live in warm water with a heavy load of nitrate, phosphate, and organics, in fact thriving under such conditions. Yellow brown and from tiny to a few inches in height, they can multiply to plague proportions. Able to sting tank mates with deleterious results, they can be controlled by adding a copperband butterflyfish, *Chelmon rostratus*, or anemone-eating shrimps, such as *Rhynchocinetes*. Neither predator is entirely satisfactory because they may not limit themselves to *Aiptasia*. Corals and other polyps may be in jeopardy. If a fish or shrimp placed in the aquarium for anemone control starts feeding on desirable specimens, the aquarist is faced with the problem of removing the offender to a new home. The anemones can regenerate easily from even a tiny piece left behind, and the problem soon returns.

Taking care not to introduce *Aiptasia* in the first place is the best solution, but this is more of a challenge than it sounds. Any individuals that go unnoticed will be producing offspring in a few months' time. Maintaining the correct conditions and keeping nutrient levels low in your minireef works against the interests of the *Aiptasia*, and may help to limit their multiplication. If you can find it, there is a nudibranch, *Dondice occidentalis*, that eats *Aiptasia* and nothing else, but no surefire solution exists.

Mantis Shrimps

Mantis shrimps can be troublesome. Living as they do in burrows or crevices within live rock, they can arrive in the aquarium uninvited and proceed to dine on fish or other invertebrates. They can be tricky to catch. It may be necessary to remove the entire rock containing the shrimps to a bucket of seawater, which will give you a better opportunity to extract them. The presence of a single small mantis shrimp in the tank is hardly cause for panic. Drastic measures should be taken only if you determine for certain that the mantis shrimp has actually done some damage. Mantis shrimps are active mostly at night, and this is a good time to observe the tank for their presence. The particular species you may have is not important. They all look basically similar, like a small shrimp or lobster, with large stalked eyes that can be rotated in all directions to search for food or recognize danger. The characteristic forelegs look like the raptorial appendages of a praying mantis (hence the name "mantis shrimp"). A mantis shrimp may lash out with these and cause a nasty cut, so do not attempt to handle it barehanded. One large species found in temperate seas is called thumb splitter by fishermen, who use them for bait.

Venomous Invertebrates

Many people not familiar with the saltwater aquarium trade will be shocked to know this, but sometimes invertebrates are imported that can cause human fatalities. While only the most irresponsible person would do so knowingly, aquarists have brought home colorful specimens without knowing what they are buying. Include yours truly in that group. I fortunately learned about the real dangers in time to avoid harm.

The stinging properties of some coelenterates reach epic proportions in a few. Fire corals *Millepora* sp., and fire anemones, *Actinodendron* sp., all both produce an excruciating, though not deadly, sting.

Among echinoderms, fire urchins, *Asthenosoma* sp., inject a venom that causes searing pain. Far more dangerous are flower urchins, *Toxopneustes* sp., capable of injecting a deadly dose of venom.

Cone snails, *Conus* sp., are predators often imported for their bright colors. Unfortunately for the aquarist, this is the largest genus of snails with well over 500 species. Some feed only on worms and will thrive in an aquarium that contains many polychaetes. Other cones feed on snails and will quickly dispatch every algae snail you have. Still others feed on fish. They pose the greatest danger because they carry a toxin specifically designed to kill their vertebrate prey. Human fatalities have resulted from the stings of several species. Cones sometimes hitchhike on live rock. Any you encounter should be removed with care. Unless you can conclusively identify the specimen, it should be humanely destroyed by placing it in a cup of water and freezing.

Undeniably, octopuses can become the most fascinating of saltwater pets, but one, the blue-ringed octopus, *Hapalochlaena*, has caused many human fatalities. Easily recognized by the pale body covered with bright blue rings, this species should be avoided scrupulously. If you see one, you might want to warn the dealer, who surely has brought it in unknowingly. No treatment exists should someone be bitten. Harboring one of these creatures is entirely irresponsible.

The fact that potentially harmful invertebrates wind up in aquarium dealers' tanks underscores the need to research any unfamiliar species before you purchase.

SUMMARY

This tour of the invertebrate realm has been necessarily sketchy. Covering thoroughly all the many creatures brought into aquarium shops would require many more pages. I provide details regarding the care of individual species in the design chapters to follow. Taxonomic information is provided in outline form in Appendixes A and B.

Information about marine invertebrates changes often. New discoveries are made by scientists and aquarists alike. New species are collected and imported by dealers hoping to woo aquarium enthusiasts with novelty. If your aquarium features invertebrates, use aquarium magazines and the Internet to keep up-to-date. Always research any unfamiliar invertebrate before purchasing.

CHAPTER 5

NUTS AND BOLTS

This chapter concerns itself primarily with the practical aspects of incorporating an aquarium into the décor of a room in your home. The basic premise of the book is that the aquarium's primary function is decorative, as opposed to, say, reproductive, for breeding a certain species of fish. To retain the aquarium's decorative value over the long term requires planning. Unlike nonliving art, the aquarium is dynamic, always changing due to the growth, maturation, and, yes, death, of its inhabitants. Anticipating these changes and making allowances for them from the beginning will maximize your enjoyment long into the future.

Built-In Installations

A built-in aquarium offers many advantages over a free-standing design. Unattractive equipment hides behind the wall. Spills and splatters mostly occur behind the tank, also. The aquarium can have its own plumbing. Equipment, such as the lighting system, can be of an industrial type—no need for an expensive finished housing. On the downside, of course, installation is a major project and the cost can be much greater than that of a more traditional, free-standing system. The cost of a built-in aquarium approximates that of a bathroom addition. This can be $15,000 or more, depending upon construction costs in your area. Only you can judge if the added expense is worth it. Although custom tanks can be any size and installation costs can be unlimited, I discuss in this section what might be possible as a do-it-yourself project on a relatively limited budget. Certain aspects of an aquarium installation may require specialized skills and knowledge. Make sure you possess these qualifications. If not, hire a professional for those parts of the project. Not only can shoddy construction hamper your future enjoyment of the aquarium, it can pose danger to you and your family, and even reduce the value of your home.

Size

A built-in aquarium should have a capacity of at least 100 gallons. Anything smaller is hardly worth it, considering the cost of building a new interior wall or cutting through an existing one. You will need at least 4 x 8 feet of floor space. The aquarium is essentially enclosed in a closet. The tank itself will be up to 2 x 6 feet, assuming you use the largest available stock size, holding about 200 gallons. Of course, custom tanks can be any size, but I will discuss what might be possible as a do-it-yourself project on a relatively limited budget.

Electricity and Water Supplies

Let's say you happen to have a closet of appropriate size that you can spare. What else must be taken into account before you begin installing the aquarium? You are going to be cutting a window into the wall; first determine if this is a load-bearing wall. If any doubt exists, consult a licensed contractor. Otherwise, you could seriously weaken the structure of your house! Next, determine if electrical service is located within the wall section to be removed. If so, you will need to reroute the wiring. This may gain you the electrical circuit you need inside the closet to supply the aquarium. On the other hand, this circuit may already be carrying all the load it can handle, and you will require new service for the aquarium equipment. In either case, I strongly recommend obtaining the services of an electrician, unless you thoroughly understand basic home wiring. Wiring in the vicinity of the aquarium should be enclosed in waterproof conduit connecting to waterproof junction boxes. Proper installation requires practice but still lies within the DIY realm if you are the handy type. All circuits must be protected by ground-fault circuit-interrupters (GFCI). This is an extremely important safety precaution. Again, consult a professional unless you thoroughly understand the nature of the work involved.

You may also need a plumber if you intend to have a laundry sink near the aquarium. Plumbing only the filtration system you can probably handle yourself, with the help of the instructions that come with the equipment. You may want to provide a drain valve as part of the filtration system. Ideally, a large tank should drain directly to a sink. If this is impossible, you can install a drain valve that can be connected to a garden hose to direct water to the nearest drain.

Floor Load

You must also make certain the floor can carry the weight. Water itself weighs 8 pounds per gallon. Water to fill the 210-gallon tank in our example, therefore, weighs almost 1700 pounds. Substrate will add more weight, not to mention the tank itself, especially if it is made of glass. You should assume the completed aquarium weighs a ton. Dividing by the tank's footprint of twelve square feet yields a load on the floor of 167 pounds per square foot. Typical building code requirements for a load-bearing residential floor call for it to support 100 pounds per square foot when the flooring is supported by wooden joists. Your floor may need shoring up to support the weight of a large tank. Fortunately, this is relatively easy to do using steel posts, cinder block columns, or similar means. Here again, you will need a contractor unless you fully comprehend the nature of the work involved.

The tank itself will need to be supported at a convenient viewing height. Space should be provided beneath the tank for installing the filter equipment. Sturdy construction using framing lumber works best. The wood can be given several coats of an exterior-grade paint to prevent water absorption.

The opening in the wall should be approximately ¼ to ½ inch larger than the outside dimensions of the tank. This ensures no undue stress will be placed on the glass as a result of a fit that is too tight. Molding frames the tank on the other side of the wall, hiding the gap. The aquarium should fit snugly against the molding all the way around. Any gaps should be filled with painter's caulk or silicone before applying finish to the molding. This step prevents dirt from accumulating between the glass and the molding. Generally, the trim on the room side of the aquarium should match the other woodwork in the room.

Apartment dwellers should limit themselves to smaller aquariums, or have the entire project overseen by a professional. Improper installation could result in great risk of damage to the levels underneath the apartment.

Lighting

The least expensive lighting system for a built-in consists of multiple fluorescent fixtures suspended on chains about a foot above the water surface. For the six-foot tank in our example, I suggest a bank of six four-foot fixtures, each holding two 40-watt lamps. This provides three rows of two fixtures each. They will extend about a foot beyond each end of the tank, but this should create no problems and will provide additional light for the work area. Ideally, electrical service for the lighting will be located on or near the ceiling, thus affording maximum protection from splashing water. Alternatively, suspended metal halide fixtures of the industrial variety can be used. You will need three of them, spaced equally along the length of the tank. Control individual metal halide fixtures, or each of the three pairs of fluorescent units, with separate timers. This enables you to vary the lighting to simulate the changing patterns that occur over the course of a day, or to temporarily create special effects for dining or entertaining. Ballasts for all of this lighting equipment will create heat. The enclosure should be vented, ideally to the outside, or at least into adjacent rooms. Passive vents through the wall, both above the aquarium and near floor level below it, can be installed during construction. Warm air from the aquarium enclosure flows out the upper vents and is replaced by cooler air from the floor. This is a simple approach that consumes no additional energy. Fan-driven vents, such as a bathroom ceiling fan, can be installed to move air from the enclosure to the outside via ductwork. For this, once again, you may need to consult a pro.

Filtration

Although many different types of aquarium filters exist, none is more satisfactory for the installation we are considering than the so-called wet/dry system popular with saltwater aquarists. I value this type of filter more for the basic plumbing scheme than for its superiority as a biological filter. In its simplest form, a second aquarium tank, known as a sump, sits underneath the main display tank. The display tank has a drain hole in the bottom, with a standpipe projecting above this drain. The height of the standpipe determines the water level within the tank. The standpipe is connected to the sump by pipes or hoses. An electric pump moves water from the sump via a pipe that reaches the top of the aquarium, where it discharges into the tank. When the pump is turned on, water from the sump causes the display tank to overflow the standpipe, completing the circuit. The total capacity of the system equals the tank capacity plus the capacity of the sump.

The standpipe inside the main tank is usually surrounded by an opaque plastic box with notches at the top over which water flows. The idea behind this design is to trap floating debris and surface film while protecting surface-dwelling fish. Some species, however, may be so inclined to dive over this waterfall that in order to exclude them you need a fine plastic mesh instead of narrow notches. Maintenance is required to keep the mesh free of obstructions such as dead leaves.

Efficient biological filtration occurs when a filter medium is placed in a box or on a tray between the tank drain and the sump, where it is showered constantly with water. Beneficial bacteria colonize this material and detoxify pollutants produced by the metabolism of the fish and plants in the display tank. When live plants grow in abundance as part of the display, much of this filtration capacity is redundant, and the filter medium can be dispensed with, although it does perform the valuable function of trapping particles of sediment.

The sump also provides a convenient location for the heater. Not only is it out of sight, it is protected from accidental damage during tank maintenance.

Accumulating biologically active debris is a further benefit of the sump. Fine particulate matter accumulates on the bottom. Thus, it can easily be siphoned out. Placing one or more baffles between the inlet side and the outlet side of the sump enhances debris collection. While the debris would be unsightly if left in the display aquarium, it is teeming with beneficial microorganisms that break down and recycle wastes, resulting in improved water quality. Saltwater enthusiasts sometimes refer to this material as magic mud in recognition of its benefits to the aquarium's ecology.

The sump can facilitate changing water, as well. By installing valves in the return line from the pump to the display tank, water can be directed either into the tank or to an external drain line. To operate, first, shut down the pump. Close the valve leading to the aquarium and open the drain valve. Turn the pump back on. When the sump is nearly empty, shut off the pump and switch the valves back to their operating positions. Refill the sump with replacement water, and then restart the pump to complete the process.

The capacity of the sump must be such that all the water in the plumbing system can drain into it without overflowing in the event of a power outage or pump failure. I suggest a sump of half the capacity of the main tank, although a much smaller sump may be enough to contain the water. Having a bigger sump makes working in it easier, increases the total water volume in the system, and minimizes any risk of overflow.

Some aquarists worry about designs that require drilling a hole in the bottom of the tank. Although a catastrophic leak is unlikely with proper workmanship, leaks do occasionally happen. You can have a truly fail-safe system by locating the sump above the display tank. In this case, the sump is called a header tank. A submersible pump located inside the display tank transfers water to the header tank. Near the top of the header tank, a drain hole allows water to escape, falling into the main tank through a connecting pipe. If the pump fails, a small amount of water drains into the display tank, and that's that. This arrangement presents additional engineering challenges, such as supporting the weight of the elevated header tank and making allowances for the lighting equipment, which must be located below the header tank and above the display tank.

Another way to eliminate the drain hole in the bottom of the display tank is to install a siphon to drain water to the sump. Unfortunately, this arrangement may also be vulnerable to problems. If the pump stops operating, water will continue to siphon into the sump until the main tank drains below the intake point. You can easily avoid such a disaster by drilling a small hole in the siphon just below the desired water level in the display aquarium. When water drains to a point below this siphon break, air rushes into the pipe and the siphoning stops.

Maintenance

Built-in aquariums are frequently simpler to maintain than their free-standing counterparts. Factors contributing to ease of maintenance include having a sink adjacent to the aquarium, valves for drain and refill, and easier access to equipment. If maintenance is easy to carry out, chances are you will stick to a regular schedule. This is crucial to the long-term success of your aquarium, regardless of its size. Just make sure your nets and the all-important algae removal tool have sufficiently long handles for the height of the tank.

Finishes

All surfaces that might be exposed to water should be protected with an exterior-grade paint or varnish. If the drywall through which the tank projects is made of Sheetrock, be certain that any exposed edges are covered. I recommend finishing the opening as if it were a pass-through or doorway prior to installing the tank itself. For the tank support structure, treated lumber can be used for an extra measure of protection against water damage.

The floor beneath the aquarium is likely to take the most abuse from spilled water. Choose from the array of flooring materials one might use in a bathroom. Sheet vinyl, vinyl tile, and ceramic tile are all good options.

Free-Standing Installations

If you cannot afford a built-in aquarium, you can have plenty of fun—not to mention impress your guests—with a skillfully done free-standing system. When making the recommendations that follow, I am assuming that one of the aquarium's main purposes is to be an artistic focal point for your living space. Some of my suggestions, therefore, merely enhance the look of the finished tank without affecting its functionality. You can cut corners on these purely decorative options to save money. Do not scrimp, however, on the recommended filtration or lighting, as doing so will make a big difference in the health and longevity of your fish. Building a successful aquarium with off-the-shelf equipment poses few problems if you know what to look for.

A free-standing tank costs a lot less than a custom built-in one, of course, but be prepared to spend around $500 and up for a complete system with a nice cabinet, proper lighting, live plants, and the fish.

Size

Free standing aquariums typically range in size from as small as twenty gallons to around 100 gallons. Standard tanks are available in sizes up to 300 gallons, but for anything much larger than 100 gallons you may spend more to set up a free-standing system than you would for a built-in. This is because a cabinet for a really large tank can cost as much as or more than building it into a wall.

Electricity and Water Supplies

I agree with the commonly given advice to choose a location for your aquarium that is away from windows and exterior doors, free from drafts, relatively stable with respect to temperature, and lacking in excessive noise or vibration. I have yet to find the perfect spot anywhere in my house, so you will probably have to compromise a bit on one or more of these criteria. Temperature stability should be the main goal. Above all, though, choose a spot with adequate electrical outlets and a sink within a reasonable distance. You are going to need electricity to operate the filter pump, lighting, and probably a heater. If not enough outlets are handy, you can always use one of those power strips that nearly everyone has under their computer desk. Do not just leave it lying on the floor. Mount the outlet strip on the wall next to the outlet or vertically inside the aquarium cabinet so the receptacles are not pointing upward, just waiting for water to spill into them. For safety's sake, purchase a power strip with a GFCI device (see above) to protect against shocks. Alternatively, replace the existing wall outlet with a GFCI receptacle (if you know what you're doing) or hire an electrician (if you don't).

Having a sink near the aquarium makes doing water changes much easier. The farther you have to lug heavy buckets, the less likely you are to do this important chore on a regular basis. One way to avoid buckets altogether is to use a drain/fill device with a garden hose. Aquarium dealers sell these gadgets. The cost is minor in comparison to the amount of labor they save. Basically, you attach the unit to a faucet, connect up a hose, and turn on the water. A valve on the unit can be set to suction water through the hose and into the sink to drain the tank. When you are finished draining, switch the valve's position, and tap water flows through the hose to refill the tank. About halfway through the refill, you can dose the tank with a dechlorinator, if you use one.

Floor Load

Floor load, as mentioned earlier, is the weight of the aquarium per square foot of footprint. In a typical frame house, floors support 100 pounds per square foot. If the tank you choose exceeds this limit, you must install additional support below to avoid an accident. A sixty-gallon hexagonal tank, for example, weighs about 600 pounds when full. Dividing by its 4.5 square-foot base gives 134 pounds per square foot. This tank would require additional support. How you position the tank relative to the floor's construction also matters. If the floor joists run parallel to the wall against which the tank sits, all the weight will be supported only by the single joist nearest the wall. On the other hand, if the joists run perpendicular to the wall, the tank will be supported by more than one joist, a sturdier arrangement.

Lighting

For free-standing tanks, the most decorative approach to lighting is an enclosed hood that matches the cabinet. For growing plants, up to four fluorescent lamps can be hidden inside the hood. Metal halide lighting can also be used, but this is overkill on anything under about seventy-five gallons, unless the tank is quite deep and you want to grow plants that demand high light levels. One drawback to any type of enclosed lighting hood is its bulkiness. The thing needs to be moved out of the way in order for any work to be done in the tank. Another issue is heat. While not a problem with fluorescent lighting on a small tank, metal halide lamps and multiple fluorescent ballasts may require forced-air ventilation of the hood to avoid overheating. This is accomplished with one or more small computer fans installed in the hood, adding to both cost and weight.

Some people may find the audible whirr of the fan annoying. If you are using plastic plants, lighting can be selected for viewing only, and you need nothing more complicated than the traditional single lamp fixture. You may want to review the discussion of lighting in chapter 2, "Bringing out the Best in Saltwater Aquariums," before shopping for equipment.

Filtration

Filtration systems that incorporate a sump offer as many advantages to a free-standing tank as they do to built-ins. The only real difference is in the size of the sump, which must fit beneath the aquarium, hidden by the support cabinet. See the section on filtration for built-in tanks, above, for more information on sumps.

If you don't want to bear the extra expense of a drilled tank and sump filter system, plenty of other options exist.

CANISTER FILTERS

In this design, the filter media are contained within a sealed canister through which water is pumped. The inlet and outlet pipes are connected to the canister by hoses. Since the only equipment in the tank are the two pipes, they can easily be hidden with plants or decorations. The canister sits underneath the cabinet.

HANG-ON FILTERS

The hang-on design is an old and reliable one, especially for smaller tanks. Water siphons out of the tank into a box that hangs from the top rim. After passing through filter media, it is pumped back into the tank over a spillway. Various brands add other features to this basic design

FILTER MEDIA

Either type of external filter can contain two basic types of media: particle and chemical. The most commonly used chemical medium is activated carbon. It excels at removing compounds that tint the water yellow, and even traps some large molecules, too. Carbon has a short life span, however, and needs regular replacement. The pores in the carbon pieces become saturated with the substances extracted from the water. Despite this, the carbon does continue to function as a biological filter, because each piece becomes colonized with beneficial bacteria. Though not absolutely necessary, carbon filtration benefits almost any tank.

All sorts of plastic and fiber products are sold as particle filter media in aquarium shops. Their function is to trap suspended debris, giving the aquarium a tidier appearance. Like carbon, a particle medium will become colonized by beneficial bacteria, and thus does double duty. In fact, this may be the main value, especially in an aquarium that lacks living plants to help with fish waste removal.

I have found that external filter media supplied as a cartridge ready to slip neatly into the canister or a hang-on box are the least trouble to work with. Periodically, any filter medium will require flushing out and/or replenishment. Many aquarists find it most convenient to do this when performing a partial water change. If you are merely rinsing the particle medium, do so in the bucket of old aquarium water. That will help to maintain bacterial activity. Because changing the carbon or rinsing the particle medium with tap water drastically reduces the population of beneficial bacteria, I recommend only replacing a portion with new medium at each maintenance time. If you are using cartridges, you can leave the old cartridge sitting in the filter box for a week or so after you install a new cartridge, in order to keep those bacteria on the job.

Undergravel Filters

In this type, the gravel on the bottom of the tank is the filter. A perforated plastic plate sits on the bottom of the tank, with standpipes that reach the surface. Water is pumped up through the standpipes by small electric pumps called powerheads. This causes more water to flow downward through the gravel bed. Each piece of gravel becomes coated with beneficial bacteria.

The undergravel filter offers the least expensive option for efficient biological filtration but has some drawbacks. First, some plants do not like water movement around their roots, which occurs if they are growing above the filter plate. This won't matter, of course, if you are using plastic. Second, the gravel bed also acts as a particle filter and will become hopelessly clogged with debris if it is not periodically vacuumed with a specially designed aquarium siphon. Despite these negatives, I have enjoyed many a tank outfitted with only an undergravel filter. Combining an undergravel filter with an external filter also works well, giving you an extra measure of pollution control.

Maintenance

Maintenance for any saltwater aquarium involves the same procedures regardless of size. In this regard, the only difference between a free-standing setup and a built-in one is convenience. Carrying out weekly partial water changes is the most essential chore. You also need to remove algae from the glass. A monthly cleaning or partial replacement of filter media is also necessary. It is more convenient, as mentioned above, to do all of this when the tank is located in its own enclosure with plumbing and a sink. Even so, with a free-standing tank, weekly maintenance takes only around an hour, even for tanks as large as one hundred gallons. The inside of the cabinet will be cramped, hindering access to the filter system. I suggest storing food, nets, and other supplies elsewhere to leave more room to get at the equipment. It will also be dark under there unless you install a work light. Battery powered closet lights work just fine. You can find one at any department or DIY store.

Finishes

Aquarium furniture manufacturers offer an impressive range of cabinets, stands, and hoods in wood, laminate, even stainless steel finishes. Choose whatever looks best with the décor of the room. You can browse the available options at manufacturer's websites, and even order online if your local dealer does not carry what you want.

A cheaper alternative, though with drawbacks, is a wrought-iron aquarium stand. In the right setting, painted wrought iron can be quite attractive. Choose a stand with scrollwork for a Victorian conservatory look, or a simple rectilinear design for more modern surroundings. The major drawback is the open space underneath, revealing all the equipment and marring the overall look of the aquarium. Many people use plants, either live houseplants or silk ones, to disguise a canister filter sitting under the tank. Rust can also be a problem. If you buy a wrought-iron stand, take the time to give it several coats of exterior paint, which will last far longer than the cursory paint job applied at the factory.

Wood stands are widely available, and have the same advantages and disadvantages as wrought iron. You can paint the wood as you prefer, using exterior paint for water resistance.

SUMMARY

Your saltwater aquarium can be a free-standing system made up of off-the-shelf components, or a custom-designed one built into a wall of your family room. Free-standing tanks are relatively affordable, under 100 gallons as a rule. A built-in aquarium is usually larger than 100 gallons and can cost as much as you can afford and then some. Built-in systems have many advantages, but you can achieve a stunning display in a small, free-standing tank with a limited budget. All you need is the right design. Large or small, the aquarium must operate safely, the floor must be able to bear the weight, and the surrounding area must be protected against water damage.

CHAPTER 6

TROUBLESHOOTING

E ven though you may follow my instructions to the letter, your aquarium may develop problems. This may occur through no fault of yours. A power outage, for example, may cause a chill (heater cannot operate) or a rise in ammonia (filtration is interrupted) or both (double whammy). Fish and invertebrates are stressed by these perturbations of their environment. A disease outbreak may be the ultimate result of any form of stress. Knowing how to cope will save *you* from becoming stressed.

Combating Diseases and Parasites in Saltwater Fish

Although two parasites (*Amyloodinium* and *Cryptocaryon*) account for the vast majority of sick saltwater fish, I will discuss other parasites, diseases, injuries, and diet problems you may have to deal with.

Amyloodinium and Cryptocaryon

Two microorganisms, one a free-swimming protozoan and the other a form of algae, are responsible for almost all of the disease problems with which saltwater aquarium enthusiasts must cope. Both of these parasites can be easily treated with copper medication, but a novice aquarist may fail to notice the telltale signs of disease until it is too late. Don't make this common mistake! Any fish that exhibits rapid, shallow fanning of the gill covers or that stays in an area of high water movement near the surface or that has any other symptom that would suggest it is having trouble getting enough oxygen, should be treated at once. Hours are important.

Amyloodinium, a rogue algae, attacks the gills, robbing the fish of its ability to extract oxygen from the water. For reef fish accustomed to water supersaturated with oxygen, this is extremely stressful. Debilitated by stress, the fish may next be attacked by *Cryptocaryon*, the protozoan parasite. If you fail to recognize that your fish is stressed, you may notice nothing out of the ordinary until little white dots, the reproductive stage of

Cryptocaryon, appear on the fish. Often, only when dots appear do inexperienced aquarists realize there is a problem and begin treatment. By then, the gills have been so eroded by *Amyloodinium* that recovery may be impossible, and the treatment fails.

Adding copper ions to the aquarium water is the only effective treatment for *Amyloodinium* and/or *Cryptocaryon*. The treatment must be carried out in a separate hospital tank if the display tank contains invertebrates. Copper is toxic to invertebrates. A 10-percent solution of copper sulfate is added to the water at the rate of one drop per gallon. This results in a copper concentration of 0.02 to 0.03 ppm. The concentration of copper should be adjusted to the midpoint of this range, 0.025 ppm. You do this by testing, adding another drop or two of solution, and testing again until the correct point is reached. Many copper medications are available commercially. Different brands may have different dosing recommendations. My suggestion is to add the dose recommended on the label, and then keep testing and tweaking to make sure the correct copper level is kept constant. Maintain the copper concentration in the hospital tank for two weeks beyond the disappearance of all symptoms. The fish should look healthy and feed normally before being returned to the display aquarium.

Brooklynella

Brooklynella so commonly affects imported wild clownfish that it is often called clownfish disease. The problem usually manifests itself within a day or two after the fish arrive in a retail shop. Clownfish infected with *Brooklynella* parasites become listless and refuse to eat; they may also show gasping behavior. Characteristically, they produce so much mucus that they appear to be sloughing off layers of skin. Commercial preparations containing formalin and malachite green treat *Brooklynella* effectively. The parasite does not respond to copper treatment. Clownfish should be medicated immediately upon discovery of the problem. Isolate them in a quarantine tank. Hatchery-produced clownfish are seldom affected by *Brooklynella*.

Lymphocystis

Lymphocystis uncommonly appears in both fresh and saltwater fish. It is usually not debilitating except in extreme circumstances. White or grayish cauliflower-like lesions appear on the fish's body and fins. Often, an injury becomes the site for development of the lesions. Thought to be the result of a virus infection, lesions may grow in size and can impede normal behavior. For example, a large lesion on a pectoral fin can prevent the fish from swimming properly. On the lips, the lesions interfere with feeding. Surgery is an effective, but risky, therapy. This is another problem best avoided rather than solved. Angelfish and butterflyfish appear to be especially susceptible. Infected fish should be isolated and the tank they were in emptied and thoroughly disinfected with bleach solution. If you keep other fish in any tank exposed to the virus, you run the risk of infecting them, as well.

Interestingly, antiviral drugs can reverse lymphocystis in large marine angelfish. Large marine angelfish feed mostly on sessile invertebrates that they nip off the reef, especially certain types of sponges. These same sponges have been found to contain antiviral compounds. Indirectly, therefore, lymphocystis is yet another condition brought on by the inadequacy of the captive diet.

Flukes, Worms, and Crustacean Parasites

Saltwater fish get all sorts of flukes, worms, and crustacean parasites both internally and externally. A home aquarist usually lacks the ability to treat these foes effectively. Professional help is required to carry out an appropriate treatment. In some cases, the problem is untreatable. Fish debilitated by parasites should be euthanized. Such infestations rarely spread from one fish to the other in the same aquarium, since the parasite usually requires an intermediate host, a mollusk, for example. It is quite unlikely that the intermediate will also be present in your tank.

You can treat one common parasite at home, black spot disease of tangs. The parasite is a flatworm that burrows under the fish's skin. The fish looks as though it has been dusted with ground pepper. Yellow tangs often develop this problem; their coloration makes an infestation especially obvious. A dip in a bucket of seawater containing a commercially available solution of picric acid is an effective remedy. Most of the time dealers treat infected fish before they are put on display because fish with black spots are avoided by customers. Nevertheless, the problem can develop in the aquarium. Catching the tangs in order to medicate them is the biggest challenge.

Bacterial Infections

Treating a bacterial disease in a saltwater fish requires identification of the causative bacteria, antibiotic sensitivity testing, and appropriate dosage with antibiotics in a timely manner. Because of these complicated procedures, attempts by amateurs to treat bacterial infections usually fail. If you suspect a bacterial infection has attacked your fish, consult a veterinarian for help.

Injuries

Fish can injure themselves, and may need some first aid. If the wound is small and not near the gills, merely painting the damaged area with a swab dipped in a mixture of one part ordinary mercurochrome and one part aquarium water usually prevents infection. Minor damage heals in a week or two. More extensive injuries may require using a broad spectrum antibiotic added to the water. Once again, you will need the assistance of a veterinarian to administer appropriate treatment.

Diet-Related Problems

A condition known as head and lateral line erosion, abbreviated HLLE, appears to be caused by an insufficiency of some important food component. It most often develops in vegetarian or mostly vegetarian fishes, such as tangs, angelfish, and damselfish. Areas around the face and gill covers lose coloration and take on an eroded appearance. The fish looks debilitated, although it may feed and swim normally. Eventually, the problem spreads along the lateral line, giving the whole fish a decidedly wretched look. HLLE can be prevented, and in mild cases reversed, by feeding a diet rich in natural seaweeds. If you plan on keeping any of the fish susceptible to this problem, make sure you avoid trouble by feeding them correctly.

Another problem develops mostly in lionfish and similar large predators that are fed on a steady diet of goldfish. This mistake in husbandry creates a severe problem likely resulting from nutritional deficiency. The symptoms are an inability to swallow and in extreme cases, open the mouth at all. There is no cure. Prevention, by feeding goldfish only now and then and saltwater fish most of the time, is the only solution to this problem.

Similarly, fish may develop mouth and jaw dysfunctions if fed exclusively on freeze-dried krill or brine shrimp. Once again, the problem seems to be irreversible once the fish is noticeably affected.

The common thread in these problems is, I hope, obvious: an exclusive diet of one food leads to health problems. Feed fresh ocean-derived food in as wide a variety as you can obtain. Save the prepared foods as a staple when nothing else is convenient. On the reef, the food is always fresh and the variety incredible.

Catching Fish

Catching fish from a well-decorated and long-established minireef can be a real challenge. Too many hiding places exist among the pieces of rock. If you try chasing the fish down with a net, you run the risk of injuring delicate invertebrates by bumping them, snagging them with the net, or knocking them off their perch on the live rock. Various kinds of fish traps offer the best option. Fish trapping can be frustrating. Fish are naturally wary of anything unusual placed in the tank, and it may take a while for them to throw caution to the winds and enter the trap to get at the bait. By the time this happens, the disease may have progressed dangerously. Another obstacle may be that sick fish often refuse to eat, rendering any bait ineffective.

Preventing Problems with Saltwater Fish

If you follow these rules, you can have fish in a minireef with low risk of having to remove them for treatment:

- Remember that if one fish has symptoms, all the fish in the aquarium require treatment. For example, *Amyloodinium* and *Cryptocaryon* both possess a free-swimming stage that spreads the infestation. Since it takes a few days for symptoms to appear, you cannot know if asymptomatic fish are infected. For this reason, a separate quarantine tank is indispensable. See chapter 3, "Making Your Aquarium Look Real," for additional information about quarantine tanks.

- Limit your fish to a few carefully selected individuals.

- Make sure the minireef has matured for several weeks before the fish arrive.

- Quarantine fish for two weeks after they are brought home from the dealer before introducing them into the minireef. New arrivals are always most at risk for problems. Already weakened from the no doubt traumatic experience of capture and shipment, a new fish may quickly be invaded by pathogenic organisms. Once the parasite succeeds in infesting the disadvantaged new arrival, trouble can easily spread to the other inhabitants of the tank. Quarantining new fish avoids this scenario, and allows for treatment of the problem without affecting conditions in the display tank.

- Maintain good water quality and provide an appropriate diet.

Invertebrate Problems

Thankfully, few parasite and disease problems plague invertebrates. About the only commonplace ones are parasitic snails and predatory flatworms.

Parasitic snails in the family Pyramidellidae often infest giant clams. The snails feed on the clam's mantle. Usually, the parasites are brought in on the clams themselves. The best way to rid a tank of these pests is to place a neon wrasse in it. Two species are available, *Pseudocheilinus tetrataenia*, the four-lined neon wrasse, and *P. hexataenia*, the six-lined version. Besides performing a valuable service, these little wrasses are colorful, harmless to other fish, and small in size. Keeping one in any tank with clams is a good precautionary measure. Placing new clams in a quarantine tank with a wrasse avoids adding the pests to your display aquarium.

The flatworm pest is *Convolutriloba*. It feeds on the soft tissues of various kinds of corals, reproducing to plague proportions if left unchecked. Readily identified by the distinctive three-pointed tail, each worm is about a quarter of an inch in length and reddish brown in color. Remove the specimen that the worms are feeding on immediately, as they often enter the aquarium on the coral itself. Transfer the specimen to a quarantine tank. A small butterflyfish can be added to the quarantine aquarium to feed on the flatworms, or the coral can be dipped momentarily in fresh water. Use distilled water to which enough alkalinity supplement has been added to raise the pH to that of the aquarium. Make sure the water is close to the same temperature as the tank. Return the specimen to the display tank only after no further sign of flatworms is present.

Environmental Causes of Disease

Several types of environmental stresses can induce disease in both fish and invertebrates, owing to the lowering of the organism's natural defenses.

Temperature Fluctuations

If the tank is getting too cool, you may need a larger heater or you may have to move the tank to a location with a stable temperature. Choose a heater that provides 5 watts or more per gallon. Keep the tank away from floor registers and outside doors. If the aquarium is too warm, the most likely culprits are the lighting system, heat shedding from the water pump, or sunlight from a nearby window. You can fix the latter problem with shades or draperies, or by relocating the tank. In the other cases, you may need a chiller. Warm water loses the capacity to hold enough oxygen for the needs of the tank inhabitants. Small aquarium chillers, though unfortunately expensive, are widely available. They are usually simple to install somewhere in the water-return line. Tank water merely passes through the chiller's heat exchanger, where it is cooled to a preset temperature. Usually only a few degrees of cooling are required to offset heat gain from equipment. The chiller operates like a refrigerator, and must have ventilation around the radiator coils. Greatest efficiency comes from forced air ventilation that carries heat outside the building.

Overcrowding

Stick to the stocking recommendations made in this book, and you should have no problems with overcrowding. Too many fish in too small a tank leads to water pollution because the biofiltration system is overtaxed. Pollution rapidly leads to stress. Crowding also increases the likelihood of aggression among the fish. Many species need sufficient space, or they may not remain peaceable toward their tank mates. Fighting is also stressful, and may leave the weaker fish injured, inviting disease.

Overfeeding

Overfeeding not only wastes food but also leads to the accumulation of uneaten food in the tank. This material decays, adding to the load on the biological filter. In effect, overfeeding creates the same undesirable condition as overcrowding: not enough capacity to meet the demand placed on the filter. Pollutants therefore accumulate to the detriment of the fish. Uneaten food is a major source of dissolved organic matter. You will observe that your protein skimmer works overtime shortly after you add food to the tank.

Medicating Unnecessarily

Beginners often make two kinds of mistakes with medications. The first is thinking that exceeding the dosage recommended on the label will lead to a quicker cure. The second is regularly adding medication as a "preventive" measure. The best preventive measure is following the rules laid down here (and in every other book on the subject) for proper care and feeding. Adding any kind of medication to a saltwater display tank can spell disaster. Medicate only when a good reason exists, and then do so in a quarantine tank, never the display aquarium. Commonly sold antibiotics will kill beneficial bacteria along with disease-causing ones. If you knock out the filter, your problems will multiply rapidly. If you conclude that only an antibiotic will save a valuable specimen, seek your veterinarian's help, and carry out the treatment in a separate tank.

Algae Problems

Under certain conditions a bloom of excessive algae growth may develop. Algae usually grow in a fish-only tank because it has no competition. Maintaining a regular routine of partial water changes, thus providing stable, appropriate conditions, deters most algae growth. Various fish and invertebrates can be added to control algae, but their efforts will not amount to much under poor water conditions; algae will grow faster than the fish can feed.

In a minireef, insufficient lighting is likely to favor less desirable kinds of algae. Usually, insufficiency results from aging lamps. Changing them solves the problem, although established algae may require physical removal. A sudden shift in the tank's "algae profile" should alert you to a potential lighting problem. If seaweeds and a sparse coating of bright green filamentous algae abruptly begin yielding territory to reddish purple slime algae or yellowish brown diatoms, check the lighting.

Excess phosphate and/or other nutrients may be fueling rampant algae growth. Purification of the tap water used for making synthetic seawater has helped many an aquarist reduce or eliminate problems.

Many utilitarian invertebrates, and, to a lesser extent, herbivorous fishes, provide a natural check on algae growth.

As with many aquarium situations, preventing undesirable algae from gaining a foothold proves easier than eliminating a bloom. Nevertheless, if you are faced with an overgrown tank, here are some steps you can take:

- Install a reverse osmosis unit to purify your tap water.
- Check to see if your seawater mix or any additive you are using contains phosphate. If so, switch brands.
- Add algae consumers such as snails, sea urchins, or herbivorous fishes.
- Physically remove as much algae as possible on a regular basis.
- Carry out more frequent partial water changes.
- Test your tank for phosphate regularly. As long as phosphate remains detectable, you will have algae.

SUMMARY

Being dynamic living systems, saltwater aquariums sometimes unexpectedly develop problems despite our best efforts. Knowing the signs of disease in fish or invertebrates and having knowledge of appropriate remedies allows you to take action before problems become too severe to correct. You will note, however, that the best insurance against trouble comes from maintaining the aquarium properly on a regular basis. Partial water changes, vacuuming debris from the substrate, cleaning algae from the glass, and keeping the lighting at the proper intensity all contribute to a healthy, trouble-free aquarium.

CHAPTER 7

BASIC SETUP PROCEDURES

Some aspects of saltwater aquarium keeping are universal. Regardless of whether the ultimate goal is a fish-only tank or a minireef tank, installation of the equipment requires the same steps. Similarly, all saltwater tanks require the active participation of beneficial microorganisms. Therefore, in the early stages of the tank's development, the procedure is focused on getting these unseen helpers established.

Tank Location

Your choice of location can greatly influence conditions in the tank. Avoid locating the tank in direct sun, for example. Sunlight may benefit corals and seaweeds, but temperature fluctuations may be excessive. A temperature swing of two or three degrees is acceptable, but the sun can quickly warm a tank to 80 degrees or more. If the only possible location receives sun, and draperies are not an option, you may need to install a chiller to maintain a stable temperature. Likewise, locating the tank in a drafty, cooler space will necessitate a heater. Perhaps the ideal spot for a free-standing aquarium would be in a conservatory or sunroom maintained in the low 70s year-round. Not only would the temperature be stable, but plenty of indirect sunlight would be available, reducing the need for artificial lighting.

Tank Support

Furniture design and craftsmanship lie beyond the scope of this book. However, your choice of support furniture can greatly affect the decorative value of the aquarium. Most people opt to purchase a stock cabinet along with the aquarium. Dealers sometimes offer discounts for doing so. Savvy manufacturers now supply cabinets in styles ranging from Shaker to stainless steel. Various stained or painted wood finishes make matching the cabinet to the rest of the room much easier.

Despite all the variety available in the marketplace, you may discover that nothing appeals to you or fits in with the room. Having a cabinet custom built may be the only way to get the look you are seeking. This, of course, is the most expensive option. Converting existing furniture, such as an antique dresser, into a suitable aquarium cabinet also requires expert skill.

Whether custom-built or off-the-shelf, the finished setup will look best if you also install a matching canopy for the lighting equipment above the tank. Proper wiring, waterproof connections, and adequate ventilation constitute the three main requirements.

Cabinet design becomes more complicated in special circumstances. Most free-standing home aquariums are set against a wall and are intended for viewing primarily from the front. A popular alternative arrangement sets the long axis of the tank perpendicular to the wall, with equipment access on one end. Personally I avoid see-through aquariums. Nevertheless, such designs lend themselves to using the tank as a room divider. Another possibility involves placing the tank in the center of the room. This is the most difficult arrangement to pull off because equipment cannot be conveniently hidden in a rear corner.

Filling the Tank

Before the tank is filled, you will need to install the background. Various backgrounds (see chapter 3, "Making Your Aquarium Look Real") can be used, but paint provides a simple, durable, and low-cost choice. With the background in place, the aquarium can be set in the cabinet in its permanent location. Using a carpenter's level, check to make certain the top of the tank is perfectly level in both directions. If not, water will exert greater pressure on the low side, increasing the likelihood of a leak. Leveling the tank may be difficult if it sits on carpet or if the floor is not level. You can compensate by inserting shims underneath the cabinet. Placing a piece of Styrofoam under the tank also helps. When filled, its weight will press down on the Styrofoam and the tank will level itself. This works for minor adjustments only.

Once the tank is in place and level, fill it with tap water. Let it sit overnight to make sure there are no leaks and that the weight does not cause any sagging of the cabinet or floor. Drain the tank and fix any problems you discover before proceeding.

How to Apply a Painted Background

Protect areas where paint is unwanted with newspaper and masking tape. Make sure to protect the interior of the tank against stray paint droplets. Thoroughly clean the glass with window cleaner, and then wipe with a lint-free cloth moistened with rubbing alcohol. Wait for the alcohol to evaporate completely. Apply two coats of exterior-grade paint from a spray can. Allow to dry according the manufacturer's directions before proceeding with the aquarium setup. After removing the masking tape and paper, carefully clean the inside of the tank using warm water to which a small amount of vinegar has been added. Rinse with clean water and dry thoroughly.

Plumbing

The most universally useful system design, as mentioned in chapter 5, "Nuts and Bolts," employs a sump underneath the tank. Other devices can be used, especially on smaller tanks, but none is as satisfactory. For most of the model designs presented later, I assume this system is used. Otherwise, I will make a specific recommendation.

Manufacturers produce many tank sizes "reef ready." Drilling the drain and installing the standpipe takes place at the factory. Surrounding the standpipe, a plastic "prefilter" hides the plumbing and allows only surface water into the drain. Narrow slots at the top prevent large objects from entering. In some designs, the return pipe passes through a second hole in the tank bottom and extends up to the top of the prefilter, paralleling the standpipe. In other designs, the return pipe passes through the tank bottom at some distance from the drain. In still others, a return hose simply loops over the rim of the tank to discharge water just below the surface. The first option is my preference. Not only does the prefilter box hide the return pipe, it also protects the pipe from being bumped. Striking the pipe with a piece of coral rock as you are aquascaping, for example, can crack the glass around the hole at the bottom as the pipe is deflected to one side.

A plastic part known as a bulkhead fitting provides a waterproof seal around the holes in the tank bottom. It consists of three components: a threaded pipe with a flange on one end, a ring nut, and a gasket. The pipe goes through the hole with the flange inside the tank. The gasket slips over the threads, followed by the ring nut. Hand tighten the ring nut until the gasket is slightly compressed against the tank. The inside of the flange has a female thread to which a standpipe or return pipe can be connected using a threaded adapter. Under the tank, the portion of the fitting extending past the ring nut has a male pipe thread to which additional pipes or hoses can be connected to transport water. All of these parts, along with instructions, come with the sump, or your dealer can advise you on the correct ones to select for the system you are assembling.

The sump tank is placed underneath the display aquarium. Water from the standpipe drains into the sump. To minimize salt creep, the sump may have a lid through which the drain hose passes. ("Salt creep" refers to the accumulation of salt crystals wherever droplets of seawater evaporate. Although it is difficult to avoid the problem completely, preventing the escape of seawater whenever possible is a good idea.) If the sump is part of a wet/dry filter, a separate box of filter medium sits on top of the sump. Water from the drain line passes over the medium before it reaches the sump. A rotating spray bar or a perforated tray distributes water evenly over the filter medium. Talk to your dealer about the pros and cons of the designs he stocks. Minireef aquariums with live rock do not require this system component. A bulkhead fitting goes through the opposite end of the sump, near the bottom. The intake of the pump connects to this fitting. The pump discharge reenters the tank via a pipe or hose that connects to the return bulkhead fitting in the tank bottom.

Next, install the protein skimmer either in the sump or adjacent to it. Locate the skimmer where it will be easily accessible for inspection and cleaning. Follow the manufacturer's directions regarding installation.

If you are using a submersible heater, install it in the sump. Place it near the bottom, where it will not be left high and dry if the water level in the sump should drop. If you are using a chiller, it will be installed in the return line between the pump and the tank. Install the chiller's thermostat sensor in the sump.

It is a good idea to lay out the equipment arrangement on paper before you proceed with installation. You will want to make sure everything can be hidden underneath the tank while remaining accessible for maintenance.

Water Movement

Sessile invertebrates benefit from strong currents that wash away wastes and bring nutrients and oxygen to them. Fish get exercise by swimming against currents. Any saltwater aquarium benefits from all the water movement you can provide, as long as it is not so vigorous as to slosh water over the rim. The return pipe from the sump discharges water in one direction only, and in a continuous stream. Natural water movement on the reef is multidirectional and intermittent. You can simulate natural turbulence by installing powerheads in the display tank. Place at least one powerhead (see page 86) toward the back of the tank with the outflow directed so it intersects that from the return pipe. The perpendicular currents collide and create turbulence. Using two powerheads, controlled by a timer known as a wavemaker, is an even better idea, though certainly not essential. Wavemakers allow the powerheads to be switched on and off on a regular schedule, creating pulsed water movement. Alternating between the two powerheads causes the motion to come first from one direction then the other. Some wavemakers permit alternation between both powerheads on, both off, or only one or the other. This results in currents of varying strength and direction.

Lighting

You can buy an aquarium control center that regulates both lighting and powerheads. These handy devices resemble the power centers sold for home computers but with built-in timers. Some units also provide auxiliary outlets for other aquarium equipment. In any event, you need a timer for the lighting system. Depending upon the size of the aquarium and the design of the canopy, you will be using fluorescent, metal halide, or a combination of both. Follow the manufacturer's recommendations regarding timing devices that are compatible with the lighting system you select. I prefer a fluorescent/metal halide combination with timers set to turn the fluorescent lamps on an hour before the metal halides and off an hour after the halides go off to simulate dawn and dusk. If you opt for moon lighting, a third timer is needed. I strongly recommend testing the lighting system and timers before filling the tank.

Testing the System

After filling the tank (see the earlier section), plug everything in and allow the equipment to run overnight. Adjust the thermostat on the heater and/or chiller, to maintain the correct temperature. Use an accurate thermometer to check the water and make adjustments to reach the target temperature. The temperature should remain constant within two to three degrees over a twenty-four-hour period.

Water should be circulating from the tank to the sump and back. The skimmer should be operating, although it will produce little, if any, foam until the tank contains salt. You will make final adjustments to the skimmer after adding the salt mix, and again later after adding live rock and fish.

Adding Salt Mix

If all goes well with your final test, it is time to add the salt mix. With no livestock in the tank, it can be used as a mixing vat. (Under no circumstances should salt mix be added to an established tank with living organisms present.) Add enough salt mix for the tank's capacity, using about 2¼ cups for every five gallons. Sprinkling in the mix by cupfuls promotes fast dissolution. After all of the mix has been added, run the system for at least twenty-four hours. Measure pH and salinity. If the salinity is too low, sprinkle in more salt mix, and test again after twenty-four hours. If the salinity is too high, remove some water, reserving it for future use, and add fresh water. Wait five minutes and check the salinity again. Repeat as needed until you reach the correct salinity. Note that reducing salinity with fresh water takes less time and effort than increasing salinity with more salt mix because you only have to wait a few minutes for the fresh water to combine with the water in the tank. Salt mix requires twenty-four hours to dissolve. The solution may clear within a couple of hours, but dissolution and equilibration to pH takes longer. I recommend waiting twenty-four hours to be sure the mix has completely dissolved.

Once you reach the correct salinity, check the pH. If it lies outside the range of 8.2–8.4 you will need a pH buffering additive to correct it. Follow the manufacturer's directions for correcting pH with any brand of additive.

Both salinity and pH should remain stable for at least twenty-four hours. This is a good time to test alkalinity, calcium, iodide, and phosphate. Doing so accomplishes two things: (1) establishes baselines for these parameters, and (2) provides an evaluation of the salt mix. Depending on the chemistry of your tap water, different

---

Really Big Tank?

Thinking about a really big aquarium? If so, its setup and stocking should be carefully planned. You will be working with many gallons of water, and several hundred pounds of rocks and sand. Some items you may want to have on hand include the following:

- Two or three large plastic garbage cans with lids
- One or more tarps for covering floors and furniture
- A hand truck for moving heavy boxes
- A box cutter
- Terry cloth hand towels
- A roll of paper towels

Use one garbage can to collect all the wet packing materials from the live rock and other debris. Use one for wet hand towels. Use the third for temporary water storage or mixing. In addition, having a helper or two makes a huge difference when working with a big tank.

brands may equilibrate to different readings. Using water purified by reverse osmosis should yield the correct values with any good brand of salt mix.

At this point, the physical and chemical environments of your aquarium have been prepared. You are ready to proceed with the fun part, stocking the aquarium with living organisms.

Aquascaping

Drain about a third of the water from the tank. Start placing rocks, live or dead, removing water if necessary to compensate for displacement. Save all seawater for topping off the tank later.

Adding Live Rock and Live Sand

You will need two pounds of live rock per gallon of water. It is imperative that the aquarium be filled with seawater at the correct salinity, pH, etc., and that all equipment is operating properly before the live rock is introduced. When the rock has been placed, add dry substrate, live sand, and/or live rock pebbles as your design dictates. With the basic reef now in place, position other decorative items, such as seashells. When all aquascaping materials have been added, top off the tank with seawater.

Aquascaping with Rock

Fish-only aquariums can be aquascaped either with live rock, dry rock, coral skeletons, or a combination of all three. Add these items before the substrate, so they will sit securely on the bottom of the tank. Also, rocks, live or dead, look more natural if partially buried.

Place a flat rock across two rocks of similar height and you've made the simplest kind of shelter for a saltwater fish. Reef fish are generally territorial, and their need for "personal space" becomes more pronounced in the confines of an aquarium. Therefore, you should provide a suitably large hiding place for each fish you plan to stock.

Besides incorporating caves and ledges into the backbone structure of your artificial reef, you can add natural enclosures such as seashells of an appropriate size. Take care to secure all tank decorations. If you build a cave, for example, make sure the supporting pieces are sitting securely on the bottom, and that the arrangement is stable. Burrowing fish can undermine rocks and cause them to tumble. Fish or invertebrates can be crushed by such a "tank-alanche" and a large rock can crack the tank if it falls. Avoid balancing larger rocks upon smaller ones. Place larger pieces on the bottom. Individual rocks should sit as they would in a natural setting, with the broadest portion of the rock down. Flat rocks serving as the roof of a cave or as an overhang must rest securely on at least three contact points of their supporting stones. Such an arrangement affords maximum stability. Try to create a natural, random arrangement, avoiding a stack that looks like a brick wall, while still keeping a stable structure. Ambitious arrangements will need securing.

Rock work can be stabilized by various means. Underwater epoxy cement, which sets even when submerged, works well to hold small rocks in position. Joints between larger pieces require reinforcing. Using a masonry bit, drill a hole in each piece and insert a length of plastic pipe to connect them like Tinkertoys, then apply cement. To drill live rock, hold it in a towel moistened with seawater while you work. Dead corals and rock should be well wetted before drilling to reduce the production of dust. Be sure to wear protective goggles and gloves. Use plastic cable ties to hold pieces in place while the cement sets. You can use the same technique to attach dead coral skeletons to a rock base, which looks a lot more natural than setting the coral on the bottom directly.

Adding Dry Substrate

In a plastic bucket, rinse dry substrate material, a portion at a time, in tap water until the water is only slightly cloudy. This will wash away dirt and the fine powder that accumulates in the bag during handling. Sometimes substrate material is contaminated with wood chips or bits of debris that will float out during the rinse. You should have approximately one to two inches of substrate.

Break-In Period

Live rock and live sand seed the aquarium with beneficial bacteria and a host of other organisms. A fish-only system decorated entirely with dead rock and sand must have a source for these microscopic helpers. When you are finished aquascaping, add a bag of commercially packaged live sand on top of the substrate, or place a few small pieces of live rock in the tank. You can also purchase cultured bacterial tank starters, but I prefer using the natural materials. The bacteria need a source of ammonia. Purchase an ammonium chloride solution made expressly for this purpose, and add it according to the label directions.

If you are aquascaping with mostly live rock, work with your dealer to schedule its arrival. If the dealer is going to cure the rock for you, all you need to do is pick it up, return home, and start aquascaping. If you are going to cure the rock yourself, you'll want a curing tank set up and running at least forty-eight hours before the rock arrives. You can use your quarantine tank for curing the rock, or set up a plastic trash can as an auxiliary tank. During the curing process, it will be periodically necessary to remove some pieces of rock for extra cleaning. Sometimes a piece of sponge or other attached organism dies producing a slimy white patch as bacteria decompose it. If you see this, take out that piece of rock and scrub off the decayed area with an old toothbrush before returning the rock to the water. (Warning, the smell can be quite offensive. This is not a task for the squeamish.) After the first week or so of curing, major die off such as this no longer occurs, and it is not necessary to do anything further except wait. Scrubbing live rock should always be done as gently as possible, and only when required. You cannot avoid removing some beneficial organisms in the process, and you do not want to eliminate them unnecessarily.

How do you know when the curing process is complete? As the rock cures, decay organisms will produce ammonia, which will be converted to nitrite by beneficial bacteria. As curing proceeds, additional bacteria will oxidize the nitrite to nitrate. Therefore, simply test the water for nitrite periodically and keep track of the results. You will see an initial rise, a peak, and then a sharp decline to zero. At that point, the curing process has run its course, usually after about two weeks. The live rock is ready to be transferred to the display tank, bringing with it all the beneficial bacteria and other organisms that will help create and maintain the minireef environment.

The same thing happens during the break-in period when only a small amount of live rock or sand is added to seed an otherwise barren tank, followed by the addition of ammonia in chemical form. Nitrite testing will reveal a peak followed by a crash as the tank's biofiltration capacity develops. Because the initial amount of bacteria is small, the break-in period for a fish-only tank takes much longer, usually about four weeks.

Settling In with Your Habitat

From this point on, you are the custodian of a living ecosystem. You must maintain the aquarium over the next several months to allow basic biological processes to develop appropriately. For about six to eight weeks, you can expect a series of algae blooms to occur. Typically, brownish diatoms and reddish purple slime algae appear first. Later, filamentous green algae supersede the earlier growths. This sequential waxing and waning of algae blooms is normal. Siphon out patches of slime algae, and use a pad to clean the glass. Do not reduce lighting in an attempt to limit algae growth. You will only prolong the process. The algae grow because the water contains compounds, such as phosphate, that stimulate their growth. Removing algae from the tank helps to export the compounds. Protein skimming also helps. You will note that the skimmer begins to produce foam during the break-in process. As microorganisms grow, reproduce, and die, they release organic compounds into the water. Some of this is taken up again by other organisms, and some is removed by the skimmer.

Eventually, the first few patches of purple coralline algae will begin to grow on solid surfaces. Coralline algae tend to grow best in moderate to dim light. Thus, new colonies often appear on the sides or back glass first. In time, several types of coralline algae will coat large areas of the glass and rocks. Use a razor blade to remove the algae from any area of the glass that you want to remain unobstructed, but leave other areas undisturbed. Coralline algae are an important component of the aquarium's ecosystem. Good coralline algae growth indicates that conditions in the aquarium are suitable for sessile invertebrates, such as corals.

Because of the inevitable algae blooms early in the life of any saltwater aquarium, it is a good idea to choose algae-eating snails as the tank's first tenants. Snails are widely available. Other possibilities include blue leg or scarlet hermit crabs. Add a few crabs or snails (don't use both) and assess the effect on the algae growth before you add more. Other utilitarian invertebrates can also be added early in the aquarium's development. These include brittle stars, small shrimps, and detritus-feeding species such as burrowing sea cucumbers. If you are working toward a fish-only display, make sure these invertebrate additions will not be eaten by the tank's eventual piscine inhabitants. If you want to dispense with invertebrates altogether, add herbivorous fish, tangs, or rabbitfishes, for example, at this point.

By the time the first critters settle in, the aquarium will be about two months old. It will have a thriving community of beneficial microorganisms, as well as utilitarian and herbivorous life forms. Once the tank has come this far successfully, you can add additional fish or invertebrates every two weeks.

With suitable lighting, you can add photosynthetic invertebrates. Hardy choices include green star polyps, leather mushroom soft corals, and disc anemones. It makes no difference how many (within reason) of these species are included, nor does it matter in what order they are added. Adding additional fish should be done with their temperaments in mind. Larger, more aggressive fish should be added last. Once established, a properly designed saltwater aquarium can thrive for many years with little attention apart from routine maintenance.

SUMMARY

When it comes to setting up a saltwater aquarium, big tanks and small ones differ only in the amount of water and materials involved. The basic procedure is the same. After readying the tank and setting it in place, install the equipment. Test the plumbing with fresh water, and make sure everything else is working properly before adding salt mix. Aquascaping comes next, using live rock and sand, or non-living materials, or a combination. Allow for a break-in period as the aquarium develops a population of beneficial microorganisms. From that point on, the aquarium will continue to mature and change for a period of months. Early on, the tank may experience a bloom of algae growth. As the developing ecosystem becomes more and more stable, you can introduce additional invertebrates and fishes about every two weeks. Although the process of stocking an aquarium can be slow, patience is rewarded with a thriving, easily maintained tank.

Part III

SALTWATER AQUARIUM MODEL DESIGNS

CHAPTER 8

BASIC LOW-MAINTENANCE DESIGNS

T he coral reef withholds the answers to many secrets. Suitable conditions for many species remain unknown. Fortunately, several mainstays of the saltwater aquarium trade have been around long enough to be well understood. By dint of their natural lifestyle, these creatures adapt quickly to the confinement and variable water quality characteristic of aquarium life. This chapter focuses on using some of these species in simple tanks for maximum decorative effect with minimal care. I have provided suggested model designs for a couple of small tanks, but the majority of ideas proposed will require a large, built-in aquarium for proper execution.

Maintenance Requirements

Maintenance of these systems requires little apart from the routine. For any of the aquariums in this chapter, here is a recommended maintenance schedule:

- **Daily:** check temperature, feed
- **Weekly:** check salinity, adjust as needed; check pH, adjust as needed; carry out 10 percent water change; clean algae off glass
- **Monthly:** check nitrate; carry out larger-than-normal water change as needed; replace detritus removal pads in filter; siphon out debris as needed
- **Semiannually:** reset system and clean decorations; carry out 50 percent water change
- **Annually:** replace lamps; service system pump

Filtration Requirements

Each of the larger systems described in this chapter requires a wet/dry filter for best results. The filter should be outfitted with a biological filtration chamber, as described in chapter 5, "Nuts and Bolts." I suggest installing a model that allows you to place a polyester fiber pad above the biofiltration medium to trap particulate matter. You should also be able to remove the biofiltration box without having to move the sump. This may mean an extra allowance for "headroom" underneath the main tank. Having a removable box facilitates storing the biofiltration medium so it will not dry out during your semiannual system reset. Keeping the medium moist ensures retention of the maximum population of beneficial bacteria. I discussed the various other advantages of this type of filter system in chapter 5, "Nuts and Bolts."

Other System Components

Control the temperature of each system by installing a heater having 5 watts of heating capacity for every gallon of water. Temperature fluctuations do not stress only the fish; beneficial bacteria may respond negatively, also.

For housekeeping purposes, nothing beats a few small hermit crabs. In fish-only tanks such as those described in this chapter, stray bits of food will invariably be missed by the fish. Hermits are expert at cleaning up, and will also feed on algae. I suggest adding any of the species mentioned on page 71 at one per fifteen gallons.

When using coral rock, allow about one-half pound of rock per gallon for the model designs in this chapter. This much rock will occupy approximately half the space within the tank, leaving the rest as swimming room. An open expanse of water shows off the fish to their best advantage.

You may have little choice when it comes to background color. Tanks designed for use with a wet/dry filter, which is what I recommend for all but the smaller systems here, come predrilled, with an overflow box permanently installed. Most of the time, the tank also has a built-in background to match the overflow. Usually, they come in black, black, and black, although some manufacturers may offer optional colors. If any of the options make sense to you, and you don't mind waiting to special order the tank, you may want to consider the background colors I have suggested. You can also order the tank with a black overflow and a clear back, to which you can apply any color of paint you desire. In this case, you may want to arrange rocks or coral to help obscure the overflow box.

The Designs

The range of creations in this chapter serves to demonstrate the breadth of possibilities for a home saltwater aquarium. Several designs even lend themselves to customization with alternative species, which I note in each model design.

MODEL DESIGN 1 | A Minimalist Look

An aquarium like this fits in with minimalist décor. Keeping the white decorations free of algae presents the biggest challenge. You may find, however, that with sufficient light the tank will grow an attractive crop of bright green, filamentous algae. If so, the look may be as pleasing as the original, stark white tank.

This aquarium is a cinch to maintain. It can serve as an introduction to saltwater aquarium keeping for an eager middle schooler. A white aquarium with black and white damselfish creates a study in contrast.

Aquarium Capacity . . . . 30 gallons

Aquascape Materials

    crushed coral rock . . . . fine grade

    coral rock . . . . 3 large pieces

Background . . . . .white

Fish

    Dascyllus sp. (see text)

Special Requirements

    A hang-on style filter incorporating a protein skimmer suffices for this tank.

Arrange the three pieces of coral rock along the length of the tank, grouping two to one side of center. Place the third piece on the opposite side of center. Add a thin layer of crushed coral rock to the bottom. A dual-lamp fluorescent fixture with 5000K or higher lamps should make this arrangement look intensely white.

Few saltwater fish surpass the humbug damselfishes in hardiness and spunk. Choose from the striped humbug, *Dascyllus aruanus*, black-tailed humbug, *D. melanurus*, or threespot humbug, *D. trimaculatus*. The latter grows too large for more than one to be accommodated in this aquarium. The other two species, reaching only about three inches, can be stocked with the idea of ending up with a pair. Place five juveniles in the tank, and a pair should form naturally after they have grown a bit. You will note that a pair has formed when two fish take over and defend a territory against the other three. At this point, you must remove the others to avoid a damaging conflict. In the event no pair forms, you will need to remove all but one fish, for the same reason. All three species produce audible vocalizations when courting or defending territory. Development of this trait should signal that the time for a new social structure has arrived.

D. aruanus and *D. melanurus* differ only in that the latter has a black tail while the former's tail is white. Both are marked in vertical black-and-white bars. *D. trimaculatus* is solid black with a white dot on the forehead and a larger white spot on each side. Aside from their aggressiveness as adults, they are ideal aquarium fish. Feed them any of the commonly available aquarium foods, making sure they receive a sizable proportion of vegetable matter. In the ocean, individuals defend a coral head and systematically kill the coral polyps to allow algae to grow. This algae "farm" supplements the damselfish's diet. Juveniles associate with large anemones sometimes, revealing their close relationship to the clownfish.

A variation on this model is to substitute a harem of blue damselfish, *Chrysiptera cyanea*, for the *Dascyllus*. Keep one large orange-tailed male with two of the smaller, all-blue females.

MODEL DESIGN 2 Cheerful Yellow

Though requiring a much larger tank, this model design resembles the previous one in that a single color repeats in several elements to maximize the effect.

Only with an extralarge tank can you display yellow tangs in something approaching a natural arrangement of many individuals. Long ranking as one of the most popular saltwater fish, with attention to their minimal needs—a continuous supply of vegetable matter and regular water changes—yellow tangs live five to seven years or more. Although reaching a diameter of nearly eight inches in the sea, aquarium specimens seldom exceed six inches.

Yellow tangs occur from Japan to Hawaii, throughout the Pacific, north of the equator. Typically, they live on outer reefs with dense coral stands, most commonly of branching genera such as *Acropora* and *Pocillopora*. They are also found in lagoons. Water depth ranges from about ten feet to over one hundred feet. Conditions in the fish's habitat are relatively constant in terms of salinity, temperature, sun exposure, and turbulence, and should therefore remain stable in the aquarium, as well.

The body of the yellow tang is disk-shaped, with a short, protruding snout filled with sharp teeth adapted for grazing. It is uniformly lemon yellow in coloration, although in darkness the fish adopts a "sleep" color pattern, pale pinkish yellow with a prominent midlateral white stripe. During daytime, the yellow coloration returns. Like all tangs, *Z. flavescens* carries a razor-sharp scale on the caudal peduncle that it uses both defensively and offensively. The scale, or *tang* (as in part of a knife), is pearly white, and consequently may be easily discerned against the background of the body. It folds into a groove on the caudal peduncle like the blade of a jackknife. Aquarists should avoid catching this or any other tang in a net. Either the net will be shredded, or the fish will become entangled and possibly injured. Common sense also suggests avoiding this razor-sharp weapon when handling the fish, as it can inflict a nasty wound.

When danger threatens, the yellow tang holds its dorsal and anal fins erect. Apparently, the function of this behavior is to make the fish look larger to a potential predator or rival. Juvenile specimens can appear twice as large as their actual size, and probably benefit more from the deception than adults do. Most *Zebrasoma* are found in relatively small groups of individuals, and this appears to be true for *Z. flavescens* over most of its range. Much larger aggregations, however, occur in Hawaii. I suggest purchasing only specimens that you know to have been collected from Hawaii. Not only are they relatively inexpensive, but also their condition is likely to be superior to that of individuals harvested in Asia.

Aquarium Capacity . . . . 180 gallons

Aquascape Materials

    crushed coral rock . . . . fine grade

    coral rock . . . . about 100 pounds, assorted sizes

    artificial branching corals . . . . yellow in color, 3 pieces, one large and two smaller

Background . . . . .black

Fish

    Zebrasoma flavescens. 9

Special Requirements

    Tangs do not like water with a heavy load of nutrients. Make sure to perform routine maintenance on schedule.

Set up this system with a large protein skimmer in the sump, and two to four 40-watt fluorescent lamps centered over the tank. Build up a wall of coral rock stretching across the aquarium, with room on all sides for swimming. Build up the ends more than the middle, and position the three pieces of artificial coral slightly off to one side of the midpoint. A big tank like this usually has two overflows, one in each rear corner. The rock wall should reach from one of these toward the opposite front corner. Black overflows with a matching black background become quite inconspicuous, and you need not hide them with more rock if you don't want to.

Run this aquarium for a month with added ammonia in chemical form. By the end of the nitrite cycle, you should start to see algae growing on the rocks. You can speed this along by adding a few algae-covered rocks from your dealer. The algae should be a bright green filamentous type. Keep the lights on continuously for another week, or until a luxuriant growth of algae develops. Then add all of the fish at the same time. Try to find juveniles, each about two inches in diameter. Monitor the water conditions for the next month, to make sure no increase in ammonia or nitrite develops. The group of tangs will establish a pecking order among themselves, and major skirmishes should remain at a minimum.

The yellow tang grazes on filamentous algae, only taking small invertebrates incidentally. Feeding them should pose few problems, as they not only crop algae from the rocks, but also greedily accept many popular and widely available aquarium foods. Numerous diets are commercially available that contain a high proportion of vegetable matter. Supplement the greens with small amounts of animal-derived foods. Always make sure the fish's stomach appears full and round. A hollow-bellied specimen needs immediate attention, as this is a sign of acute starvation. Grazing species typically feed continuously during the daylight hours. While it is not usually possible to feed them continuously in captivity, two or three daily feedings, along with natural algae growth, should suffice. Do not make the mistake of feeding yellow tangs exclusively on terrestrial greens such as lettuce or spinach. While such foods are acceptable from time to time, the fish's nutrition will be incomplete without ocean-derived veggies.

The hardiness of the yellow tang is legendary, but it is quite susceptible to declining water quality. This is to be expected, considering that their preferred habitat is constantly replenished from the open sea. Failure to carry out regular partial water changes is often responsible for problems. The fish develop reddish inflamed patches on the skin, a sure sign that water conditions are well below optimum. Whether this is due to the accumulation of dissolved organics, metals, some other substance, or a combination, the condition responds favorably to a large water change. Activated carbon filtration will not by itself remedy the problem. Left untended, a tang that exhibits the inflammation will often develop *Cryptocaryon*, *Amyloodinium*, or a combination of both of these parasitic infestations. Without immediate improvement in water quality, and a regimen of medication, fatalities often result.

Aquarium spawning of the yellow tang is likely impossible, but the phenomenon has been observed in the sea on repeated occasions. Generally, they spawn in groups around sunset, milling about, their activities increasing until a female dashes toward the surface with one or several males in pursuit. Eggs and sperm are released, fertilization occurs, and the developing embryos are left to fend for themselves.

To customize, you could substitute the schooling bannerfish, *Heniochus diphreutes,* for the yellow tangs. It even reaches about the same size. Feed this species on an assortment of foods in small pieces suitable for its small mouth.

MODEL DESIGN 3 Regal Tang Showcase

Regal tangs, *Paracanthurus hepatus*, go by a variety of other common names, including hippo tang and blue tang. They present more of a challenge to the aquarist, and thus do best in a species tank such as the moderately large one suggested for this model design.

Aquarium Capacity . . . . 75 gallons

Aquascape Materials

    crushed coral rock . . . . fine grade

    coral rock . . . . a few large pieces

    branching coral skeleton . . . . a large piece, artificial or natural

Background . . . . .pale blue, or a photo

Fish

    Paracanthurus hepatus 3

Special Requirements

    Tangs do not like water with a heavy load of nutrients. Make sure to perform routine maintenance on schedule.

The regal tang is a distinctive true blue color with a yellow tail. A sickle-shaped black bar on the side completes the dramatic appearance of this handsome fish. It is found almost exclusively in association with the stony coral *Pocillopora eydouxi* on the seaward side of the reef. When disturbed, the fish has a habit of wedging itself into the coral, lying flat on its side. Its propensity to do this in the aquarium has given pause to more than one novice aquarist. Unfortunately, too many of these fish have been collected by poisoning the entire coral head. This is a good candidate for cyanide, so know your supplier before you purchase.

The coral preferred by the regal tang is favored by collectors, and you should have little trouble locating a piece of skeleton. The species bears stout, somewhat flattened branches, rounded at the ends. It is sometimes identified as cat's paw or big toe coral. Any similar coral that grows as a rounded cluster of branches will do just fine. Create a base for the coral by placing rocks a few inches to one side of the middle of the tank. Place the big coral skeleton on top. If you can find a photo background of dense coral growth, this is a good tank for it. In that case, choose a coral skeleton that matches one in the background.

Follow the instructions given in the previous model design for conditioning the tank. Regal tangs eat considerably more animal matter than other tangs, and their captive diet should reflect this.

Here's an idea for customization: Instead of the somewhat fussy regal tang, this aquarium could house a large school of green chromis, *Chromis viridis*. This greenish blue damselfish spends most of its time in open water, ready to feed on plankton, and adapts quickly to captivity.

MODEL DESIGN 4   Colorful Community Tank I: Large

In this and the following model design, I present my suggestions for tanks that are both easy to maintain and filled with color and movement. The "large" and "small" designations are somewhat arbitrary. You could combine these species in a variety of ways and still end up with a successful community aquarium.

This model design exemplifies an old rule of thumb about mixing various species of saltwater fish: choose fish as diverse in coloration and lifestyle as possible. Doing so helps avoid conflicts due to overlapping needs. Fish should not have to constantly compete for the same food items or territories. The threadfin butterflyfish (*Chaetodon*) picks constantly for small invertebrates. *Siganus*, the foxface, eats primarily algae. Beware, this species has venomous spines, similar to those of the spotfin lionfish (*Pterois*). The lionfish feeds on live crustaceans and will swallow nearly any small prey. The harlequin tuskfish (*Choerodon*) and the Picasso triggerfish (*Rhinecanthus*) eat just about anything.

Aquarium Capacity . . . . 120 gallons

Aquascape Materials

    crushed coral rock . . . . fine grade

    coral rock . . . . assorted pieces

    branching coral skeletons . . . . artificial or natural

Background . . . . .pale blue or black

Fish

    Chaetodon auriga 1

    Siganus vulpinus 1

    Choerodon fasciatus. 1

    Rhinecanthus aculeatus 1

    Pterois antennata 1

Special Requirements

    Owing to the necessary absence of invertebrate scavengers and herbivores, the aquarium will need regular maintenance to remove algae and should have a large biofilter to handle the waste from these large, hungry fishes.

To get this community going, aquascape the tank with rocks and coral so as to provide multiple retreats. If each fish can retire to its own space, interspecies aggression will be minimized. Giving precise instructions as to how to do this challenges my ingenuity, as positioning each rock needs to be judged as the construction evolves. I can only repeat my advice to have a trial run or two with dry rock.

Another longstanding rule of thumb says that to mix fish of different temperaments successfully, place the more docile species into the tank first. For this assortment, I suggest starting with the butterflyfish, although *C. auriga* usually demonstrates a lot of spunk for a member of its genus. Follow it with the lionfish. You may need to train the lionfish to eat dead food by first tempting it with live foods. If other fish are present, they may intimidate the lionfish and thus get all the food. The butterflyfish, however, is unlikely to be interested in a large feeder minnow or crab. Wait until you have a noticeable growth of filamentous algae before introducing the foxface to this tank. It will spend most of its time grazing, swimming to and fro. Make sure you regularly feed it with sea veggies of all kinds. None of the other fish likely will pay much attention to the vegetarian fare.

When the first three species settle in, you can add the other two, about two to three weeks apart. It makes little difference which one you add first, as both are bold and unlikely to be intimidated by the other fish. The harlequin tuskfish is collected in Australia and elsewhere, and is known for its bright blue canine teeth. Boldly marked with white and red vertical bars and light blue highlights, it is a hardy, vigorous species that feeds readily on a variety of aquarium foods. Ditto the Picasso triggerfish, with its tan and pearly white body marked with blue, black, and yellow in a "modern art" pattern. Though individual fish sometimes have behavior problems, if added last and given plenty to eat, the Picasso trigger ranks among the best of its clan for captivity.

Potential substitutes can be found within any of the families represented in this community. Other butterflyfishes can stand in for the threadfin. Numerous larger wrasses can replace the harlequin tuskfish, and any species of *Pterois* will do. Instead of the foxface, you could keep a big tang, such as *Zebrasoma veliferum*. Other docile triggerfishes can be added instead of the Picasso trigger, for example, *Xanthichthys auromarginatus*, the bluechin trigger.

MODEL DESIGN 5 | Colorful Community Tank II: Small

This would be my tank if I were interested in lots of bright color and relatively little care in a package compact enough for an office or bedroom. It is also the only model design in this section that calls for live rock, itself a fascinating aquarium subject.

Something of a hybrid between a fish-only aquarium and a minireef, this model design features three of the all-around best saltwater fish. The live rock can be of any variety you find attractive. Determine, with the help of your dealer, the optimum conditions for the type of live rock you select, and equip the aquarium accordingly. At minimum, you will need 160 watts of fluorescent lighting and extra powerheads to increase water movement.

Aquarium Capacity . . . . 75 gallons

Aquascape Materials

    crushed coral sand . . . . coarse grade

    live sand . . . . about 10 pounds

    live rock . . . . 50 pounds

Background . . . . .black

Fish

    Gramma loreto 3

    Oxycirrhites typus. 1

    Centropyge argi. 3

Invertebrates

    Lysmata amboiensis 1

Special Requirements

    Provide reef tank conditions of lighting, water movement, and salinity.

The royal gramma (*Gramma*) frequents ledges, under which it often rests upside down. If possible, select a flat piece of live rock that can be used to create a ledge in your aquascape. Choose a single large fish and two smaller ones. This is likely to give you two females and a male. Two males may not get along, as will be evidenced by their mock battles. Each fish opens its capacious jaws as wide as possible, and pushes with them against the similarly gaping maw of the adversary. Such encounters end with the defeated interloper retiring to a crevice in the rocks, eventually to leave the area altogether. In the aquarium, the loser will have no place to go, and the interaction can escalate to a serious fight. Separate the two males as soon as you notice the jaw-jousting behavior. Perhaps you can trade the losing male for a female specimen.

The longnosed hawkfish (*Oxycirrhites*) prefers to perch in a prominent spot, alert to the slightest movement of potential prey. Plan to place a tall chunk of rock near the center of the tank, where the hawkfish can show off his picnic tablecloth pattern of red and white checks.

The angelfish (*Centropyge*) will patrol the entire tank. As with the grammas, choose one larger specimen and two smaller. This will, in all likelihood, result in a harem, the normal arrangement for *Centropyge*. These fish all start life as females. As they mature, larger and more robust individuals develop into males. The technical term for this phenomenon is *protogynous hermaphroditism*, and it is more commonplace among marine fish than you might think. In placing the rock, leave open space near one end of the tank to give these beautiful fish room to swim. They will benefit from filamentous algae growth occurring naturally within the tank.

All three fish species snatch food from the water column, and all three will take a wide variety of aquarium foods. Brine shrimp, mysid shrimp, live rock organisms, and chopped frozen diets all suit them. Offer a variety, including some products containing seaweed.

I suggest including two or three brittle stars as scavengers. Hermit crabs may be destructive to live rock organisms. Herbivorous snails might compete with the *Centropyge* for available food. The scarlet cleaner shrimp (*Lysmata*) will do a bit of scavenging, as well as remove dead tissue and parasitic organisms from the fish.

Equip this tank with a minireef filtration system, including a sump with an efficient protein skimmer. Use metal halide lighting if you wish, allowing you to add photosynthetic invertebrates later. The pygmy angel may nip occasionally at corals or clams but seldom does extensive damage. Once the equipment is up and running, add the live rock and live sand, and run the aquarium for a month before adding the fish. Start with the grammas, add the hawkfish about two weeks later, and finish up with the angels. You must add the group of angels all at once, or you risk problems. If you add a single fish, it may not tolerate subsequent additions of others. You can avoid the problem altogether by including only one pygmy angel in your community. Add instead a pair of tank-raised clownfish, your choice of species. Then add the single angelfish last.

With either livestock option, this aquarium should be a stunning display after about a year. Remember that maintenance needs is the same as for a reef tank.

So many small community fish are imported these days, picking some substitutes for this tank is easy. Any of the dottybacks (*Pseudochromis*), for example, can take the place of the gramma, although unless you have a mated pair they will fight, so you can keep only one. That would leave room for a goby, such as *Gobiodon okinawae*, the yellow coral goby. The small, spunky flame hawkfish (*Neocirrhites armatus*) can replace its cousin. And various species of *Centropyge* are available.

MODEL DESIGN 6 Common Lionfish

Lionfish, genus *Pterois*, adapt quickly to captivity. With a suitably large tank and a proper diet, a lionfish can live fifteen to twenty years in your home.

Aquarium Capacity . . . . 120 gallons

Aquascape Materials

    crushed coral rock . . . . fine grade

    coral rock . . . . a few large pieces

    coral skeleton . . . . artificial or natural, 5 pieces, assorted

Background . . . . .black

Fish

    Pterois volitans. 3

Special Requirements

Marine fish must provide most of the diet. Supplemental feedings of shrimp, crabmeat, or shellfish are beneficial. Occasionally feed live guppies or goldfish, depending upon size of lionfish.

Lionfishes are members of the scorpionfish family, Scorpaenidae, so named because all members possess venomous dorsal and pectoral fin spines. For defensive purposes, the spines erect automatically when the lionfish feels threatened. Should a predator be foolhardy enough to swallow the lionfish anyway, the inside of its mouth will be stung severely, hopefully encouraging the predator to spit out the lionfish before too much damage is done. I have been stung once, by a dwarf lionfish (*Dendrochirus zebra*). The intense, burning pain was followed by an angry red welt that itched like the devil for several days afterward. For me, this was much like being stung by a wasp. In others, the pain may be much more severe, requiring medical attention. Fortunately, one rarely hears of an aquarist being stung. Lionfishes are not particularly aggressive; the spines operate only defensively. Contacting the spines causes a reflex in the fish that drives the spine into the intruder. The lesson: Always make sure you can see the lionfish when your hands are in the tank.

Pterois volitans, the common lionfish, is also sometimes known as the black volitans lionfish. Growing to over a foot in length within about five years, it needs a large aquarium. Otherwise, it is probably the best aquarium choice in its family, spending most of the time in the open and feeding readily on a variety of frozen, fresh, and live seafoods. An eight-inch specimen can easily swallow a three-inch tank mate, so beware.

Although there are some obvious differences, all the lionfish species have essentially the same color pattern. Probably this has to do with their similar lifestyles. Since they are sit-and-wait predators, the coloration probably serves to camouflage them against the backdrop of alternating light and shadow on the reef. The basic body color in all species is pearly white. Vertical wavy bars of reddish orange and chestnut brown cover the length of the body. Dark brown blotches and spots usually mark the fins, making them blend with the body and the background. All species have greatly enlarged pectoral fins, which flare out behind the fish's head when it is excited. The resemblance of the fins to a lion's mane is the source of the common name for the group. Besides making the lionfish appear larger to a predator, the pectoral fins are sometimes used to herd smaller fish when the lionfish is hungry, steering them within striking range.

The mouth of any lionfish is a remarkable structure. It is capable of opening suddenly to a surprisingly large gape. The lionfish waits in ambush for a suitable fish or crustacean to swim into range, then its mouth pops open like a trap. This causes a rush of water toward the lionfish, and the hapless prey is sucked in. Special crushing teeth in the lionfish's throat dispatch the victim quickly so its struggles won't harm the lionfish. The corpse is then swallowed whole. All of this takes only a moment. A six-inch lionfish can dispatch five feeder fish in seconds.

The common lionfish only rarely shows aggression toward members of its own species, so three specimens should get along nicely in the roomy tank suggested for this model design. Install a large protein skimmer in the sump, and make sure you keep up with water changes. The hearty lionfish appetite guarantees the aquarium will have a heavy load of pollutants. Other than that, these fish are a cinch to keep and make great pets. They will learn to recognize you, becoming agitated when you approach the tank. They won't bother snails, so you might want to keep about a dozen in the tank to control algae. Using a long-handled tool to remove algae from the glass makes sense, to avoid the venomous spines.

Any *Pterois* can be substituted. Make sure all have a spot to shelter, or there may be trouble.

MODEL DESIGN 7 An Eel's Lair

Of all the big fish found in aquarium shops, few inspire the attention enjoyed by eels. People seem to find eels either repulsive or adorable; no one seems to be on the fence about them. Here's a model design that can be scaled for any eel you are likely to encounter.

Aquarium Capacity . . . . 40 to 120 gallons

Aquascape Materials

    crushed coral rock . . . . fine grade

    coral rock . . . . a few large pieces

    branching coral skeletons . . . . artificial or natural

Background . . . . .black

Fish

    Moray eel . . . . 1 (see text)

Special Requirements

    Eels excel at finding a way to escape the tank. Make sure the aquarium is securely covered.

Acanthurus sohal

Amblyeleotris wheeleri

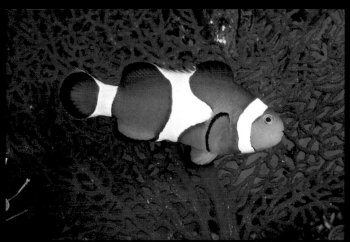

Amphiprion ocellaris

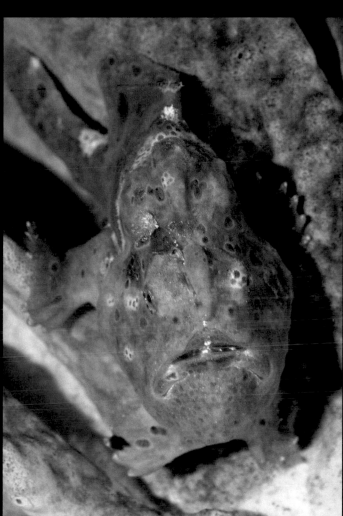

Antennarius maculatus

Assessor flavissimus

Calloplesiops altivelis

Centropyge argi

Centropyge bicolor

Centropyge bispinosus

Centropyge loriculus

Chaetodon auriga

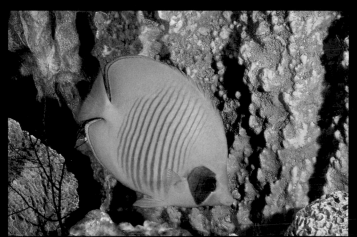

Chaetodon semilarvatus

Chromis cyanea

Chrysiptera parasema

Cirrhilabrus rubriventralis

Coris gaimard

Cryptocentrus cinctus

Dascyllus melanurus

Gobiodon okinawae

Gomphosus varius

Gramma loreto

Hippocampus erectus

Gymnomuraena zebra

Nemateleotris decora

Opisthognathus aurifrons

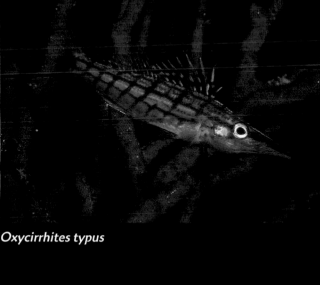

Oxycirrhites typus

Paracanthurus hepatus

Pholidichthys leucotaenia

Pomacanthus arcuatus

Pomacanthus asfur

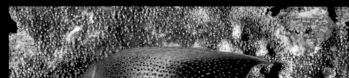

Pomacentrus alleni

Premnas biaculeatus

Pseudanthias pleurotaenia

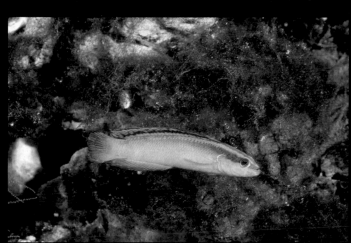

Pseudochromis porphyreus

Pterosynchiropus splendidus

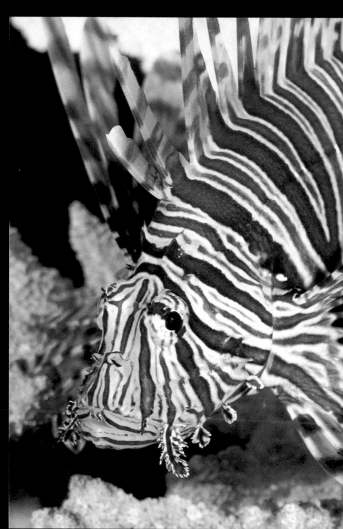

Pterois volitans

Serranocirrhitus latus

Serranus tabacarius

Siganus vulpinus

Sphaeramia nematoptera

Synchiropus picturatus

Thalassoma duperryi

Zebrasoma flavescens

Catalaphyllia jardinei

Colochirus robustus

Elysia crispata

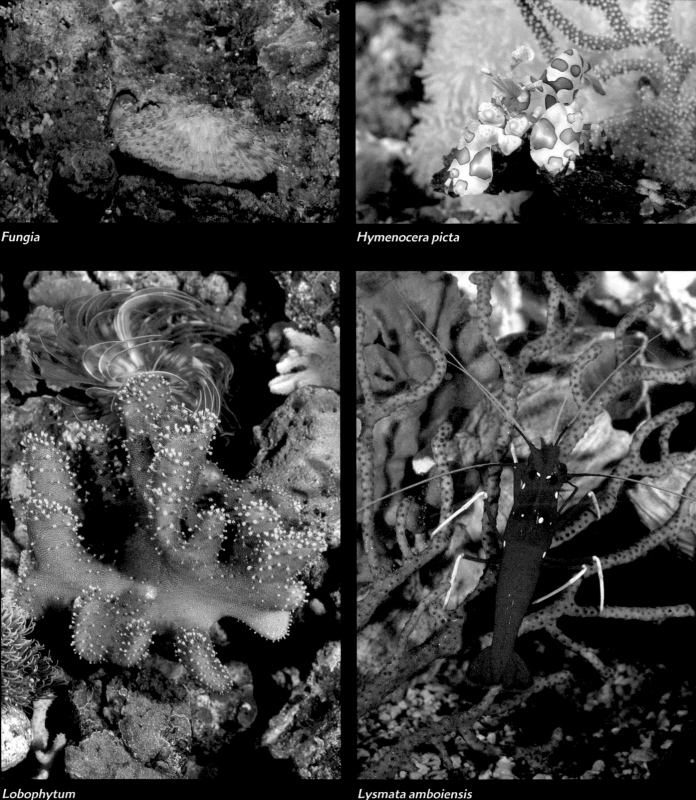

Fungia

Hymenocera picta

Lobophytum

Lysmata amboiensis

Ophioderma brevispinum

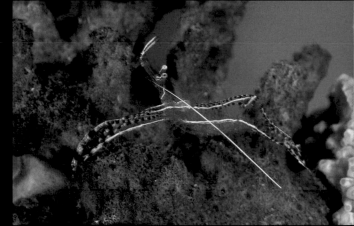

Periclimenes pedersoni

Phymanthus crucifer

Pseudocolochrius violaceus

Stenopus hispidus

Thor amboiensis

Trachyphyllia geoffroyi

As a group, moray eels make good aquarium pets. Some get very large and should not be placed in a small tank. Four commonly available species and their tank requirements are:

- *Enchelycore pardalis*, Hawaiian dragon moray eel, 55–75 gallons
- *Echidna nebulosa*, snowflake moray eel, 40 gallons
- *Gymnomuraena zebra*, zebra moray eel, 120 gallons
- *Gymnothorax meleagris*, comet moray eel, 55–75 gallons

Although the alternative suggestions for eels are given above, many other eel species can be found in dealers' tanks. Resist the temptation, however, to purchase a ribbon eel (*Rhinomuraena* sp.). It seldom feeds in captivity.

A moray eel needs a lair in which to retire. Direct your aquascaping efforts toward this end. Place a cairn of rocks off-center in the aquarium, positioning them to create a deep cave. Select pieces carefully, keeping in mind the final arrangement you want and the scale of the aquarium. Building a moray cave offers the ideal use of silicone adhesive and/or portland cement to construct a stable arrangement of rocks. For a truly professional look, try the following technique. Work with the model design on a tabletop to get the positioning right before you assemble it permanently in the aquarium.

Start by placing chunky, flat-bottomed rocks a few inches apart on the tank bottom, forming the first tier of the artificial reef. You can carry the rock structure around the ends of the tank toward the front, creating a greater sense of enclosure. Next, position secondary pieces to create two walls with a gap between them. The gap should open in the direction facing the viewer and should lie near the center of the tank, though not exactly in the middle. Across the top of the gap lay a flat piece to form the roof of the cave. You can fill some of the open space with coral skeletons positioned naturally on either side of the gap in the rocks. Once all the rock is placed, add the substrate to about an inch deep. With any luck at all, your moray will settle into the artificial cave and peer out from the gap you provided.

Morays vary in their temperament and willingness to feed in captivity. Of the four species mentioned, the zebra moray may be the most reluctant to accept aquarium fare. You can tempt it at first with live crustaceans, such as small crabs or shrimp. It does not normally feed on fish but can be trained as a juvenile to take fish meat from the end of a feeding stick. With this or any other moray, impaling the food on the end of a bamboo skewer and gently moving it in front of the moray usually works to get it to eat dead foods. Snowflake morays adapt quickly, and may not even need the training period.

The dragon moray may refuse to eat for an extended period. In the ocean it eats mostly fish but will also take crustaceans. Offering live fish and/or shrimp may tempt it to start eating in its new home. The comet moray seldom needs encouragement to start eating and readily takes both living and dead seafood items. Nevertheless, it too may fast for long periods after being relocated. Provided you find no problems with water conditions, the hunger strike should cause no alarm. Just be patient and keep offering food about once a week. After a month or more of sulking, the eel will start eating. You will then be surprised at how greedily it accepts your twice-weekly offerings. Now and then any eel may stop eating again, only to resume after a few weeks. No one knows why.

I suggest installing a small spotlight trained just below the mouth of the cave. You want the viewer to experience the classic moray pose, open-mouthed, body partly extended from its hiding place. The eel, that is, not the terrified viewer.

For sheer shock value, choose the Hawaiian dragon moray. It has a habit of waiting just inside its cave, then lunging out suddenly when someone comes too close. Combined with its Halloween color scheme and its fearsome mouth full of needle-sharp teeth, this behavior seldom fails to impress. The comet moray also settles quickly into an aquarium cave, though its dental equipment lacks the scary quality of some of its relatives. The all-around best moray is probably the snowflake. Readily available from Hawaii, it reaches only about two and a half feet in length, the smallest of the four species included here. The zebra moray can approach four feet in length. You can try combining different species of moray in the same tank, though cannibalism is not unheard of. Good choices for a pairing would be the snowflake and comet morays. In a suitably large tank, a moray eel can be kept with fish too large for it to consume.

MODEL DESIGN 8 Polka Dot Grouper

I hesitate to include this fish because it has been overfished in many parts of its range, both for the aquarium and as a food fish. For a truly bulletproof tank subject, however, this big grouper is hard to best.

Aquarium Capacity . . . . At least 75 gallons, preferably larger

Aquascape Materials

    crushed coral rock . . . . fine grade

    coral rock . . . . a few large pieces

    coral skeletons . . . . artificial or natural

Background . . . . .see text

Fish

    Chromileptes altivelis . . . . up to 3

Special Requirements

    None

Start this fish in a large tank, and you won't be faced with a crisis when it outgrows a smaller one. Few species adapt so quickly to captive care. The juveniles are almost too cute to resist, with their bold pattern of black polka dots on a white background and their bobbing swimming pattern. They grow quickly, feeding gluttonously on anything and everything, eventually exceeding two feet in length. Like most groupers, *C. altivelis* lies in wait and then lunges at its prey, swallowing it whole. Also called panther grouper, barramundi cod, pinhead grouper, and humpback grouper, it gets along well with its own kind and with other species, although it cannot be trusted to spare any fish it can swallow.

The polka dot grouper requires a place to retire in order to feel comfortable. Aquascaping should conform to this need. Build a cave as described in the previous model design for moray eels. Apart from that, tank decoration is immaterial. The fish show up well against a plain black background, but you could create a whimsical look with a polka dot background. Using a stencil, paint the dots first, allow them to dry, and then paint over them with the background color. You could duplicate the grouper's pattern of black dots on white, or do the reverse.

Such a greedy appetite requires plenty of biofiltration and protein skimming. Add herbivores, such as sea urchins, which the fish will ignore. They will help to control algae and consume uneaten food. Remember that urchins absolutely require water of full strength salinity, though the grouper tolerates some variation from optimum. Carry out partial water changes on schedule, keep the filter serviced, and this fish will likely thrive in your care for fifteen years or more.

For an alternative to this model design, another large grouper or a boisterous triggerfish such as *Balistapus undulatus* will thrive in this tank.

MODEL DESIGN 9 Nocturnal Fish

You need only enough lighting to observe the behavior of the fish and invertebrates in this model design. The ideal arrangement includes a bright white, 5000K fluorescent lamp paired with a red one. The white lamp is used only for maintenance and to observe the aquarium during daytime, while the red lamp illuminates the night scene.

Aquarium Capacity . . . . 55 gallons

Aquascape Materials

    crushed coral rock . . . . fine grade

    coral rock . . . . about 40 pounds, assorted sizes

    branching coral skeleton . . . . a large piece, artificial or natural

Background . . . . .black

Fish

    Apogon cyanosoma 5

    Apogon maculatus 1

    Sphaeramia nematoptera 3

Ophiocoma sp. 2

     or *Ophioderma* sp. 2

Eucidaris tribuloides 1

Special Requirements

The low light level means little algae growth, so make sure the sea urchin gets a bit of seaweed now and then.

The inhabitants I have selected for this tank number among the most durable species found in the aquarium trade. *Apogon maculatus*, the flame cardinalfish, lives in the Caribbean and tropical West Atlantic. This area also provides most of the brittle stars you are likely to encounter, as well as *Eucidaris*. The flamefish spends more of its time in hiding than the other two species suggested for this model design. It is coral pink in color with a large, dark eye and two black spots on each side of its body. It may be aggressive toward its own kind or similarly colored species.

Sphaeramia, one of the standards of the aquarium trade, is known as the pajama cardinalfish because someone fancied its white posterior with pinkish polka dots looked like pajama bottoms. The middle region of its body is crosshatched in black and pearl, while the anterior portion is brassy yellow. The large eye is red. Add all three specimens simultaneously, and allow them to sort out their own pecking order. Aggression rarely leads to anything serious.

Apogon cyanosoma, attractively patterned in alternating blue and orange stripes, it also has large eyes. It will learn to feed during the daytime more easily than the other two.

None of these fish gets much longer than about four inches, and all thrive on a varied diet of typical aquarium foods. Make sure to include foods advertised to contain color-enhancing components, which help to keep the red and orange pigments looking vibrant.

For aquascaping this tank, try to find slablike pieces of coral rock that can be stacked to form ledges. Also, create caves by leaving a couple of openings in the structure big enough to accommodate any of the cardinalfish. Cave construction using coral rock is an art that benefits from practice. Lay everything out on a table and try different configurations before permanently installing the rock work in the tank. For maximum stability, you may need to secure some pieces with silicone.

From time to time, unusual nocturnal species appear in shipments. The pineapplefish, *Cleidopus gloriamaris*, an Australian native, is a fascinating prospect for this model design. It has proved hardy in captivity when fed live foods.

Some fish attract our attention because of their bright coloration, others because they behave in an unusual way. The subject of this tank wins us over with weirdness.

Aquarium Capacity . . . . 40 gallons

Aquascape Materials

    crushed coral rock . . . . fine grade

    coral rock . . . . a few large pieces

    coral skeletons . . . . artificial or natural (optional)

Background . . . . .black

Fish

    Antennarius maculatus 1

Special Requirements

    You may need to feed live fish for a while until the frogfish becomes accustomed to feeding in captivity.

How about a fish that fishes? The clown frogfish does so quite successfully. One of its dorsal fin rays has been modified into a fishing pole, the *illicium*, complete with lure. When the frogfish is hungry, it extends the illicium, dangling the lure enticingly in the direction of any potential prey it detects. Hidden by effective camouflage consisting of a blotchy, brown and white pattern and tufts of skin that look like encrusting organisms, the frogfish remains motionless on the bottom most of the time. When it succeeds in attracting a fish within range, it explodes into motion and engulfs the hapless victim in its huge mouth. It then resumes its patient wait. If fed about twice a week on live fish or strips of fish fillet, the frogfish thrives in a small aquarium, reaching an ultimate size of about four inches. Because frogfish spend so much time motionless, a small aquarium accommodates them nicely. Even a much larger specimen could be housed in the forty-gallon tank in this example.

You do not need much in the way of decoration for this aquarium, only a few rocks for the frogfish to blend into. If you choose to add a coral skeleton, you may want to select an artificial piece in a color that pleases you. Keep the entire setup simple and make sure you do regular water changes.

Several other frogfish species appear in aquarium shipments from time to time. Dealers will sometimes label them as anglerfish. They are interchangeable in terms of their aquarium care, although reaching different adult dimensions. Try to get a positive identification, so you will know what to expect. In addition, no shortage exists for weird and wonderful marine fish. You might consider the black and neon green convict eel, *Pholidichthys leucotaenia*. A burrower, it is hardy and long-lived.

MODEL DESIGN 11 Shark!

Too many sharks collected for the aquarium wind up outgrowing their tanks. A commonplace example is the nurse shark, which reaches about nine feet, requiring an aquarium the size of a swimming pool. The little shark featured in this model design barely exceeds three feet.

Aquarium Capacity . . . . 210 gallons

Aquascape Materials

    coral sand. . . . . coarse grade

    coral rock . . . . a few large pieces

    coral skeletons . . . . artificial or natural (optional)

Background . . . . .pale blue or black

Fish

    Chiloscyllium plagiosum 1

Special Requirements

    Plan on having plenty of seafood available.

The number of fish fans who want a shark never fails to surprise me. Sharks can be a challenge to maintain, and most of them grow way too large. The diminutive bamboo sharks, however, remain small, under four feet, and can reproduce in captivity. Feeding them poses no challenge. They eat any and all seafoods. Impale the food on the end of a stick. You don't want fingers included in the shark's captive diet!

C. plagiosum, the white-spotted bamboo shark, may dig in the substrate, undermining your aquascaping. Because it lacks a bony skeleton, the little shark can be seriously injured by falling rocks. It spends a lot of time on the bottom, so I suggest leaving mostly an open expanse of sand, with only three to five large pieces of rock strategically placed.

Keeping a shark is a big responsibility. They can live a long time and become accustomed to life in captivity. Be prepared for it to hide for a while after you bring it home. Perform maintenance regularly, taking no chances that your shark might develop an illness. Sharks may react negatively to attempts at medication.

For this model design, only small sharks should be considered. The brown banded bamboo shark (*Chiloscyllium punctatum*) can stand in for its cousin, but the adult is not as attractive as the white-spotted.

CHAPTER 9

BIOTOPE TANKS

Any display of reef fish impresses with bold colors and constant motion. For sheer fascination, however, minireef aquariums offer more than any fish-only tank can. Defining what, exactly, constitutes a minireef depends upon whom you ask, but a typical example features sessile invertebrates and live rock. Fishes, if included, are species that will leave the invertebrates alone. Beyond that basic pattern, aquarists have set up everything from minireefs devoted to different color forms of the same coral to aquariums seeking to duplicate the look of an actual reef biotope. The latter approach forms the basis for this chapter.

Reef Biotopes

Coral reefs develop in characteristic ways in response to environmental patterns. Different water depths, sub-surface topography, and levels of turbulence primarily determine which types of sessile invertebrates and seaweeds can live in a particular spot. These varieties, in turn, influence the other types of animals that can coexist in the same area. Although the limits of a particular fish species' range are somewhat diffuse, factors such as the presence of a preferred food item may cause certain species to congregate in one area and not another. Choosing a given biotope as the model for an aquarium gives us plenty of options. Let's examine the different kinds of reef biotopes.

> # Invertebrate Names
>
> I have endeavored, with the help of references, to apply a plausibly correct scientific name, in some cases to the species level, for invertebrates likely to be encountered in aquarium shops. I do so with the caveat that identification of many marine invertebrates, corals and their relatives especially, simply cannot be done merely by comparing the specimen in question to a picture in a book. Most of the time, positive identification requires microscopic examination. Even then, coming up with a name can be vexing, because so much of the taxonomy is in disarray. Material for doctoral theses for years to come lies waiting on every patch reef. That said, we cannot have a useful discussion about reef invertebrates without using *some* name for the different types. For this reason, most of my identifications are to genus only. I use species names only when there is widespread agreement that the scientific name for a certain "trade" species is correct. Further complicating matters, scientific names may change when research sheds new light on relationships. Be alert to this possibility when comparing information from different references. The inhabitants of less than 10 percent of Pacific reefs, for example, have been scientifically catalogued.

Major Reef Types

Charles Darwin was the first to describe specific reef types formally. Later researchers have added some to his original three.

- Barrier reefs: Separated from the shore by a wide channel, barrier reefs develop along the edge of the continental shelf. The organisms found on the seaward side often differ markedly from those in shoreward waters.

- Fringing reefs: Barrier reefs that hug the shore are usually called fringing reefs. The channel is absent, and coral growth may be exposed at low tide. Many saltwater aquarium species are collected from this, the most common type of reef.

- Atolls: When fringing reefs encircle an island and the island subsequently subsides under the ocean, an atoll is formed. These ring-shaped reefs have a central lagoon area with species that thrive in bright shallow water.

- Patch reefs: Separate from the main reef structure, patch reefs develop for a variety of reasons. Any suitably stable spot may be colonized by corals, and a new patch reef begins. Research has shown that certain key "founder" species typically start building the patch reef, and the biotope then becomes more complex and the reef framework grows.

- Bank/barrier reefs: Along the Florida Keys, reefs run parallel to the shore as with barrier reefs, but the intervening channel is narrow and shallow compared to other barrier reefs. The term *bank/barrier reef* is sometimes used to describe this unique topography.

Zonation

On a given reef, patterns of coral zonation can be recognized. Certain corals tend to be found in certain areas of the reef. Factors influencing zonation include depth, especially as it affects penetration of sunlight, and water movement, whether forceful or relatively calm. Other local conditions, such as exposure of the reef at low tide or the increases in salinity and temperature that occur in shallow lagoons, further demarcate zones of diversity. First walking along the shore, then wading, and finally swimming, let's explore each of the major zones.

TIDE POOL

Tide pools form when a tide recedes and water remains in depressions waves have sculpted in the soft coral rock. Various species routinely find themselves trapped in these pools with no option but to wait for the return of the tide. Even though the tropical sun can heat the water, increase salinity by evaporation, and thus lower the oxygen content, tide pools may be remarkably diverse. As a rule, the larger the pool, the more diverse it is. Excavations along highway U.S. 1 in the Florida Keys have created some spectacular man-made tide pools.

IRON SHORE

When no beach exists and waves break directly upon rocks, we have an iron shore. Even in this harsh environment, corals and other organisms thrive, clinging tenaciously to the substrate.

LAGOON

Moving further seaward, we encounter the lagoon, a shallow, relatively calm and sediment-lined area, where collectors take many aquarium animals. Corals adapted for growing on soft sediment or sand, *Catalaphyllia* and *Fungia*, for example, grow here, along with dozens of sponges, soft corals, anemones, crustaceans, and echinoderms. Because nutrients become concentrated in the lagoon, plankton flourishes, feeding millions of hungry mouths. Certain portions of the lagoon accumulate a thick blanket of mud. Turtle grass, *Thalassia*, takes root in the sediment and covers acres. The turtle grass beds provide yet another biotope, exploited by such familiar creatures as *Condylactis* anemones and the giant seahorse, *Hippocampus erectus*.

MANGROVE SWAMP

Sometimes the shore edge of a lagoon is fringed with mangrove trees, creating yet another biotope. The mangrove's prop roots extend into the ocean, sheltering vast numbers of tube worms, sponges, and other invertebrates. These areas also act as fish nurseries, with juveniles of many species found there. Like the lagoon, because of its accessibility from shore, the mangrove swamp provides many aquarium species.

BACK REEF SLOPE

Paddling further out, we find that the bottom begins to slope upward, and the amount of coral growth increases noticeably. We have reached the back reef slope, where, protected from the fury of the open ocean by the reef itself, another rich community of fish and invertebrates appears. Growth-forms, both delicate and massive, appear among the corals.

REEF FLAT

At the top of the back reef slope, the bottom levels out again, often only a few feet below the surface of the sea. We have reached the reef flat and could wade again, except our feet might be cut to ribbons by the thousands of corals. Calm shallow water under the blazing sun may allow a coral garden to develop, or, on occasion, this zone is strikingly empty, strewn with coral rubble from the reef crest. Coral gardens sometimes grow so close to the surface that they are left high and dry at low tide. Corals from such areas often have bright pigments that protect them from the sun's harsh rays.

REEF CREST

Corals found on the reef crest, where waves break across the reef's highest point, often grow as branching forms highly prized by some aquarists. Often brightly colored, reef crest corals thrive on high levels of sunlight and pounding currents.

UPPER FORE REEF

Surmounting (somehow) the reef crest, we arrive in the clear water of the open ocean as the reef drops away below our feet. Up here, where the shallow water permits maximum light penetration, we find the greatest abundance and diversity of both invertebrates and fishes. Here we might see a shoal of *Pseudanthias* or *Chromis* numbering in the thousands. Stony and soft corals, sponges, gorgonians, and dozens of other encrusting species vie for space in the sun. On and among them, crustaceans, worms, echinoderms, and small colorful fish seek shelter and food. Tangs, angelfish, butterflyfish, and wrasses patrol back and forth, feeding on algae and invertebrates. Here and there, lionfish, groupers, and other predators may lurk. In this reef zone, most experienced saltwater aquarists find great inspiration.

DEEP FORE REEF

Light becomes more and more dim as we (hopefully now wearing scuba gear) descend the face of the reef. With each fathom of descent, we find new species. In deep water, corals become thin and flat, spreading out to capture what little light is available. Some favored aquarium fish live here, including the flame angelfish (*Centropyge loriculus*) and blackcap basslet (*Gramma melacara*).

Captivated, we might be tempted to spend hours on the deep fore reef, but it is time to return to the surface. The dive boat waits above. Soon, at home, we can begin to recreate in an aquarium one of the reef's memorable sights.

System Components

Each of the model designs described in this chapter assumes a uniform set of specifications for the aquarium system that varies only with respect to the size of the tank. See chapter five, "Nuts and Bolts," for additional details on filtration and lighting systems.

Filtration

The filtration system should be of the sump type, including a protein skimmer. Aquascaping consists of live rock. A sand bed lies on the bottom of the tank, and it has been seeded with live sand. For some model designs, the sump can be used as a refugium.

Lighting

Each model design requires lighting appropriate to the biotope being modeled. Bright shallow waters generally call for metal halide lighting. Deeper, dimmer habitats can manage with fluorescent. Do not attempt to maintain photosynthetic invertebrates under inappropriate lighting regimes.

Water Movement

For all sessile invertebrates, the importance of water movement has been well established. Public aquariums and large private installations often employ surge-producing equipment, such as dump buckets, that are too bulky or too messy for home use. At present, devices that control multiple powerheads to produce variable flows appear to be the best option for smaller systems.

Maintenance Considerations

No getting around it, a minireef aquarium requires more maintenance than a basic fish-only system. Nevertheless, many aquarists find the rewards worth the additional effort. Be realistic about your ability and willingness to perform critical maintenance functions.

Food Production

Strange as it may sound, more captive saltwater creatures starve to death than die of disease. Many a failed system could have been saved with better attention to nutrition. Suspension feeding invertebrates, in particular, may fail to receive adequate nourishment and perish within a year. Avoid needless waste by planning ahead for a continuous food supply before you commit to a tank of such species, or even a single specimen. I have provided tips on food cultivation in chapter 2,"Bringing Out the Best in Saltwater Aquariums." Eric Borneman's *Aquarium Corals* and Ron Shimek's *Marine Invertebrates* provide detailed recipes for coral foods and information about feeding specifics in invertebrate groups, respectively.

Cultivating live foods for your aquarium can be as much fun as the aquarium itself, but to do it consistently you will need a permanent work space for the purpose.

Water Changes

Invertebrates, corals in particular, demand water chemistry approaching the norms of the sea. Regular partial water changes help to remove accumulating pollutants and restore valuable trace elements. Attention to this aspect of maintenance requires both time and a way to prepare seawater. Your plan should include both, if you hope to have a successful minireef.

Monitoring

A test and tweak routine ensures that the crucial factors of salinity, calcium concentration, alkalinity, and pH remain optimal at all times. If you are unprepared for weekly monitoring of these parameters, consider a more basic aquarium design.

Supplementation

The aquarium must have additions of distilled water to compensate for evaporation. Calcium will require replenishment if your corals are to grow new skeletal material. Buffer may be needed to maintain alkalinity. Consider automating these procedures to the extent possible, providing greater consistency of water chemistry over time.

The Designs

For my money, the most enjoyable saltwater tanks are those that reflect a specific biotope in a particular part of the world. It's okay, though, to combine species from diverse locations, provided the aquarium you create satisfies their lifestyle needs. Many coral reef biotopes develop similarly, regardless of the part of the globe in which they occur. This no doubt stems from the precise requirements of corals themselves and the stability of conditions in reef-friendly environments. As a result, we find the same ecological roles being filled by similar organisms in reef and near-reef biotopes around the world. Seahorses, for example, are likely to turn up among sea grasses irrespective of longitude.

MODEL DESIGN 12 Anemonefish

Undoubtedly the most popular aquarium specimens, anemonefishes have introduced many aquarists to saltwater. Hardy, relatively small, accepting a variety of aquarium foods, and exhibiting bright colors and interesting behavior, anemonefishes have the added advantage of wide availability of captive-propagated stock. Thanks to the efforts of pioneers such as Martin Moe, anemonefish became the first saltwater aquarium fish to be propagated in commercial quantities. Building on the techniques of early hatcheries, entrepreneurs now produce many other types of saltwater fish, as well.

Anemonefish distinguish themselves by their habit of associating with large sea anemones. Adult anemonefish rarely stray more than a meter's distance from the host anemone. In the cruel sea, doing so means certain death at the hands of a predator. Their unique dependence upon giant sea anemones has resulted in an equally unique way of coping with the problems of reproducing the species while avoiding inbreeding. All anemonefish start life as males. When a breeding female dies, her former "husband" rapidly develops into a functional female, and then one of the juvenile males takes the role of breeding male. This arrangement guarantees that once an anemone is occupied by an anemonefish clan, a female fish will always be present. Every anemone successfully occupied thus continues to be used by generations of the occupying fish species. No member of the clan need embark on a dangerous excursion to find and attract a new female. The anemonefish lifestyle has not only achieved the goal of species survival, but has led to the evolution of some twenty-eight species of anemonefishes that are distributed throughout the Indo-Pacific region.

In the aquarium trade, four species of anemonefishes tend to dominate the market. *Amphiprion ocellaris* is arguably the most popular and widely available member of its clan. Another, *A. percula*, is often confused with *A. ocellaris*. In many shops, the fish labeled Percula Clownfish is probably *A. ocellaris*. The two differ only in morphological details apparent to hair-splitting ichthyologists. Their similar color pattern of bright orange with white bars edged in black led to the common name for *A. percula*, "clownfish" to be applied not only to *A. ocellaris* but to all members of the group. Thus, in aquarium parlance *clownfish* and *anemonefish* are synonyms.

Amphiprion ocellaris, whose correct common name is false clown anemonefish, ranges from Southeast Asia to the Philippines, Indonesia, and northwestern Australia. An unusual color variety, completely dark brown or black, is found near Darwin, Australia. This species associates with the carpet anemones *Stichodactyla gigantea* and *S. mertensi* and with the so-called radianthus anemone, *Heteractis magnifica*. It is found in water up to fifty feet deep on the outer reef or in a shallow lagoon. It adapts readily to aquariums, with or without a host anemone.

Amphiprion frenatus, the tomato anemonefish, occurs in all countries bordering the South China Sea, including the Philippines, Indonesia, and Singapore, from which locations most aquarium specimens were once imported. Juveniles are red with two vertical white bars, one just behind the eye and the second encircling the middle of the body. In the adult, the midbody bar is lost, and the red coloration on the flanks darkens to black. Intermediate specimens are red with the single anterior white bar. Associating most often with the bubble tip anemone, *Entacmaea quadricolor*, *A. frenatus* usually accepts any anemone available to it in the aquarium. In nature, it also inhabits the leathery anemone, *Heteractis crispa*. This anemone is found in water up to about thirty feet deep in lagoon areas. Hence, this is where the anemonefish lives, as well. Aside from a tendency to become aggressive toward tank mates when mature, *A. frenatus* is an ideal aquarium fish.

Amphiprion melanopus, known both as the cinnamon anemonefish and the red and black anemonefish, may also become somewhat aggressive as it matures, especially toward other anemonefishes, which it no doubts looks upon as a threat to its possession of the host anemone. It associates with *Entacmaea quadricolor*, and *Heteractis crispa*. It ranges from Indonesia eastward to the Marshall Islands, inhabiting the waters of numerous archipelagos. Juveniles are red orange with a white bar behind the eye and a black spot on the upper body behind the dorsal fin. With maturity, the black spot enlarges to cover most of the rear two-thirds of the body, leaving the tail red orange.

Clark's anemonefish, *Amphiprion clarkii*, has often been misnamed sebae anemonefish by aquarium dealers. (The true *A. sebae* is far less common.) That confusion could occur between these similar species is not surprising when one considers that numerous color forms of *A. clarkii* exist, depending in part upon the geographic location it inhabits and in some cases by the host anemone. For example, the individuals living in a Mertens' carpet anemone, *Stichodactyla mertensi*, are often completely black except for white bars behind the eye and at midbody. Among these dark color forms, the tail can be white or yellow, depending upon the geographic location. Color forms apparently become easily established in this wide-ranging (Persian Gulf to Japan and western Pacific archipelagos) species, as it may be orange, yellow orange, or black with numerous variations in between. All specimens have the two white bars, and some may have a third bar on the caudal peduncle. It associates with a variety of anemone species in nature, and will even accept an Atlantic pink-tipped anemone (*Condylactis gigantea*) as a surrogate host in the aquarium.

Because they normally spend their lives in the restricted area near the host anemone, anemonefishes are "preadapted" to captivity. They are undemanding in their requirements, needing only appropriate water conditions and a suitable diet (flakes, frozen foods, brine shrimp, and algae) to thrive, and even spawn, in aquariums as small as thirty gallons. The anemone need not be present.

Always buy captive-propagated anemonefishes, as they adapt better to the aquarium than their wild-caught counterparts. They are long-lived, surviving to the age of fifteen years, possibly older, with proper care. They are colorful, and their charming swimming behavior attracts interest from fish watchers of all ages. Anemonefishes are tolerant of less-than-perfect water conditions, and thus afford the beginner a chance to make an occasional mistake without disastrous consequences. Perhaps best of all, anemonefishes are readily accessible and reasonably priced.

Aquarium Capacity . . . . 30 gallons

Life Support . . . . .live rock, live sand, protein skimmer/box filter combination

Lighting . . . . .one 30-watt fluorescent lamp

Background . . . . .black

Decoration . . . . .plastic anemone reproduction

Special Requirements . . . . .none

Fish (Choose a mated pair of one species.)

> *Amphiprion clarkii*

> *Amphiprion frenatus*

> *Amphiprion melanopus*

> *Amphiprion ocellaris*

> *Amphiprion percula*

Invertebrates

> Algae snails. 3

> Brittle stars. 1

> *Lysmata amboiensis* (optional) 1

Even a younger aquarist should have no trouble setting up and maintaining this simple system. I cannot guarantee that the fish you select will accept the artificial anemone as host, but it is worth trying. After painting the background, place the tank on its support and install the combination protein skimmer/box filter. Fill the tank with seawater and start the filter running. The water should be quite clear the following day. Add one inch of sand on the bottom. Use coarse coral sand and seed it with a small amount of live sand, or use all live sand. Arrange the larger pieces of live rock toward the back of the tank, roughly in a U-shape, open to the front for viewing. You can use the type of live rock known as base rock, since primarily its function is practical rather than decorative. Place the artificial anemone near the center of the open area. Run the system for a month before adding a pair of anemonefish. If you select one-inch captive-propagated individuals, you should have a mated pair in six months or so. Feeding and maintenance for this model design consist of the basics: twice-daily feedings with a variety of seafoods and prepared frozen diets containing algae, and regular partial water changes. The pair will likely remain with you more than ten years and may spawn regularly. The scarlet cleaner shrimp (*Lysmata*) lives about three years.

MODEL DESIGN 13 Anemonefish II

This model design mimics the previous one, with the exception that the artificial anemone is replaced with a living surrogate, *Condylactis gigantea*, a hardy species sometimes accepted by an anemonefish with no other option.

Aquarium Capacity . . . . 30 gallons

Life Support . . . . .live rock, live sand, protein skimmer/box filter combination

Lighting . . . . .two to four 30-watt fluorescent lamps

Background . . . . .black

Decoration . . . . .none

Special Requirements . . . . .the anemone needs reef water conditions and moderate current

Fish (Choose a mated pair of one species.)

　　Amphiprion clarkii

　　Amphiprion frenatus

Invertebrates

　　Algae snails. 3

　　Brittle stars. 1

　　Condylactis gigantea . . . . 1 to 3

　　Lysmata amboiensis (optional) 1

In caring for this aquarium, the goal is to keep the anemone happy. It contains zooxanthellae, thus thriving best under bright illumination. Hardy, abundant, and beautiful, *Condylactis* often proves acceptable to the two anemonefish species suggested for this tank. It is also far easier to care for than their natural host anemones. *Condylactis* likes to sit with the column wedged into a rock crevice or in deep sediment. The former situation is more easily met simply by placing two *more or less* flat pieces of live rock close together and depositing the anemone between them. Place the rocks near the center of the aquarium, where light will be abundant. Installing powerheads to provide crosscurrent water movement should keep the anemone satisfied. You should see the tentacles waving gently. Never aim the powerhead directly at the anemone. Position rocks strategically to deflect some of the force of the water. Set the tank up as described in the previous model design. Run it for two weeks with only the live rock and sand, then add the anemone and observe it for another two weeks to make sure it is adapting. Feed it once or twice a week with a small amount of any of the foods you are stocking for the fish. When you are satisfied the tank is ready, as evidenced by stable water parameters and a thriving, fully expanded anemone, introduce the *Amphiprion* pair.

MODEL DESIGN 14 Anemonefish III

If you feel ready for the challenge of keeping a host anemone with a pair of anemonefish, this model design is for you. The anemones that host anemonefish are such popular aquarium subjects, and yet so widely misunderstood. One should consider their special needs in detail before committing to creating an aquarium for them. Continued importation of host anemones by the aquarium trade may be ecologically damaging. Biologists observe that survival of larvae is rare. They encounter few small individuals of any anemone species. The rate at which immature forms survive to adulthood is known as a species' recruitment rate. Low recruitment rates characterize species that are long-lived. Anemones live to be quite old. Many of the larger ones are over a century in age. Unfortunately, such long-lived creatures often survive only a few months in captivity. Larger individuals probably constitute brood stock. Each one collected means fewer larvae to replenish the reef. Further, removal of the anemone reduces the population of anemonefish, also, because the anemone host is essential to anemonefish survival.

I recommend that aquarium hobbyists select only *Entacmaea quadricolor* as anemonefish host. It is the most abundant host anemone in nature. It occurs from the Red Sea to Samoa. It is host to many species of anemonefish. Most importantly, it can be propagated in the aquarium. This anemone settles into the aquarium quickly, preferring to attach to a rock or other solid object with its column protected. It needs bright illumination, water conditions appropriate to corals, and regular feeding with small pieces of seafood.

Since dealers continue to import host anemones, you should learn to identify and avoid them. *Heteractis aurora*, beaded anemone, has ribbed tentacles with swellings that are often a contrasting color. It hosts seven anemonefish species. *Heteractis crispa* hosts eleven species. The column has a tough, leathery feel. In the aquarium trade, it is usually known as the sebae anemone, but some books may list it as the leathery anemone. *H. crispa* possesses short white tentacles tipped in magenta. *Heteractis magnifica*, magnificent sea anemone, often labeled ritteri anemone, hosts ten anemone species. It ranks as the most difficult host anemone to maintain. Another species *H. malu*, known variously as white sand anemone or delicate anemone, hosts only one anemonefish species. It is less commonly imported than the others. *Stichodactyla gigantea*, the giant carpet anemone, hosts seven anemone species. It can be separated from the other two *Stichodactyla* species by longer tentacles, often strikingly colored. *Stichodactyla haddoni*, Haddon's carpet anemone, "saddle carpet" in the aquarium trade, sports short tentacles frequently in two colors, giving the oral disc a mottled appearance. Six anemonefish species associate with it. Mertens' carpet anemone, *Stichodactyla mertensi*, is called Sri Lanka carpet by aquarium dealers. Sometimes bright green, its stubby tentacles are uniform in color. Often, a contrasting ring of purple pigment encircles the mouth. This species holds the oral disc size record for anemonefish hosts, and can be over three feet in diameter. *Macrodactyla doreensis* is known as long tentacle anemone, often abbreviated LTA. Recognize it by the red column topped with bluish gray verrucae. The long tentacles, gray, bluish, or pinkish in color, often twist into a spiral shape. It hosts only three anemonefish species in nature.

Entacmaea quadricolor, called the bulb, bubble tip, or maroon anemone in the aquarium trade, holds the record for anemone species hosted at thirteen. The inflated tips of the tentacles, looking something like the nipple on an old-fashioned glass baby bottle, make it unmistakable. Unlike most other aquarium anemones, it commonly reproduces by asexual reproduction, simply dividing to form two offspring. Aquarists have exploited this tendency to produce captive-propagated specimens, which are now widely available.

This model design pairs a captive-propagated *Entacmaea* with hatchery-raised anemonefish.

Aquarium Capacity . . . . 50 gallons

Life Support . . . . .live rock, live sand, standard reef filtration

Lighting . . . . .four 30-watt fluorescent lamps

Background . . . . .pale blue

Decoration . . . . .none

Special Requirements . . . . .the anemone needs reef water conditions and a brisk current

Fish

   Premnas biaculeatus, gold-striped form, mated pair

Invertebrates

   Algae snails. 5

   Serpent stars 2

   Entacmaea quadricolor. 1

Try to find the rose form of *Entacmaea* and the gold-striped form of *Premnas*. Both the orange pink of the anemone and the maroon and gold of the anemonefish show up best against a pale blue background. The tank must be at least fifty gallons to support not only the large anemone, but also the anemonefish, capable of reaching six inches in length. Install powerheads to supply current, as described in the previous model design.

Also as it is described in that model design, run the system with only the live rock and sand for two weeks, then add the anemone and evaluate its condition for two more weeks before bringing home the anemonefish.

Because *Entacmaea* likes its column buried in a deep crevice, you should place two relatively massive pieces of live rock close together near the center of the tank to accommodate it. Handle the anemone very gently, placing it in the crevice without applying any force. If you are lucky, within a few hours it will settle itself in and expand its tentacles. Wait a few days before feeding it, then give a small piece of shrimp or fish.

You could add a few harmless invertebrates such as a couple of yellow sea cucumbers, *Colochirus robustus*, to this display to create additional interest. Cleaning shrimps, such as *Lysmata amboiensis* or *L. debelius*, would also be at home in this aquarium. Add color by choosing serpent stars, such as *Ophioderma*, that often turn up in shops in shades of green, orange, and red. Two pretty species imported from the tropical Atlantic are *O. appressum* and *O. rubicundum*.

MODEL DESIGN 15 Royal Gramma

I confess a favorable prejudice toward the royal gramma. It comes from the Caribbean region, and it is usually available from East Coast wholesalers. It is among the least demanding of saltwater fish, thriving under any reasonably conscientious maintenance program. Apart from a tendency to feed on smaller shrimp, it never bothers invertebrates, leaving open numerous possibilities for creating an interesting community. Males may exhibit aggressive behavior, but a group can share a tank. Typically, they remain close to each other, taking shelter upside down under an overhang. When it does occur, male to male aggression rarely leads to a damaging fight. One fish always backs down and moves out of the winner's territory. Several three-inch adults can live within a tank four feet in length.

The royal gramma was one of the first marine fishes to be introduced into the aquarium trade, arriving in the 1960s. The bright yellow body appears as if the fish were held by the tail and dunked in purple paint, the colors blending about two-thirds of the way toward the tail fin. A few yellow scales form lines that merge with the purple anterior. There is a black dot on the purple dorsal fin, and the paired fins are also purple. Yellow streaking decorates the head. *Gramma brasiliensis* is slightly larger than *G. loreto* and lacks the yellow lines on the head. Although not often seen in the trade, the Brazilian gramma is a good aquarium fish, despite a tendency to aggressiveness toward tank mates, and especially toward other *G. brasiliensis*. Keep only one or a mated pair.

Royal grammas have been bred successfully in captivity. Mated pairs can be obtained by keeping one larger fish (or one previously identified as male) in a tank with several smaller individuals. The fish will pair off naturally. When ready to breed, the male builds a tube-shaped nest slightly larger than his body, using pebbles, seaweed, and bits of debris. Sometimes, the pair chooses a hole or cave, placing stones in front of the opening to restrict access, presumably for the protection of the developing eggs. A strand of seaweed placed in the nest serves as a substrate upon which the female deposits her eggs, which are immediately fertilized by the male. He guards the nest until the fry hatch, in about a week. The pair will spawn repeatedly, producing successive batches of fry every few days. Fortunately for aquarists, the fry can be raised on a captive diet, making them easy for hatcheries to produce. Nevertheless, most specimens still come from wild populations.

Royal grammas may be found in association with coral heads, hence the optional inclusion of *Montipora*, a relatively easy stony coral, to this biotope. Most commonly, however, large numbers of royal grammas are found where the vertical relief of the reef is most dramatic. Here, they hide under ledges or in cracks, darting out to snatch plankton from the water column. Duplicating this habitat in the aquarium poses few problems.

Aquarium Capacity . . . . 75 gallons

Life Support . . . . .live rock, live sand, standard reef filtration system

Lighting . . . . .two to four 40-watt fluorescent lamps

Background . . . . .black

Decoration . . . . .none

Special Requirements . . . . .additional powerheads needed to provide current for the optional coral

Fish

    Gramma loreto . . . . up to 5

    Gobiosoma oceanops. . . . . 3, optional

Invertebrates

    Algae snails. 8

    Brittle stars and/or serpent stars 5

    Stenopus hispidus. 1

    Montipora. . . . . 3 to 5 specimens, optional

Arrange the live rock across the back of the aquarium to form a wall with open spaces here and there. These facilitate water circulation as well as provide hiding places for the royal grammas. Each individual needs its own little spot if you want aggression minimized. As with other model designs, allow the system to run for at least two weeks with only live rock and sand, then add the invertebrates, and run a while longer before adding the fish. Stocking gradually minimizes the likelihood of problems.

Montipora comes in bright colors and adapts readily to aquarium care, provided the basic needs for any coral are met. Beginners who want experience with small-polyp stony corals often choose this genus. It is readily available because fragments can grow quickly to produce new colonies. Don't include other coelenterates in the tank, as they may cause harm to the *Montipora*.

The live rock for this model design, about sixty to eighty pounds in all, should consist largely of base rock to minimize costs. Select several showier pieces to place near the top of the wall where they will be seen. Royal grammas are unlikely to bother any invertebrates they cannot eat, so you could add others besides those mentioned. Any medium-sized cleaning shrimp can be substituted for the *Stenopus*, for example.

Clear shallow water and relative calm characterize the lagoon. Here live some of the most lovely species collected for the aquarium. Lagoons often have a floor of sediment with tiny patch reefs dotted here and there. This diversity of topography and bottom type result in a correspondingly diverse fauna and flora.

Aquarium Capacity . . . . 75 gallons

Life Support . . . . .live rock, live sand, standard reef filtration

Lighting . . . . .two 150-watt metal halide lamps

Background . . . . .deep blue

Decoration . . . . .none

Special Requirements . . . . .reef water conditions and moderate current

Fish

    Calloplesiops altivelis 1

    Gobiodon okinawae 5

    Pseudocheilinus tetrataenia 1

       Or *Pseudocheilinus hexataenia*. 1

Invertebrates

    Algae snails. 7

    Brittle stars. 3

    Trachyphyllia 3

       Or *Cynarina* 3

    Lobophyllia 1

    Tridacna crocea. 3

Seaweeds

    Penicillus. 5

    Udotea 1

    Cymopolia barbata . . . . 1 clump

       Or *Halimeda* . . . . 1 clump

Few marine fish can compare with the comet grouper (*Calloplesiops*) in terms of hardiness and ease of care. It is rarely afflicted with parasites, even when other fish in the tank are. In a well-established reef community with plenty of live rock and live sand, the comet can find plenty to eat even without the attention of the aquarist. Its only drawback is a tendency to hide for a long time, even several weeks, after relocation. The primary requirement for success, therefore, is the presence of an adequate cave into which the comet can retire.

Keep the comet cave in mind as you select live rock for this model design. You are going to build a small patch reef at one end of the tank, arranging it so the comet can move in. The rest of the tank will be left open. You will need at least three pieces of rock to make a base, then a fourth one for the top of the cave. Add up to three smaller pieces around the bases of the larger ones to help balance the composition. Place a one- to two-inch layer of sand on the bottom, surrounding the bases of the live rock. Use as much live sand as feasible. You want to establish a thriving population of small organisms as quickly as possible. Once the live rock has been placed, create a "forest" of calcareous seaweeds across the open area of the sand. Choose an assortment of varieties from those suggested, or if you prefer use only one species. Make sure the holdfast is present on *Penicillus*, *Udotea*, and *Halimeda*. Poke a hole in the sand with your finger and gently place the holdfast, burying it at the same depth it was growing, as evidenced by the bits of substrate still clinging to the holdfast and stalk. *Cymopolia* lies in clumps on the bottom, often unattached. Leave room among the groups of plants to place the specimens of *Trachyphyllia*.

While *Trachyphyllia* normally sits in sediment, *Lobophyllia* forms dome-shaped colonies attached to rock. Since the two cannot be allowed to come into contact, lest *Trachyphyllia* sting its tank mate, place the *Lobophyllia* specimen atop the live rock. That should keep it a safe distance from the other coral. Either of these large-polyp stony corals adapts well to aquarium care. They make good starter corals. Moderate but not forceful current helps them feel at home. *Trachyphyllia*, open brain coral, is a single, large polyp. The skeleton is a simple cone that sits, pointed end down, in sediment. As a result of this growth form, it is easily collected without damage, which may help to explain why aquarium specimens do so well. *Cynarina*, button coral, is also a single large polyp and can serve as a stand-in for *Trachyphyllia*. Another open brain coral, *Lobophyllia*, possesses "teeth" at the margin of the colony, which are lacking in *Trachyphyllia* or *Cynarina*. *Lobophyllia* colonies are groups of polyps, another difference from the other two genera.

Tridacna crocea typically inhabits shallow water and so can contribute its beautiful blue and green colors to this lagoon aquarium. Unfortunately, it is among the more difficult members of its genus. Ideally, purchase a specimen already attached to a piece of live rock, and place pieces of rock on either side of the clam. It lives on hard-bottom areas, often wedged into a crevice. You could substitute another species of clam, as the most commonly available ones live in shallow water and should do well under the same conditions recommended for *T. crocea*.

Both the corals and the clams need food. You can feed small bits of seafood to the corals. Try different products to see which ones are acceptable, then offer them in rotation to provide a balanced diet. They may be seen to consume particles of food added for the fish. The giant clams will benefit greatly from phytoplankton additions four or five times a week. Other plankton substitutes, as well as organisms produced by the live rock and live sand, should provide a diet on which the invertebrates will thrive.

Homegrown Bounty

The importance of microscopic and near-microscopic invertebrates that reproduce within the aquarium can scarcely be overstated. For many kinds of showy, colorful invertebrates, these organisms are an essential component of the diet. Live rock and live sand play numerous roles in the ecology of the aquarium, with food production being one of the major ones. In addition to tiny invertebrates, *Eurythoe*, a small orange bristleworm, usually becomes established in live sand. It performs valuable service as a scavenger as well as provides food for certain fish and crustaceans. Snails may deposit eggs that are eaten by other organisms, added value to their usefulness as algae grazers. Numerous sessile invertebrates may release their larvae, periodically providing yet another substitute for plankton. Spawning fish are likely to lose eggs or fry to other larger creatures in the same tank. While not likely to supply all of the aquarium's dietary needs, homegrown foods such as these likely provide valuable nutrients lacking in processed aquarium foods. Creating a refugium in the sump of your system helps maximize production of a host of food organisms.

Wait at least a month for the sand bed and live rock to seed the aquarium before adding the clams and corals. Keep the lights on a regular twelve-hour schedule, and make sure the calcium level remains at 400 ppm or above. Three types of inhabitants in this tank build a calcified skeleton: the seaweeds, the clams, and the corals. Without adequate calcium and correct alkalinity, they will not fare well.

When all the invertebrates have been added, the wrasse (*Pseudocheilinus*) and gobies (*Gobiodon*) can come next. The wrasse will help protect the clams from parasite damage, as it feeds on the tiny snails that often enter the aquarium attached to a clam host. As added benefits, either species of *Pseudocheilinus* is colorful, active, and hardy. Add the comet grouper last, and remember not to fret if it lies low for a long while.

The gobies are naturally short-lived. Expect only a couple of years or three. The neon wrasse likely will live about five years. Follow proper maintenance procedures, and the comet grouper will grace your blue lagoon for many years. The corals and clams have much longer life spans and should survive more than one generation of fish inhabitants. Carefully planned and thoughtfully executed, this relatively simple reef tank will charm your family and guests.

MODEL DESIGN 17 Turtle Grass Bed I

My first encounter with a turtle grass bed went badly. Trying to make my way through the knee-deep bottom sediment, I was stung by tiny hydrozoans growing on the leaves of the turtle grass. Fortunately, the experience did not deter me from returning time and again to the turtle grass to observe and collect the many creatures living there. For many species of marine fish, the grass beds serve as a nursery. Certain invertebrates may be more abundant in turtle grass than elsewhere in the reef environment. You can set up this tank using real turtle grass, but the plant can be challenging to establish in an aquarium. Plastic reproductions of the freshwater plant *Vallisneria* make a fine substitute.

Aquarium Capacity . . . . 50 gallons

Life Support . . . . .live sand, standard reef filtration

Lighting . . . . .one 150-watt metal halide lamp

Background . . . . .light green

Decoration . . . . .live turtle grass or plastic *Vallisneria*, two or three pieces of live rock

Special Requirements . . . . .reef water conditions and moderate current

Fish . . . . .none

Invertebrates

    Algae snails. 5

    Brittle stars. 2

    Condylactis gigantean 5

    Elysia crispata . . . . 1 (optional)

        Or *Elysia ornata*

    Anemone shrimp (see text)

Seaweeds

    (optional, see text)

Fish are omitted from this model design for two reasons: most of the species found in turtle grass would outgrow the tank, as they only live there when small, and small fish would eventually be captured by the anemones.

Arrange the pieces of live rock to form a small outcrop near one end of the tank. The live sand bed should be deep, up to four inches, for live turtle grass. If you use plastic plants, add only about two inches. If you use live sand only to seed a bed consisting mostly of plain sand, allow the system to mature for a month with only the plants and/or seaweeds before adding the more delicate invertebrates. You can add algae snails as soon as algae begins growing on the glass, but start with only two snails and build up the population gradually. As soon as you see that most of the algae are being consumed, stop adding snails. Add the brittle stars next, and then wait about two weeks before adding the anemones.

The *Caulerpa* species will grow vigorously under the bright illumination. Start with a small clump, and allow the seaweed to grow naturally among the grass plants. You may want to allow the seaweed to almost cover the bottom before adding anything else except snails. Then arrange the clumps of *Halimeda* randomly, keeping them near the center of the tank, where they will receive plenty of light. You must maintain calcium and alkalinity levels in order for *Halimeda* to survive.

If you add the optional *Elysia*, you must have a continuously replenished supply of seaweeds to satisfy its appetite. *Elysia* is a remarkable sea slug. It does not consume the entire seaweed but rather sucks out the contents of individual cells in the seaweed's upright blades. In this way, it not only obtains food directly, but also co-opts the green chloroplasts. These somehow are retained in the animal's body, where they remain viable and continue to photosynthesize, providing the slug with carbohydrates even when it is not feeding. The chloroplasts tint the animal green. If the slug is not getting enough to eat, it digests its stored chloroplasts, and the green fades to pale tan. *E. crispata* will accept several seaweeds as food, including *Caulerpa*, *Halimeda*, and *Sargassum*. *E. ornata* feeds exclusively on *Bryopsis*.

The Florida pink-tipped anemone (*Condylactis*) may be extremely abundant in turtle grass beds. Gently place them in a small depression scooped out in the sand. Hopefully, they will remain in place, expanding their tentacles fully within a day or so. Individual anemones are usually pale with pink tips on the tentacles. Some individuals are entirely pink. Mix or match these color morphs as you wish. Make sure the anemones are fed regularly with a small piece of shrimp or fish even though they possess zooxanthellae. A shrinking anemone is a starving anemone. Do not confuse the normal contraction of the anemone with shrinking. Normal changes in size and shape occur over the course of a day. If the anemone begins to shrink, this will be noticeable when its tentacles are fully expanded.

Condylactis hosts a number of interesting little shrimps. You could include one or several of them in this tank. *Periclimenes pedersoni*, *P. yucatanensis*, and *Thor amboiensis* are all good choices. Release the shrimp from its transport bag near the anemone, and it should hop right on. Don't try to place more than one shrimp on each anemone, unless you obtain a mated pair. *P. pedersoni* exhibits cleaning behavior, and *P. yucatanensis* may also be a cleaner. *Thor* is not a cleaner but is found on anemones and some corals worldwide. It should be kept in groups of three or more per anemone. All these shrimps probably obtain part of their nutrition by feeding on the host anemone's mucus and/or its tissues. Therefore, add them to the tank only if your anemones are larger specimens, say four inches across the expanded tentacles or larger.

Maintenance of this aquarium is relatively simple, since very little food is added in comparison to a tank with fish. Perform regular water tests to make sure the alkalinity and calcium levels are correct, adding supplements if necessary, and otherwise maintain normal reef water conditions. Feed the anemones two or three times a week. Now and then, feed the tank live newly hatched brine shrimp, phytoplankton, or some other plankton substitute.

MODEL DESIGN 18 Seahorses

Seahorses rank among the most engaging animals in the sea. As seahorse expert Dr. Amanda Vincent likes to say, "It's the only fish that holds your hand." Seahorses wrap their prehensile tails around stationary objects, and will use your fingers for that purpose when you have your hands in the tank. Although they are cute and fascinating, seahorses present significant challenges as aquarium specimens. Don't try this model design unless you are prepared to provide your "herd" with live foods on a daily basis.

All seahorses live in grass beds on the continental shelves worldwide. Some twenty-odd species occur in both the temperate zone and the tropics. Threatened by onshore development and overfishing, seahorse populations have dwindled in many locations. Thus, aquarists should make sure they are prepared for the work required to maintain seahorses in captivity. Although hardy under correct water conditions, seahorses absolutely require a reliable supply of living foods. Enticing them to accept nonliving foods is possible but only with plenty of patient effort. Further, providing a varied, balanced diet means having more than one type of live food available. Suitable foods include marine fish larvae, baby guppies, tiny grass shrimp, and adult brine shrimp. If you can provide these in some combination, you can keep seahorses.

Aquarium Capacity . . . . 30 to 50 gallons

Life Support . . . . .live sand, standard reef filtration

Lighting . . . . .two to four fluorescent lamps, or one 150-watt metal halide lamp, depending upon tank size

Background . . . . .light green

Decoration . . . . .live turtle grass or plastic *Vallisneria*, two or three pieces of live rock

Special Requirements . . . . .reef water conditions and moderate current

Fish

    Hippocampus erectus . . . . up to 6

Invertebrates

    Algae snails. 5

    Brittle stars. 2

    Lysmata amboiensis . . . . 1 to 3

        Or *Stenopus hispidus* . . . . 1 or a mated pair

Seaweeds (optional)

    Halimeda . . . . 6 clumps

    Caulerpa prolifera . . . . 1 clump

      Or *Caulerpa mexicana* . . . . 1 clump

    Penicillus . . . . 7 individuals

Set up this tank as in the previous model design. Use the live rock to create a patch reef toward one end of the tank, hiding the filter intake. Add the sand bed. Space grass plants randomly, leaving plenty of room in between. Decorate the foreground area with *Penicillus* and *Halimeda*. Arrange the *Caulerpa* toward the rear of the tank; it will grow toward the light and create a nice backdrop after a few weeks. After the seaweeds establish themselves, add the snails and brittle stars. You will need to add food three or four times a week for the brittle stars, since there won't be much for them to scavenge from the seahorse diet. About a week later, add your choice of shrimps. Continue feeding so both brittle stars and shrimps obtain enough to eat.

Now start setting up your live food facilities. How you do this depends upon the actual foods chosen. If you are very lucky, your local dealer may be able to supply all the foods you need, saving you the trouble of growing your own. You can find information about culturing all sorts of live foods in reference books and online. In any case, once you have a food supply, add the seahorses to the tank. If you choose from randomly collected individuals, select an equal number of males and females, in the hope that they will form pairs. If possible, obtain one or more already mated pairs that were collected together. Males can easily be distinguished from females by the fleshy brood pouch on the belly of the former. (Yes, in seahorses, it is the male that becomes pregnant. Perhaps that explains why these fish seem to be more popular with women than with men.) Seahorses form strong pair bonds and remain faithful to a single partner. If one member of the pair dies (or is harvested by a collector) the remaining seahorse will seek out a new mate. For this reason, pairing in the aquarium is relatively easy.

Feed seahorses several times a day simply by adding the swimming food to the tank and letting nature takes its course. Healthy seahorses may spawn for you after they have been in the aquarium long enough to settle in. After an hours-long courtship dance, they mate, and the female transfers eggs to the male's brood pouch, where they are fertilized. The baby seahorses develop into miniature versions of the adults before being expelled as the male gives birth. The male undergoes a true pregnancy, with a placenta-like structure forming to nourish the offspring. Newly hatched seahorses, unfortunately, are even more of a challenge to feed than adults, although dedicated enthusiasts have enjoyed much success.

You can train seahorses to eat nonliving foods if you have sufficient patience. It is first necessary to get them accustomed to the presence of your fingers or a pair of long forceps. Then you feed them for a while with a favorite live food grasped in the fingers or forceps. Once the seahorse is used to eating this way, you can try switching to a nonliving substitute food. Eventually, many seahorses get with the program, though not all. You can find plenty more information about seahorse care at *www.seahorse.org*.

MODEL DESIGN 19 Indo-Pacific Upper Fore Reef

This is the model design that many reef tank enthusiasts aspire to. The corals found in this high-energy environment demand plenty of light and water movement but will reward you with a stunning exhibit.

Aquarium Capacity . . . . 120 to 180 gallons

Life Support . . . . .live rock, live sand, standard reef filtration

Lighting . . . . .two to three 150-watt metal halide lamps, depending upon tank size

Background . . . . .pale blue

Decoration . . . . .none

Special Requirements . . . . .calcium above 400 ppm, alkalinity at about 4 Meq/L, very low levels of nitrate, phosphate undetectable, correct water movement (see text)

Fish

    Pseudanthias bicolor. 7

        Or *Pseudanthias pleurotaenia* 5

    Sphaeramia nematoptera 5

    Gobiodon, any species. 5

Invertebrates

    Algae snails. 10

    Brittle stars. 5

    Lysmata amboiensis . . . . 1 to 3

        Or *Lysmata debelius* . . . . 1 or a mated pair

Corals (see text)

    Acropora sp.

    Pocillopora sp.

    Montipora sp.

    Seriatopora sp.

    Porites sp.

Due to the aggressiveness of some corals toward others, it is important to gather all the information you can about a particular specimen before adding it to this aquarium. If you choose only captive-propagated coral specimens, rather than those collected from the wild, you are more likely to find details of the coral's growth requirements. Captive-propagated corals have adapted to aquarium conditions, and should fare better than their wild counterparts. For these and other reasons, always choose captive-propagated corals if possible. *Acropora* and *Pocillopora* species generally rank as more demanding in comparison to *Montipora*, *Seriatopora,* and *Porites*.

The corals suggested for this model design will not thrive with lax water movement. You can add several powerheads controlled by a wavemaker (see page 100) to create turbulence. If you have a built-in tank, you have the option of creating much better water movement with a surge device. You can find a design for one in Borneman's *Aquarium Corals*. A surge device more closely approximates the bulk movement of water over the fore reef than does the directional flow from a powerhead.

Although they obtain nutrition from photosynthesis by their zooxanthellae, corals need to be fed. Normal healthy corals expand their polyps and can be observed feeding when an appropriate food, such as live brine shrimp nauplii, is added. Microplankton substitutes, such as rotifer cultures and various concoctions of finely divided particulate foods should be added to the tank several times a week.

Successful care of the branching corals of the fore reef is as much art as science. In this realm perhaps more than any other, the advice and examples of successful aquarists is invaluable. Fortunately, the Internet makes such information readily available at the click of a mouse. Assimilate all you can, then apply what works for others to your own situation. As you gain experience and your corals thrive and grow, you will be in a position to add your knowledge to the ever-accumulating pool of coral husbandry techniques.

Coral Taxonomy and Growth Patterns

As a rule of thumb, you should ignore any species designations given to the corals offered by aquarium dealers. The color and colony form of individual corals develop as a result of the specific conditions of light and current under which the coral grows, rather than as a result of strict genetics as are the shapes and colors of many familiar animals. Without knowing from where and under what circumstances a given coral originated, assigning a species name is effectively impossible. This need not be a drawback, however, as we are less concerned with the coral's name than with its growth requirements. In the case of corals cultivated from fragments, requirements can usually be obtained from the supplier of the specimens. For wild-collected corals, much can be inferred from the form and color of the colony. Typically, branched forms and bright colors are associated with shallow water and vigorous currents, while platelike forms and subdued colors develop in deeper waters. The supreme test, though, is how well the coral fares under conditions you provide. Always observe a new coral specimen carefully for the first few weeks to determine if it is "happy" where you've placed it. Don't hesitate to relocate corals that are doing poorly, as often different lighting or current pattern will turn things around. Remember, however, that lighting shifts must be done gradually, or the coral will be stressed, defeating your purpose in relocating it. It may, for example, be necessary to shade the coral for a week or two in its new location, then expose it gradually to longer and longer periods of bright lighting. Finally, the shade can be removed altogether.

MODEL DESIGN 20 | Indo-Pacific Fish Community I

This model design is really more of a "formula" for creating a harmonious community of saltwater fish. I call it the Chinese menu approach, as in "choose one from column A and one from column B." In the confines of the aquarium, reef fish will exhibit aggression toward each other unless chosen with care. Two basic rules apply here:

Unless you know for certain that the species tolerates its own kind or you have a mated pair, never place two individuals of the same species in the same tank.

Choose only one member of any given fish family to add to your display. Combining two species of, for example, butterflyfishes, entails much more problem potential than combining one species of butterflyfish with one species of wrasse.

Aquarium Capacity . . . . 55 gallons

Life Support . . . . .live rock, live sand, standard reef filtration

Lighting . . . . .two to four fluorescent lamps

Background . . . . .black

Decoration . . . . .dead coral skeletons, seashells, plastic reproductions

Special Requirements . . . . .reef water conditions and moderate current

Fish

    Centropyge sp. . . . . 1 or a harem (see text)

    Forcipiger longirostris 1

    Oxycirrhites typus. 1

    Paracanthurus hepatus 1

    Halichoeres chrysus 1

Invertebrates

    Small hermit crabs 6

You will need about fifty pounds of live rock. Purchase cured rock if at all possible, or cure it yourself as described on page 103. Have the tank and filter system up and running before adding the rock. I won't try to give precise instructions for live rock placement, since everything depends upon the size, shape, and orientation of individual pieces. Try to create a stable reef wall that contains numerous gaps and openings through which fish can swim and water can freely move. To determine the natural orientation of a piece of live rock, study the types of organisms growing on it. Green algae, for example, are a sure sign that side of the rock was facing the light. Most encrusting organisms that derive food from the water currents will be on the top and sides of the rock. The underside of the rock may be pale, or there may be colonies of purple encrusting algae and/or sponges located there. Common sense also suggests that the broader, heavier part of the rock was the base.

Once the rock is in place, add the substrate material. Remember that live sand should always be added on top of quarry sand. If you choose to add additional decorations, place them next. Try not to overdo this part of the aquascape. A single well-chosen dead coral skeleton or seashell will ultimately look better than a jumble of multiple pieces. Because you want to leave room for the fish to swim front and center, keep most of the aquascape in the rear half of the tank.

Go ahead and add the hermit crabs when you add the live rock. They will help to clean up algae growth and detritus as the tank goes through its break-in period. After two weeks to a month, you can begin adding fish. Always add the larger, more aggressive species last. From the list of species suggested for this tank, I'd suggest beginning with the regal tang (*Paracanthurus*). If you add the optional dead coral, this fish will likely spend most of its time near the coral or among its branches. Add the dwarf angelfish (*Centropyge*) next. If you go with a harem of two females and one male, I suggest omitting the butterflyfish (*Forcipiger*) to avoid overstocking beyond the capacity of the biofilter. Finish off the tank with the wrasse (*Halichoeres*), the hawkfish (*Oxycirrhites*), and the butterflyfish, in that order.

The recommended species are all hardy and easy to feed. If you add new fish only about once every two to three weeks, feed them well, and keep the tank properly maintained, this community should give you few problems while providing plenty of color and movement.

MODEL DESIGN 21 Indo-Pacific Fish Community II

This is a larger version of the foregoing model design. When it comes to larger fish, the compatibility rules mentioned above apply wholeheartedly. A big angelfish or wrasse can do significant damage to a tank mate in short order.

Aquarium Capacity . . . . 180 gallons

Life Support . . . . .live rock, live sand, standard reef filtration

Lighting . . . . .three 150-watt metal halide lamps

Background . . . . .black

Decoration . . . . .dead coral, shells, artificial reproductions

Special Requirements . . . . .reef water conditions and moderate current

Fish

    Pomacanthus sp. 1

    Chaetodon sp. . . . . 1 or a pair (see text)

    Coris gaimard 1

    Chromis viridis. 7

        Or *Chromis vanderbilti* 7

    Siganus vulpinus 1

Invertebrates

    Small hermit crabs 12

Angelfish (*Pomacanthus*) are particularly intolerant of potential competitors, that is any other angelfish or fish of any species if similar in color to the angelfish. Choose from among the following species, blue ring (*P. annularis*), emperor (*P. imperator*), or Koran (*P. semicirculatus*). Likewise, members of the closely related butterflyfish family may not tolerate each other in the aquarium, despite the observation that many travel in pairs on the reef. Good choices include: threadfin (*Chaetodon auriga*), saddled (*C. ephippium*), raccoon (*C. lunula*), or copperband (*Chelmon rostratus*). The gaudy clown wrasse (*Coris gaimard*) won't abide another male clown wrasse in the neighborhood. You could substitute a dragon wrasse (*Novaculichthys taeniorus*), lyretail wrasse (*Thalassoma lunare*), or yellow wrasse (*T. lutescens*). Instead of either *Chromis* species, you could include a school of bannerfish (*Heniochus diphreutes*). The foxface (*Siganus*) can be replaced by a tang, such as powder blue (*Acanthurus leucosternon*), powder brown (*A. japonicus*), sailfin (*Zebrasoma veliferum*), or the old standby yellow (*Z. flavescens*). Be aware that the two *Acanthurus* species often fare poorly, probably because of improper collecting and handling practices. Be certain of the integrity of your source for either of these species.

In terms of setting up, breaking in, and stocking, follow the instructions given for the previous model design.

MODEL DESIGN 22   Soft Corals and Seaweeds

An aquarium based on a shallow water lagoon habitat can take many forms. This model design focuses on the numerous varieties of soft corals available. Soft corals lend themselves to captive propagation, and this should be your primary source of specimens.

Aquarium Capacity . . . . .50 to 120 gallons

Life Support . . . . .live rock, live sand, standard reef filtration

Lighting . . . . .two to four fluorescent lamps, or three 100-watt metal halide lamp, depending upon tank size

Background . . . . .light green

Decoration . . . . .none

Special Requirements . . . . .reef water conditions and moderate current

Fish

    Assessor flavissimus 1

        Or *Assessor macneilii* 1

    Chrysiptera cyanea . . . . 1 or a harem (see text)

        Or *Chrysiptera parasema* . . . . 1 or a harem

    Cirrhitichthys oxycephalus. 1

    Paracheilinus octotaenia 1

Invertebrates

    Algae snails. 5

    Brittle stars. 2

    Lysmata amboiensis . . . . 1 to 3

        Or *Stenopus hispidus* . . . . 1 or a mated pair

    Sarcophyton sp.

    Litophyton sp.

    Lobophytum sp.

    Cladiella sp.

    Sinularia sp.

Seaweeds

    Halimeda . . . . 6 clumps

    Caulerpa sp. 2 or 3 clumps

Seaweeds and soft corals go together well because they like similar conditions of bright illumination and moderate current. The various shades of green seaweeds nicely complement the yellows and tans of the soft corals, too. You should install a good skimmer, as both seaweeds and soft corals release organic compounds into the water. Soft corals can be aggressive, sometimes without touching each other. I suggest you choose a single genus from among those listed, and stock the tank with several specimens of this one type. Soft corals frequently occur in large stands of a single species. By limiting yourself to one genus, not only will you avoid potential interactions, but also the tank will accurately represent a natural biotope.

Because the *Caulerpa* quickly spreads, it is not necessary to use decorative live rock. Base rock will do, as it provides biofiltration but does not cost as much as the showier rock types. Arrange the live rock to create two patch reefs, one larger than the other, on either end of the tank. These will undoubtedly be claimed as territories by the *Assessor* and the damselfish (*Chrysiptera*). When the rock is in place, add the sand. Let the tank settle in for a few days before adding the seaweeds. Use any species of *Caulerpa* you like, or a combination of several. Drape them attractively over the lower portions of the patch reefs, allowing them to extend into the open space between. Space the clumps of *Halimeda* randomly in the open space, as well. Wait three weeks for the seaweeds to establish themselves before continuing.

Add the algae snails, brittle stars, and one or two soft coral specimens together. Do not be concerned if the soft corals remain contracted for a while. This is a normal reaction. Sometimes, the polyps do not emerge for days at a time. As long as the colony looks healthy otherwise, nothing should be amiss. Continue adding specimens every two or three weeks until you have achieved the arrangement you want. Some specimens can be placed on the rocks; others can sit directly on the sand. Most likely, the soft corals will already be attached to a small piece of rock, which makes them easy to position as you wish. You can add the shrimp at any time. During the stocking period, feed the shrimp and brittle stars a couple of times a week, and carry out all usual maintenance procedures.

After six to twelve weeks you can begin adding fish. Start with the wrasse (*Paracheilinus*). Follow with the *Assessor*, the *Chrysiptera*, and finally the hawkfish (*Cirrhitichthys*). You should end up with a total of five fish for a 50-gallon tank, or twice that many if you go with the 120-gallon tank. For the smaller system, add either the *Assessor* or the *Chrysiptera*, but not both, and skip the hawkfish.

Only add a harem of *Chrysiptera* if you have set up a large tank; otherwise keep only one. Males and females can be distinguished by the larger size and more aggressive behavior of the male. He will tolerate females, but not another male, in his territory. Work with your dealer to make appropriate selections. In the case of *C. cyanea*, males have a colorful, often orange, tail. In females, the tail fin is clear.

If you set up a large tank and include the hawkfish, choose *Stenopus* rather than *Lysmata*. The latter may be preyed upon by the hawkfish, but it is unlikely that the larger, more aggressive *Stenopus* will meet this fate.

MODEL DESIGN 23 Jawfish

Few saltwater fish can compete with yellow-headed jawfish for sheer entertainment value. Skittish at first, they require patience from the aquarist until they become accustomed to captivity. Once settled in, they are hardy and extremely charming to watch.

Aquarium Capacity .55 gallons

Life Support . . . . .live rock, live sand, standard reef filtration

Lighting . . . . .two fluorescent lamps

Background . . . . .blue

Decoration . . . . .none

Special Requirements . . . . .deep sand bed with pebbles and shell fragments, reef water conditions, and moderate current

Fish

    Opisthognathus aurifrons 5

Invertebrates

    Algae snails. 5

    Brittle stars. 2

Seaweeds (optional)

    Halimeda incrassate. 6

        Or *Penicillus*. 6

        Or *Udotea*. 6

        Or *Avrainvillea*. 6

        Or *Rhipocephalus*. 6

I have selected a tall tank for this model design to accommodate a deep sand layer on the bottom while leaving room above. Jawfish need a bed of substrate material at least six inches deep in which to construct a burrow. To maximize the available space, use a few strategically placed pieces of live rock in the display tank because the jawfish may burrow beneath them. If you want more rock for biofiltration, it can always be placed in the sump. The excavations of the jawfish will keep the substrate moved around, minimizing the possibility of dead spots where debris might decay.

Select good-quality coarse coral sand for most of the substrate, mixing it with pebbles and shell fragments. Add live sand on top to seed the aquarium with beneficial organisms. Add the snails and brittle stars when the sand and rock are in place and the tank has settled for a few days. Wait a month before adding the fish. They should all go in at the same time.

Jawfish are particularly prone to leaping out of the tank, especially when they first arrive. To minimize problems, turn out the lights and handle the shipping bags as little as possible during the acclimation period. The jawfish will immediately dive under rocks and probably remain hidden for a while after they are introduced. Cover the tank well, leave the lights off, and do not disturb the tank further for a few days. Soon, one or more fish will emerge from hiding and begin constructing a burrow.

The jawfish uses its large mouth to burrow into the substrate. Typically, the burrow is about twice as deep as the fish is long. Thus, a three-inch fish needs six inches of substrate depth. Once the burrow is finished, the fish spends most of its time in a vertical position, tail hidden inside the burrow, alert to any movement in the vicinity that might indicate a predator or a potential meal. It snatches small organisms from the water column all day, that is, while not spending time making additions and improvements to the burrow. The fish piles up small shells, pebbles and other trophies near the entrance to the burrow. It is not above raiding a neighbor's collection in order to seize a prize specimen. I have had no luck in figuring out what attracts a particular fish to a certain item, but this behavior seems to be an important part of the social interaction within the colony. Other than petty theft, the crime rate in a jawfish colony is low. Aggressive interactions seldom occur and are limited to mouth gaping and mock battles.

Jawfish have spawned in captivity. Males and females spawn in the privacy of his burrow, and the male incubates the eggs in his mouth.

Once all the fish have a burrow and are feeding normally, you can plant a selection of the listed seaweeds, burying the holdfast in the substrate. Group them near the center of the tank where the illumination is brightest. The seaweeds are added last to avoid their being uprooted during burrow construction by the jawfish. Remember that appropriate calcium and alkalinity levels are essential for cultivation of these calcareous seaweeds.

Aside from their propensity to jump, jawfish present few challenges. Carry out routine maintenance, of course, and feed them a varied diet of chopped seafoods and frozen preparations.

MODEL DESIGN 24 | Filter-Feeding Invertebrates

Here's an aquarium for the enthusiast willing to dedicate plenty of effort to its care. Don't try this one unless you are prepared to culture the necessary foods on a regular basis.

Aquarium Capacity . . . . 90 gallons

Life Support . . . . .live rock, live sand, standard reef filtration

Lighting . . . . .two fluorescent lamps

Background . . . . .black

Decoration . . . . .none

Special Requirements . . . . .good water movement and plenty of particulate foods

Fish

    Serranocirrhitus latus 1

Invertebrates

Brittle stars. . . . . 3 to 5 small ones

Lysmata amboiensis . . . . 1 to 3

Protula magnifica

Sabella sp.

Sabellastarte magnifica

Leptogorgia miniata

Swiftia exerta

Tubastrea sp.

Pseudocolochrius sp.

With the exception of the snails and brittle stars, all of these invertebrates need twice daily feedings with a plankton substitute. Very little is known about the nutritional requirements of most of these organisms, and you should experiment with various foods. All will benefit from foods deposited in their vicinity with a bulb baster. The large polyps of *Tubastrea* should be fed individually.

Different species of filter feeders remove different sizes of food particles. While adult brine shrimp may be acceptable to the *Tubastrea*, the annelids (*Protula*, *Sabella*, *Sabellastarte*) probably take particles the size of bacteria. For this reason, do not use a protein skimmer on this tank, rely instead on regular partial water changes to remove dissolved organic matter from the system. Otherwise, certain food items may be skimmed out.

This is an appropriate tank in which to arrange the live rock as a cave, with a U-shaped wall along the back and sides, and some flat pieces for the roof. You will probably need to attach pieces of rock to each other or to a support structure, in order to create a stable arrangement. See the suggestions for doing this on page 102.

Set up the aquarium as described for others in this chapter, first adding rock and sand and allowing the system to mature for several weeks before beginning to add invertebrates. As usual, add the brittle stars early, and stock individual invertebrate specimens about two weeks apart over a period of several months. Once the invertebrates have all been added, you can introduce the optional sunburst anthias (*Serranocirrhitus*). This fish is hardy, easy to feed, and should thrive on many of the planktonic foods added for the invertebrates. The aquarium will generate plenty of interest without it, however, if that is your preference.

Several types of filter-feeding invertebrates continue to be offered in aquarium shops, despite the near impossibility of maintaining them successfully for any length of time. Learn to recognize and avoid such specimens. Among coelenterates, several genera, including *Dendronephthya*, *Nephthea*, *Stylaster*, and *Gorgonia*, usually starve, surviving only a few weeks or months in captivity. Among annelids, the inarguably lovely Christmas tree worm, *Spirobranchus giganteus*, typically meets a similar fate. The worms live in colonies embedded in

Reef Supports

Often the live rock just cannot be arranged as you want it and remain stable. In these situations, supporting the rock on a framework of plastic pipe may solve the problem. Spend some time thinking about the final look you want, then construct a support with lengths of pipe and the appropriate fittings. A simple support for a cave, for example, might consist of a structure built like a table, with legs at each corner. The table top holds up the roof of the cave. If you cannot find the fittings you need for a particular configuration, drill small holes in the pipes and secure them with plastic cable ties (also known as zip ties). You can use cable ties to attach pieces of rock to the support, also. You can find other ideas for building with live rock in reference books and online.

Porites coral. Not only must the worm receive adequate amounts of particulate food, the coral must also be maintained. If the coral dies, the worms shortly follow. Among arthropods, anemone crabs, *Neopetrolisthes*, need both a plankton substitute and an anemone host in order to survive. Most aquarists are surprised to discover the crab is a filter feeder. Do yourself a favor and avoid disappointment by leaving these species to professional aquarists.

Besides the constant attention to feeding, this tank needs routine maintenance to keep the water quality high. If you cannot commit the necessary time, choose another model design. For the aquarist who makes the effort, this can be a remarkably gaudy tank, since most of the organisms suggested are brightly colored.

MODEL DESIGN 25 | Hawaii

Some of the best saltwater aquarium fish come from Hawaii, but little if any collecting of invertebrates is allowed. Therefore, this model design relies on the fish for most of the show.

Aquarium Capacity .125 gallons

Life Support . . . . .live rock, live sand, standard reef filtration

Lighting . . . . .two to four fluorescent lamps

Background . . . . .black or dark blue

Decoration . . . . .dead coral skeletons, seashells, plastic reproductions

Special Requirements . . . . .reef water conditions and moderate current

Fish (choose from among the following)

    Acanthurus achilles. 1

    Apogon cyanosoma 3

Centropyge loriculus	1 or a harem
Or *Centropyge potteri*	1 or a harem
Chaetodon kleini	1
Or *Chaetodon miliaris*	1
Ctenochaetus hawaiiensis	3 to 5
Zebrasoma flavescens	3 to 5
Gomphosus varius	1
Heniochus acuminatus	1
Pervagor spilosoma	1
Thalassoma duperryi	1

For this aquarium, a standard wall of live rock extending across the back will offer maximum visibility of the fish. As with some other model designs, leave openings between the rocks to allow for water circulation and fish movement. Provide extra water movement with powerheads. These fish, in particular *Acanthurus achilles* and *Thalassoma duperryi*, need plenty of current.

Wait three weeks after the rock is in place before you begin adding fish, then space your additions two weeks apart. Start with the cardinalfish (*Apogon*). Next, add the butterflyfishes (*Chaetodon, Heniochus*) one at a time. Follow with the groups of tangs (*Ctenochaetus, Zebrasoma*). The filefish (*Pervagor*) can go in after the tangs, followed by the wrasses (*Gomphosus, Thalassoma*). Finally add the Achilles tang (*Acanthurus*).

You cannot keep all these fish together in this one tank, so choose the ones you like best to total ten to twelve specimens. The tangs and angelfishes need plenty of vegetable matter in their diet, some of which they will crop from the rocks. All the others need a varied diet of seafoods.

While you can use plastic reproductions of various invertebrates to take the place of unavailable Hawaiian specimens, they are optional. In fact, you may think the tank looks best with only the live rock as a backdrop for the colorful fish. Because of its relative ease of care and abundant color and movement, this model design might be a good choice for a busy household, or even a commercial installation in a restaurant. Take care to maintain correct levels of calcium and alkalinity, and you should be rewarded with a good growth of encrusting purple and mauve coralline algae on the rocks and glass. The tangs will help to keep these areas free of filamentous green algae. Coralline algae are an important reef component in Hawaii, where some reef structures consist entirely of these organisms.

MODEL DESIGN 26　Convict Blenny

This tank is "bulletproof" and an ideal choice for those who want a long-term relationship with just a few fish. You can keep a pair of specimens together in the same tank, and they may well spawn. Rearing the offspring has not, to my knowledge, been accomplished.

Aquarium Capacity . . . . 50 gallons

Life Support . . . . .live rock, live sand, standard reef filtration

Lighting　. . . . . .two to four fluorescent lamps

Background　. .black

Decoration　. . . . . .none

Special Requirements . . . . .reef water conditions and moderate current

Fish

　　Pholidichthys leucotaenia . . . . 1 or a mated pair

　　(also see text)

Pholidichthys, commonly known as the convict blenny, burrows into the substrate in the transition zone between the reef itself and the adjacent areas of rubble. The juveniles look nothing like the adults, and instead mimic the coloration of the coral catfish, *Plotosus*. This is an example of Batesian mimicry, wherein a harmless species achieves protection by looking like a noxious one. *Plotosus* possess venomous fin spines that can inflict a painful sting. Predators learn quickly to avoid them, and the juvenile *Pholidichthys* benefits from this aversion.

As with other burrowers, *Pholidichthys* needs a deep layer of substrate composed of a mixture of sand, shell fragments, and rubble. With even minimal attention to water quality maintenance, you can keep these fish for many years. They are not aggressive toward anything too large to eat and can be combined with a variety of other fishes and invertebrates, if you so desire.

Establishing this tank is routine. Add the rock and sand, then wait three weeks before you add the fish. You can also follow one of the other model designs in this section, replacing one or more of the suggested fish with *Pholidichthys*. See, for example, Model Designs 20, 21, and 22.

MODEL DESIGN 27 Easy Corals

Looking for ideas for a stunning reef tank that won't challenge your skills too much? This one is basically the same as Model Design 19 but with corals more typical of back reef zones than the fore reef. These latter types of corals, mostly large-polyp (LPS) varieties, are in general easier to keep than the high energy SPS corals.

Aquarium Capacity . . . . 120 to 180 gallons

Life Support . . . . .live rock, live sand, standard reef filtration

Lighting . . . . .two to three 150-watt metal halide lamps, depending upon tank size

Background . . . . .pale blue, light green, or black

Decoration . . . . .none

Special Requirements . . . . .calcium above 400 ppm, alkalinity about 4 Meq/L, very low levels of nitrate, phosphate undetectable

Fish

  Centropyge bicolor. . . . . 1 or a harem

     Or *Centropyge flavissima* . . . . 1 or a harem

  Meiacanthus atrodorsalis 1

  Ecsenius bicolor 1

     Or *gravieri*

  Nemateleotris, any species 1

     Or *Ptereleotris microlepis* 3

  Pomacentrus alleni 1

  Signigobius biocellatus . . . . mated pair (see text)

     Or *Valenciennea puellaris* . . . . 1 or a mated pair

Invertebrates

  Algae snails. 10

  Brittle stars. 5

  Lysmata amboiensis . . . . 1 to 3

     Or *Lysmata debelius* . . . . 1 or a mated pair

Corals (see text)

Blastomussa sp.

Cynarina sp.

Caulastrea sp.

Favia sp.

Fungia sp

Galaxea sp.

Herpolitha sp.

Hydnophora sp.

Trachyphyllia sp.

Catalaphyllia sp.

Euphyllia sp.

Plerogyra sp.

Physogyra sp.

Lobophyllia sp.

Turbinaria sp.

Not all the corals listed can be successfully maintained together in one tank. Several, including *Catalaphyllia*, *Euphyllia*, *Physogyra*, and *Plerogyra*, produce long sweeper tentacles capable of inflicting a damaging sting to any potential competitor within reach. And virtually any two corals can damage each other if they are placed so close together that they touch. Study photos to determine which corals you like best. Make sure to place all specimens so they have plenty of room between them. Space is the most valuable commodity on the reef. Once a larval coral settles into a suitable spot, it will defend itself against all comers. With millions of years of practice, some of them have become quite adept, indeed.

A harem of dwarf angels (*Centropyge*) consists of one male and two or more females. Males are always larger than females, so the best approach is to place one large and two small individuals in the tank simultaneously. *Meiacanthus atrodorsalis* is one of the fanged blennies. Armed with venomous fangs, these little fish viciously bite the inside of a predator's mouth, hoping to be spit out. They are usually successful. They may bite you, too, so handle with care. The other blenny suggestions, *Ecsenius bicolor* and *E. gravieri*, are called combtoothed blennies because they have numerous tiny teeth they use to scrape filamentous algae from solid surfaces. Keep only one specimen per tank, as they are territorial and will fight with competitors. Two dart-fishes are suggested, any of the *Nemateleotris* species or *Ptereleotris heteroptera*. Either one requires a suitable shelter into which it can quickly retreat when it perceives danger. *Nemateleotris magnifica*, *N. decora,* and

N. helfrichi all look so gorgeous you may have trouble choosing between them. It's one per tank, however, as they don't get along. *Ptereleotris* can be kept in a small group.

The remaining two species, *Signigobius* and *Valenciennea*, can be a challenge to keep. Both feed by taking up a mouthful of substrate, "chewing" to extract any small edible organisms that might be present, and spitting out the sand and gravel. It may be difficult for them to get enough to eat unless the tank has a mature, active sand bed. *Valenciennea* is arguably the more attractive of the two, but *Signigobius* is so interesting I would choose it over its cousin. *Signigobius* is always found in pairs, and should not be maintained singly, as this seems to be extremely stressful. It is known as signal goby in the aquarium trade, but the semaphore-like dorsal fins with their huge eyespots are not used for signaling. Instead, they help the goby deceive potential predators into thinking it is a crab. Coupled with the slow, jumpy movements of the fish as it grazes the bottom, the deception apparently works quite well. Experienced aquarists capable of supplying its needs may also want to consider devoting a species tank to *Signigobius*.

Setup and maturation of this aquarium should follow the same schedule suggested for Model Design 19. Unlike the branching corals in that model design, not all the corals in this aquarium will be placed atop the live rock. *Cataphyllia, Cynarina, Fungia, Herpolitha,* and *Trachyphyllia* should all sit on the substrate. *Fungia* and *Herpolitha* are capable of movement and will eventually topple if placed on rocks. The others are adapted to sitting in soft sand or sediments. *Cataphyllia*, in fact, is typically buried with only the tentacle crown above the substrate. Perhaps one reason these corals are easy to keep has to do with this mode of life. They can be collected without damage. Other corals must be pried or broken from the reef, a procedure likely to result in injuries.

Although these corals need careful attention to water quality, proper lighting, and regular feedings with a plankton substitute and small bits of seafood, many aquarists have found them to be hardy and rewarding aquarium subjects. Your likelihood of success will be enhanced if you stock this, or any coral reef aquarium, gradually. Think in terms of months, perhaps even a couple of years, to achieve a truly striking exhibit.

MODEL DESIGN 28 *Pseudochromis*

This family of pint-size relatives of the sea basses has so many good aquarium species, you may want to set up several small tanks so you can exhibit more than one variety.

Aquarium Capacity . . . . 30 gallons

Life Support . . . . .live rock, live sand, standard reef filtration

Lighting . . . . .two to four fluorescent lamps

Background . . . . .black

Decoration . . . . .none

Special Requirements . . . . .reef water conditions and moderate current

Fish

    Pseudochromis aldebarensis . . . . 1 or a mated pair

        Or *Pseudochromis diadema*. . . . . 1 or a mated pair

        Or *Pseudochromis flavivertex* . . . . 1 or a mated pair

        Or *Pseudochromis fridmani* . . . . 1 or a mated pair

        Or *Pseudochromis paccagnellae* . . . . 1 or a mated pair

        Or *Pseudochromis porphyreus* . . . . . . 1 or a mated pair

Invertebrates

    Algae snails. 2

    Brittle stars. 1

    Lysmata amboiensis 1

    Soft coral (see text)

    Giant clam (see text)

Also called dottybacks, the many species of *Pseudochromis* generally remain under four inches in length. All are territorial and somewhat aggressive, and they may attack fishes much larger than themselves if they feel threatened. They are ideal for a small tank such as this one. If you can obtain a mated pair, they spawn readily in captivity. Many species are captive-propagated specimens. You should seek these out whenever possible.

With the possible exception of very small shrimps, dottybacks leave most invertebrates unmolested. You could include any of the smaller soft corals in this tank, for example. Among the more interesting choices might be *Anthelia*, *Cespitularia*, or *Xenia*. These all spread across rocks and other surfaces, polyps arising densely from a sheet of tissue connecting all members of the colony. Of particular interest are the species that exhibit pulsing movements. Called waving hand or pulse corals, they are quite popular and often available from propagators. No one is sure why they pulse, and sometimes they refuse to do so for no apparent reason. Aside from this quirk, they are hardy and easy to keep with bright light and proper water conditions. Most are thought to derive nearly all their nourishment from their symbiotic zooxanthellae.

Similarly dependent upon zooxanthellae, but also requiring particulate food, any of the species of *Tridacna*, the giant clams, will make a colorful and interesting addition to this tank.

Set up the aquarium in the manner described for others, adding the rock and sand first, then waiting for several weeks before introducing other specimens. Then, start with the utilitarian invertebrates and continue adding specimens about every two weeks until the tank is stocked. It makes little difference in what order you add them. The dottyback should go in last. Because the soft corals grow and spread rather rapidly under good conditions, this tank should take on a mature, natural look in a relatively short period of time.

You will need to add a plankton substitute on a regular basis for the clams. Dottybacks will feed greedily on any type of seafood chopped into pieces of appropriate size or frozen commercial preparations.

MODEL DESIGN 29 Dragonets

When first you see a dragonet, you will find it hard to resist. Both commonly available species are some of the most flamboyantly colored fish on the reef. Alas, they can be very challenging to keep due to their specific food requirements. This model design is only for experienced aquarists who are up to the challenge.

Aquarium Capacity . . . . 50 gallons

Life Support . . . . .live rock, live sand, standard reef filtration

Lighting . . . . .four fluorescent lamps

Background .black

Decoration .none

Special Requirements . . . . .reef water conditions and moderate current

Fish

   Pterosynchiropus splendidus . . . . 1 or a mated pair

      Or *Synchiropus picturatus* . . . . 1 or a mated pair

Invertebrates

   Algae snails. 5

   Brittle stars. 2

   Lysmata amboiensis . . . . 1 to 3

   Corals, soft corals, and/or giant clams (see text)

Seaweeds (optional)

   Halimeda . . . . 6 clumps

   Penicillus. . . . . 7 individuals

      Or *Udotea*. 7 individuals

You may think fifty gallons is a lot for a fish that barely reaches six inches in length. This much space or more is necessary, however, in order to provide a steady supply of the tiny benthic invertebrates that constitute the sole food source for the dragonets. An active live sand bed, plenty of live rock, and a mature reef tank are prerequisites. Plan on having the aquarium set up for at least a year before you add the dragonets.

Male and female may be distinguished in either species by the much longer dorsal fin of the male, with its greatly elongated first spine. He also tends to be bigger. You can keep a pair together, or even one male of each of the two species, but two males of the same species will fight.

Dragonets ignore invertebrates other than their tiny prey, so you can decorate this tank with an assortment of corals, soft corals, and/or giant clams. Check some of the other model designs in this chapter for suggestions, bearing in mind that different types of corals and soft corals may be incompatible in close quarters. Also, avoid anemones, which eventually will catch and eat the dragonets. Follow the stocking plan suggested for Model Design 19. If the tank has a productive sand bed, the fish should show no signs of losing weight after a few weeks in the aquarium.

MODEL DESIGN 30 | Florida Keys Garden

Some of my fondest memories include the time I spent in graduate school working in the Florida Keys. This model design recreates one of my favorite underwater scenes, located just offshore near Grassy Key.

Aquarium Capacity . . . . .90 gallons

Life Support . . . . .live rock, live sand, standard reef filtration

Lighting . . . . .three 100-watt metal halide lamps

Background . . . . .pale blue or green

Decoration . . . . .none

Special Requirements . . . . .reef water conditions and moderate current

Fish

    Amblycirrhitus pinos 1

    Apogon maculates 1

    Centropyge argi. . . . . 1 or a harem

    Gobiosoma oceanops. 3

       Or *Gobiosoma evelynae* 3

    Serranus tabacarius 1

       Or *Serranus tigrinus* 1

Invertebrates

    Algae snails. 5

    Brittle stars. 2

    Ricordea florida. 1

    Phymanthus crucifer 5

    Palythoa sp.

    Zoanthus sp.

Seaweeds (optional)

    Halimeda . . . . 6 clumps

    Caulerpa sp. . . . . 1 clump

    Penicillus. . . . . 7 individuals

    Udotea . . . . 7 individuals

    Cymopolia barbata . . . . 1 clump

Include among your live rock selections several pieces with attached polyps of *Ricordea florida*. It is a false coral, slow growing, tolerant, and comes in bright shades of green, blue green, and orange. Captive-propagated specimens are sometimes available. They are likely to adapt better than wild-harvested individuals. The flower anemone (*Phymanthus*) occurs commonly in shallow inshore waters, with its column completely buried in the sand or sediment. Relying on both its zooxanthellae and its sticky tentacles to obtain food, it is capable of withdrawing completely out of site when disturbed. The two sea mats (*Palythoa*, *Zoanthus*) also can commonly be found in shallow, quiet water. CAUTION: sea mats should all be considered toxic and should only be handled while wearing plastic gloves. Do not keep sea mats if you have small children in the house.

The varying shades of green and interesting shapes of the seaweeds greatly enhance the look of this aquarium. *Cymopolia* is my favorite. It looks like multiple strings of white beads with a bright green pom-pom at the tip of each strand.

Start this aquarium with live base rock arranged so as to leave an open area near the center of the tank for the garden. Leave room to place the *Ricordea* rocks on top once the aquarium has matured a bit. The sea mats, too, will be supplied attached to pieces of rock. Leave room around the perimeter of the open space, and use these specimens to edge the garden. As usual, wait about two to three weeks from the time the base rock and live sand are added to begin adding other specimens. Start with the utilitarian invertebrates, then add specimens every two weeks or so. Plant the seaweeds in the center space, and place individual anemones randomly among them. Dig a shallow depression in the sand with your fingers and gently place the anemone in it. The anemone should settle in and bury itself within a day or two.

When all the invertebrates and seaweeds have been added, you can start stocking the tank with fish. Add one or two specimens every two weeks, in the following order: *Gobiosoma*, *Apogon*, *Serranus*, *Amblycirrhitus*, and *Centropyge*. The gobies are cleaners and will help to keep the other fish free of parasites. *Apogon maculatus* is nocturnal and will spend the daylight hours under a ledge or in a crevice. Make sure you add food before turning out the lights so this fish will get enough to eat. The minibass (*Serranus*) lies in ambush and will take up residence in an appropriate cave or crevice. Feed daily with small pieces of seafood. The hawkfish (*Amblycirrhitus*) will perch on the rocks here and there, motionless until food is available, at which time it will snatch nearly anything edible from the water. Besides feeding on filamentous algae, the dwarf angel (*Centropyge*) will take small bits of most aquarium foods. In a ninety-gallon tank, these fish should form a harmonious community.

MODEL DESIGN 31 | Octopus

Surely the most intelligent and interesting invertebrates, octopuses have a mixed record of success in home aquariums. Devoting a tank to one can be a fascinating experience or a frustrating chore. This model design should start you on the path to the first outcome.

Aquarium Capacity . . . . 30 gallons

Life Support . . . . .live rock, live sand, hang-on filter with built-in skimmer

Lighting . . . . .two fluorescent lamps

Background . . . . .black

Decoration . . . . .none

Special Requirements . . . . .reef water conditions and moderate current

Fish

   none

Invertebrates

   Octopus joubani 1

The dwarf octopus from Florida and the Caribbean is the best choice for captivity. Adults are about six inches from tentacle tip to the top of the head. Virtually every specimen collected is female. Males generally live only long enough to mate with a single female, and then die shortly thereafter. Indeed, females never survive more than a few weeks past the hatching of their eggs. Since nearly every female collected has been fertilized, expect to see egg production, brooding, and eventual death of your specimen. Although she will occupy your aquarium for at most a year, a dwarf octopus will never cease to amaze you with her intelligence and skill.

Any octopus requires a cave in which to retire. When setting up this tank, arrange pieces of rock to form a cave, locating the main opening so you can peer in to observe the octopus at home. Feeding is simple. Octopuses are predators that hunt at night, leaving the cave at dusk to seek out hapless crustaceans or mollusks. *Octopus joubani* greedily accepts small living crabs and shrimp. After a few weeks in captivity, she will learn to take nonliving foods from the end of a feeding stick.

I recommend against adding any other mobile invertebrates, such as snails, brittle stars, or shrimps to the tank, as they may simply become dinner for the octopus. Sessile invertebrates, such as soft corals, can be included if you wish. If you go this route, pay special attention to water changes, since the octopus can produce a lot of waste, potentially taxing the filter system.

Although they are generally hardy in a properly maintained aquarium, octopuses often fall victim to the living room carpet. Master escape artists, octopuses can squeeze through an opening the size of their eye. In the case of *O. joubani*, this would be a hole slightly smaller than the diameter of a pea. Keep your tank well covered and its occupant well fed. Many aquarists believe an octopus is more likely to roam if it is hungry.

Eventually, your octopus will spend more and more time inside the cave. Take a close look and you are likely to see a clutch of eggs attached to the ceiling of the cave, with the mother guarding them zealously. She constantly fondles the eggs, aerating them with jets of water from her excurrent siphon. You can actually see the young octopuses developing within the eggs. When they hatch, they will be miniature versions of their mother, and just as hungry. Prone to cannibalism, young octopuses must be placed in solitary confinement if you intend to rear them. This is one reason they are not cultivated for the aquarium trade. They also need plenty of live foods small enough for them to subdue. This limits their diet to such things as live brine shrimp and baby guppies, and probably guarantees they will develop nutritional deficiencies. Mortality is extremely high, no doubt another reason tank-raised octopuses do not appear in stores.

Hormonal changes in the brooding mother octopus suppress her desire for food. Most likely, this adaptation prevents her from feeding on her own offspring. Unfortunately, she does not regain her appetite after the eggs hatch and her duties have ceased. Within a short while, she dies of starvation.

Despite its short life span, an octopus is a fascinating aquarium subject. The eyes, which look a lot like the eyes of vertebrates, seem to be sizing you up as you peer through the glass, leading you to wonder who is watching whom. The skin can take on a wide range of colors and textures, which not only provide the octopus with camouflage, but also conveys its emotional state: reddish brown when agitated, pale when fearful, greenish brown when at rest. Place an unfamiliar object in the tank, and the octopus cannot resist inspecting it. Place a small shrimp in a corked bottle and drop it in the tank, and the octopus will manipulate the bottle until she figures out how to hold it with some of her tentacles while extracting the cork with others. Do this a second time, and the octopus will immediately remember how to remove the cork.

MODEL DESIGN 32 False Corals

Most false corals do well in moderate to low current and can thrive on less light than most stony and soft corals can. Thus, they are an ideal choice for a simple reef tank that won't do too much damage to your pocketbook.

Aquarium Capacity . . . . 30 gallons

Life Support . . . . .live rock, live sand, standard reef filtration

Lighting . . . . .two to four fluorescent lamps

Background . . . . .black or dark blue

Decoration . . . . .a few seashells

Special Requirements . . . . .reef water conditions and moderate current

Fish

    (see text)

Invertebrates

    Algae snails. 5

    Brittle stars. 2

    Lysmata amboiensis 1

    False corals . . . . 3 to 5 assorted varieties (see text)

The taxonomy of false corals, also known as disc anemones, mushroom corals, or mushroom polyps in the aquarium trade, is in something of a shambles, and none of the names applied to them in the aquarium literature may be correct. This should pose few problems for you, however, since they all require the same basic care. Moderation in all things seems to suit them best. They prefer lower light levels and gentler currents than most of the sessile invertebrates kept in reef tanks.

Individual false corals are discs ranging from dime-size to half dollar–size. They have either short, stubby tentacles or no tentacles at all. In some, the tentacles are branched at the tips; while in others, the tips of the tentacles are a contrasting color. Many different colors and patterns occur, including red, blue, and fluorescent green in stripes, swirls, dots, and squiggles. These many variations probably explain why invalid species names have frequently been assigned to the group. As long as they do not touch each other, the different varieties can live together in one aquarium. They often reproduce by splitting off daughter polyps from the margin of the disk, so the aquarium eventually becomes heavily populated with them.

False corals are typically supplied as small colonies of five to twenty individuals attached to a chunk of live rock. Keep this in mind when purchasing rock for the initial setup of this aquarium, and be sure to leave room. Otherwise, setup and maturation of this tank should proceed as suggested for the others in this chapter, with a waiting period of two weeks to a month after the live rock and live sand have been added.

Various small fish can share the tank with false corals, including dottybacks, neon wrasses, flasher wrasses, and gobies. Leave out the fish, however, if you add the giant false coral, *Amplexidiscus fenestrafer*. This atypical species grows to the size of a dinner plate and specializes in feeding on clownfish in its natural habitat because it mimics a large sea anemone. In the aquarium, it will catch and eat many kinds of small fishes.

MODEL DESIGN 33 Red Sea I

Red Sea fishes have traditionally been scarce and expensive in the U.S. aquarium trade. Their beauty and hardiness, however, have made them popular with aquarists despite the cost.

Aquarium Capacity . . . . 180 gallons

Life Support . . . . .live rock, live sand, standard reef filtration

Lighting . . . . .three150-watt metal halide lamps

Background . . . . .black

Decoration . . . . .coral skeletons, seashells, plastic reproductions

Special Requirements . . . . .salinity at 36 ppt, reef water conditions, and moderate current

Fish

      Zebrasoma desjardini. 1

         Or *Zebrasoma xanthurum* 1

      Pomacanthus asfur 1

         Or *Pomacanthus maculosus* 1

      Pseudochromis springeri 1

         Or *Pseudochromis flavivertex* 1

      Chaetodon semilarvatus 3

Invertebrates

    none

For a truly regal aquarium, this one will be hard to beat. It is unlikely you will be able to find Red Sea live rock, so make do with a decorative rock from another source. Arrange the rock to create a pinnacle on one end of the aquarium connected to a lower mound near the opposite end by an arch spanning the middle. You will need to construct a framework of PVC pipe to support the arch. Follow normal procedures after the rock and sand have been added, and allow the tank to mature for a month before you start stocking it with fish. Add the diminutive *Pseudochromis* first, followed by the three golden butterflyfishes (*Chaetodon*). Next, add the angelfish (*Pomacanthus*), and finish off the tank with the tang (*Zebrasoma*). All these fishes are robust and somewhat aggressive, so watch carefully for territorial squabbles each time you place a newcomer in the tank.

Other than those on the live rock, no living invertebrates are recommended for this tank. Red Sea invertebrates are difficult to come by and may be harassed or eaten by one or the other of the fishes. If you want additional color, use empty seashells, dead coral skeletons, or plastic reproductions.

You can expect to spend about $3,000 for the fish to stock this aquarium.

MODEL DESIGN 34 Red Sea II

The Red Sea fishes suggested for this model design were omitted from the previous one because of their aggressive dispositions. These bad boys are best enjoyed in solitary confinement.

Aquarium Capacity .50 gallons

Life Support . . . . .live rock, live sand, standard reef filtration

Lighting . . . . .two to four fluorescent lamps

Background . . . . .light blue

Decoration . . . . .dead coral, seashells, plastic reproductions

Special Requirements . . . . .reef water conditions and moderate current

Fish

　　Acanthurus sohal

　　　Or *Rhinecanthus assassi*

Set up this aquarium as described in the previous model design, using proportionately less live rock. After the maturation period, it is ready for a fish. Either species should prove easy to maintain, with the *Acanthurus* needing considerably more vegetable matter in its diet than the triggerfish. This aquarium would make a striking exhibit for a business office.

Some people would award the queen angelfish the title of "Most Beautiful Fish on the Reef." If you agree, this model design should delight you.

Aquarium Capacity . . . . 210 gallons

Life Support . . . . .live rock, live sand, standard reef filtration

Lighting . . . . .three 150-watt metal halide lamps

Background . . . . .pale blue or black

Decoration . . . . .coral skeletons, seashells, plastic reproductions

Special Requirements . . . . .reef water conditions and moderate current

Fish

    Holacanthus ciliaris 1

    Acanthurus caeruleus 1

    Chromis cyanea. 3

    Pomacanthus arcuatus. 1

        Or *Pomacanthus paru* 1

    Thalassoma bifasciatum . . . . 1 or a small group (see text)

Invertebrates

    Algae snails. 5

    Brittle stars. 2

    Lysmata amboiensis . . . . 1 to 3

        Or *Stenopus hispidus* . . . . 1 or a mated pair

Seaweeds (optional)

    Halimeda . . . . 6 clumps

    Caulerpa prolifera . . . . 1 clump

        Or *Caulerpa mexicana* . . . . 1 clump

    Penicillus. . . . . 7 individuals

This is another model design in which the live rock supplies a backdrop against which the gorgeous colors of the fish are displayed. If you want to create a complicated design with arches and so forth, fine, but the fish will nevertheless steal the show.

After setup and maturation, add fish in the following order: *Chromis*, *Thalassoma*, *Acanthurus*, *Pomacanthus*, *Holacanthus*. If you want to keep a group of wrasses (*Thalassoma*), you will want one male and several females. The female looks nothing like the male, which is emerald green with a turquoise head. The bright yellow females are known as banana wrasses in the aquarium trade. You may have to ask your dealer to special order them for you. In the case of the two angelfish species (*Pomacanthus*, *Holacanthus*) and the Atlantic blue tang (*Acanthurus*), juveniles will adapt better to captivity than adults will. In all three cases, the juveniles do not resemble the adults at all. With proper care and a varied diet, though, they should grow and assume the normal adult coloration in a few years' time.

You can scale down this model design if you like by eliminating some of the fish. Keep only one angelfish, skip the tang, and this community would fit nicely in a 125-gallon aquarium.

CHAPTER 10

Small Tanks

Many aquarium books (including mine) warn beginners about setting up a marine tank that is too small. Typically, the suggestion is to set up the largest tank your space and budget can accommodate. While it is true there are many advantages to larger tanks, reef aquarium keepers have discovered that wisely designed small tanks can indeed succeed.

Special Considerations for Small Tanks

Among the more common problems associated with small tanks is a propensity toward temperature instability. With the same amount of heat, a small volume of water changes temperature faster than a larger volume. Thus, big tanks tend to heat up and cool down more slowly, maintaining a stable temperature as the room temperature changes. Similarly, a given fish will pollute a small-volume tank more quickly than a larger one. The fish excretes wastes proportional to the amount of food it consumes. The fish's waste, therefore, will be more diluted in a larger volume of water, and thus take more time to build up to harmful levels. Similarly, respired carbon dioxide has less impact on the pH of the tank when the water volume is greater.

The foregoing should immediately suggest the key to a successful small tank: test and tweak on a weekly basis (or more often if possible), and perform partial water changes religiously. Common sense should also prevail in the selection of inhabitants for small aquariums: they need to be small, as well. Keeping a grouper, for example, in a twenty-gallon tank guarantees problems when the grouper outgrows its surroundings. By the same token, keeping a dozen gobies in a tank better suited to a single specimen will lead to disaster.

With careful planning, conscientious maintenance, and common sense, you can create an interesting and beautiful aquarium even in a tiny tank. Consider the following important points as you develop your design:

- Locate small tanks in an area of the house where the temperature remains relatively constant.

- Provide enough light for photosynthetic invertebrates. Doing so poses fewer problems for a small tank because of the restricted surface area and depth. Compact fluorescent lighting has revolutionized small aquarium illumination.

- Use a hang-on box filter with built-in skimmer for tanks in the ten- to twenty-gallon range. A sump or an external protein skimmer may not be practical for a small tank. For smaller systems, use the built-in filter that comes with the aquarium, and rely on water changes to take the place of skimming.

- Avoid adding large filter-feeding invertebrates. They can pose a great challenge in a small aquarium. It is difficult to supply enough food without overwhelming the system with pollutants.

- Keep the fish population to a minimum in a small tank. At most, a pair of three-inch fish could be safely kept in twenty gallons. One or two individuals of a tiny species, such as some gobies, might be OK even in a five-gallon system.

- Consider using only live rock and sand. Live rock and live sand play crucial roles in small tanks as in larger ones. A beautiful small tank can be created containing these materials alone.

For some highly desirable saltwater species, a small tank may be the best way to exhibit them. Animals that would quickly be lost in a large aquarium become the focus of a tiny one. Several of the model designs in this chapter exploit this principle.

Nanotanks

Anything smaller than about five gallons may be called a nanotank. Aquarium manufacturers have offered several such systems in recent years, and they have acquired a devoted following. Small enough to sit on a desk, with all necessary components built in, nanotanks offer the opportunity to enjoy a reef aquarium with minimal investment of money or effort. Thoughtfully done, a nanotank can be a real "jewelry box," stocked with a wealth of diminutive invertebrates.

The Model Designs

Anything presented in miniature seems to whet our interest. When something unexpectedly small is offered up, few can resist the temptation to exclaim, "How cute!" Aquariums are no exception to this rule. Each one suggested on the following pages encapsulates but a few threads of the intricate tapestry that is a coral reef. All the featured life forms demonstrate complex and interesting relationships for which reefs are famous.

MODEL DESIGN 36 *Bartholomea* and Friends

The curlicue sea anemone, *Bartholomea annulata*, plays host to several types of crustaceans. These relationships form the basis for a unique biotope aquarium.

Aquarium Capacity . . . . 20 gallons (high)

Life Support . . . . .live sand, live rock, hang-on filter with skimmer

Lighting . . . . .one to two fluorescent lamps

Background . . . . .pale yellow green

Decoration . . . . .none

Special Requirements . . . . .reef water conditions and moderate current

Fish

    none

Invertebrates

    Algae snails. 2

    Brittle stars. 1

    Bartholomea annulata 1

    Alpheus armatus . . . . 1 or a mated pair

    Periclimenes yucatanensis . . . . 1 or a mated pair

        Or *Periclimenes pedersoni* . . . . 1 or a mated pair

        Or *Thor amboiensis* . . . . 3 to 5

Seaweeds (optional)

    Halimeda incrassate. . . . . 3 to 5

        Or *Penicillus*. . . . . 3 to 5

        Or *Udotea*. 3 to 5

Set up this tank with most of the live rock located to one side, leaving an open space near the center of the tank for the anemone. The tall tank design allows *Bartholomea* to expand to its full height without restriction. The seaweeds, in any combination of species, should be planted in the sand on the end opposite the live rock.

Place the live rock so it hides the filter equipment, and add the sand after the rock is in position. Allow the tank to run for a couple of weeks before adding the utilitarian invertebrates. Introduce the anemone next, giving it another two weeks to settle in. Feed it a small piece of fish or shrimp about every three days. It will contract after feeding, subsequently expelling a waste pellet in a day or two. Remove the waste as soon as you see it. Feed the anemone again when it is fully expanded.

Once you have the anemone established in the tank, add its symbiotic partners. The *Alpheus* shrimp should be added last. This will avoid its preying on one of the other shrimps, should they not immediately move into the anemone's tentacles. Once all the invertebrates have been added, this aquarium should be relatively trouble free with proper maintenance.

MODEL DESIGN 37 *Condylactis* and Friends

The primary distinction between this tank and the *Bartholomea* aquarium is the need for proper lighting for the anemone. *Bartholomea* lack zooxanthellae and lighting is thus immaterial to its well-being. This model design is a miniature version of the sea grass bed tank described in the previous chapter.

Aquarium Capacity . . . . 20 gallons (long)

Life Support . . . . .live sand, hang-on filter with built-in skimmer

Lighting . . . . .two to four fluorescent lamps

Background . . . . .light green

Decoration . . . . .plastic reproductions of *Vallisneria*, or living *Caulerpa prolifera* to simulate sea grass, two or three pieces of live rock

Special Requirements . . . . .reef water conditions and moderate current

Fish

   none

Invertebrates

   Algae snails. 2

   Brittle stars. 1

   Condylactis gigantean . . . . 1 to 3

   Thor amboiensis. 5

Seaweeds (optional)

     Caulerpa prolifera . . . . 1 clump

     Penicillus . . . . 5 individuals

Use the plastic if you must, but I think the *Caulerpa* looks much better. Add it when you add the live sand and live rock. Use the rock to build a tiny patch reef, placing it to hide the filter, which can be located anywhere along the back of the tank. Add the sand next, then arrange the strands of *Caulerpa* so they will grow into a carpet over the open space around the rock. Although *Caulerpa prolifera* most closely resembles sea grass, feel free to substitute any other *Caulerpa* species. Plant the *Penicillus* in a stand, spacing them about an inch apart in the brightest area of the tank. You will need to make sure calcium and alkalinity levels are maintained if you expect the *Penicillus* to thrive. It must have calcium to construct its supporting skeleton.

As usual, run the tank for about two to three weeks, add the snails and brittle star, then run another week or two before adding the anemone(s). Feed the anemone every three days, as described in the previous model design. When the anemone appears to be settled in, add the sexy shrimps (*Thor*). If you choose to add more than one anemone, you can place a different shrimp species, such as *Periclimenes yucatanensis* and *P. pedersoni*, in each one.

MODEL DESIGN 38 *Heliofungia* and Friends

Built along the same lines as the previous two tanks, this model design showcases the fascinating mobile coral and the delightful sexy shrimp.

Heliofungia, known in the aquarium trade as plate coral, was once thought to be extremely difficult to keep. Now that we know what it needs, many aquarists exhibit it successfully. Looking like a large anemone, the coral is unique in its ability to move slowly about the bottom. It needs regular feedings in order to thrive.

Aquarium Capacity . . . . 20 gallons (long)

Life Support . . . . .live rock, live sand, hang-on filter with built-in skimmer

Lighting . . . . .two fluorescent lamps

Background . . . . .deep blue

Decoration . . . . .none

Special Requirements . . . . .reef water conditions and moderate current

Fish

    none

Invertebrates

    Algae snails. 2

    Brittle stars. 1

    Heliofungia 1

    Thor amboiensis. . . . . 3 to 5

Arrange the live rock along the back of the tank, extending it down the sides toward the front. Leave the majority of the bottom area open for the coral to roam about. Add the sand after the rock is in place. Let the aquarium mature for two or three weeks, then add the algae snails and brittle star. Wait another two to three weeks before adding the coral and shrimps. The two can be added simultaneously. Seaweeds are omitted from this model design because they can exude organic matter that irritates the coral.

Sexy shrimp, by the way, are so named because of their habit of raising the abdomen and shaking it. You may or may not be forgiven for playing a recording of "Shake Your Booty" while showing off this tank to friends.

MODEL DESIGN 39 Goby and Shrimp

A twenty-gallon tank can become home to any of the many species of gobies that associate with certain snapping shrimps. Always purchase the shrimps and gobies together, if possible. Known matches are included in the species list.

Among the most fascinating relationships in the sea, the partnership between certain gobies and certain alpheid shrimps makes a great subject for a small aquarium exhibit. The shrimp and goby (or a mated pair of gobies) live together in a burrow excavated by the shrimp. Because it is unable to construct a burrow, the arrangement permits the goby to exploit areas of the bottom that otherwise would remain unavailable to it. With real estate on the reef in high demand, this gives the goby an advantage over competitors restricted to hiding in natural crevices in the reef. The shrimp may benefit from the habitual digging by the goby, which stirs up small organisms on which both can feed. More important from the shrimp's point of view is the role of the goby as a danger detector. The shrimp is blind, giving it an obvious handicap in terms of avoiding predators. When the two venture forth from their shared quarters, the shrimp keeps one antenna perpetually in contact with the goby. When the fish senses a possible threat, a flick of its tail signals to the shrimp that it is time to seek shelter, and both retreat to the burrow. Both the shrimps and their goby partners are attractively marked in bright colors, making them a hit with observers.

Aquarium Capacity . . . . 10 to 15 gallons

Life Support . . . . .live rock, live sand, hang-on filter with built-in skimmer

Lighting . . . . .two fluorescent lamps

Background . . . . .black

Decoration . . . . none

Special Requirements . . . . .reef water conditions and moderate current

Fish

Cryptocentrus cinctus . . . . 1 or a mated pair

    Or *Amblyeleotris guttatta* . . . . 1 or a mated pair

    Or *Amblyeleotris randalli.* . . . . 1 or a mated pair

    Or *Amblyeleotris wheeleri* . . . . 1 or a mated pair

    Or *Stonogobiops nematodus* . . . . 1 or a mated pair

Invertebrates

    Algae snails. 2

    Brittle stars. 1

        Or *Alpheus ochrostriatus* (see text)

        Or *Alpheus rapicida* (see text)

        Or *Alpheus randalli* (see text)

Arrange the live rock in two stacks on either end of the tank. Make one stack larger than the other to create asymmetrical balance to the composition. Add a thick sand bed, and scatter small live rock pebbles on top. With luck, the goby and shrimp will build a burrow in the open area between the two rock stacks.

Follow the instructions given for the previous model designs: add utilitarian invertebrates two weeks after the rock and sand, followed by the goby and shrimp after another two weeks. If you prefer, small hermit crabs, such as *Clibanarius tricolor*, can be substituted for the snails.

MODEL DESIGN 40   Harlequin Shrimp

One of the most beautiful and hardy invertebrates for a small tank, *provided* you feed it live sea stars. They are particularly fond of *Linckia* species but will accept others. The common *Echinaster* species of the tropical Atlantic and Caribbean can be used, for example.

Aquarium Capacity . . . . 10 gallons

Life Support . . . . .live rock, live sand, hang-on filter with built-in skimmer

Lighting . . . . .one to two fluorescent lamps

Background . . . . .pale blue

Decoration . . . . .none

Special Requirements . . . . .reef water conditions and moderate current

Fish

    none

Invertebrates

    Algae snails. 2

    Hymenocera picta . . . . 1 or a mated pair

Seaweeds (optional)

    Caulerpa, any species . . . . 1 clump

Since the main attraction in this tank is the shrimp, avoid creating an elaborate live rock structure, behind which it may decide to hide. Instead, choose a large specimen of live rock with colorful encrustations and place it near the back of the tank. Add the sand, and then surround the front of the rock with the seaweed. When two weeks have passed, add the snails, followed a week or two later by the shrimp. Add a small feeder starfish three days after the shrimp arrives. You should see the shrimp begin feeding immediately. Watch the tank carefully for the next few weeks to determine when the starfish has ceased to be of interest to the shrimp, signaling the time for a replacement.

In a fascinating example of cooperative behavior, a pair of harlequin shrimps will work together to overturn a large starfish, enabling them to get at the tube feet underneath. If you only have one shrimp, select small starfish, or place them near the shrimp, upside down, to facilitate its feeding.

Take care to add feeder starfish as if they were specimens. They are quite sensitive to improper salinity or poor water conditions, more so than is the shrimp. Acclimate carefully, or the prospective food may succumb and fall apart before the shrimp derives any benefit from it.

MODEL DESIGN 41 Boxing Crab

If ever there were an invertebrate perfect for a tiny tank, this is it. Hardy and undemanding, the boxing crab would be completely lost in a larger tank. Its reclusive nature dictates minimizing places it could hide out of sight.

Aquarium Capacity . . . . 5 gallons or less

Life Support . . . . .live rock, live sand, equipment supplied with tank

Lighting . . . . .compact fluorescent lamp, or light source supplied with tank

Background . . . . .black

Decoration . . . . .none

Special Requirements . . . . .reef water conditions

Fish

Invertebrates

   Algae snails. 1

   Lybia sp. . . . . 1 or a mated pair

As with the previous model design, this tank works best with a single piece of live rock. Otherwise, the crab may spend most of its time hiding in the spaces between pieces. The tiny anemones clutched by the crab probably derive food as a result of the messy habits of the crab. This anemone has not been seen other than in the crab's possession, raising questions about how, for example, it manages to reproduce. It is possible that the relationship benefits only the crab, since the anemone, albeit well-fed, may not be able to complete its life cycle once drafted into service. Clearly, though, the relationship benefits the crab. It may brandish its anemones as weapons, or use them as mops to collect food particles.

Set up this simple tank as described for the other small tanks in this chapter, waiting several weeks before you add the crab and its anemones.

MODEL DESIGN 42 Decorator Crab

This is a good tank for a desktop. The main attraction is found in the Gulf of Mexico and never fails to delight viewers with its remarkable camouflage behavior.

Aquarium Capacity . . . . 5 gallons or less

Life Support . . . . .live rock, live sand, equipment supplied with tank

Lighting . . . . .compact fluorescent lamp, or light source supplied with tank

Background   . . . . .black

Decoration . . . . .none

Special Requirements . . . . .reef water conditions

Fish

Invertebrates

   Algae snails. 1

   Podocheila reisi 1

You will need to replace some live rock periodically because the crab will remove encrusting organisms and attach them to specialized bristles on its carapace. The attached invertebrates and bits of seaweed provide perfect camouflage, as the crab habitually chooses items from its immediate vicinity. When the crab molts, its wardrobe is shed along with its exoskeleton, requiring it to go "shopping." It may select items from its old exoskeleton and reattach them or choose a whole new ensemble from whatever is at hand (or chela). Hardy and easily fed on various kinds of seafood, the decorator arrow crab enhances its camouflage by moving with studied slowness, lest it attract the attention of a hungry fish.

Set this tank up along the same lines as the others described in this chapter.

MODEL DESIGN 43 Elysian Fields

This strikingly beautiful sea slug can be a challenge to keep. I recommend this small tank for experienced aquarists only.

Aquarium Capacity . . . . 20 gallons (long)

Life Support . . . . live rock, live sand, hang-on filter with built-in skimmer

Lighting . . . . two to four fluorescent lamps

Background . . . . black

Decoration . . . . none

Special Requirements . . . . reef water conditions, gentle current

Fish

    none

Invertebrates

    Algae snails. 1

    Elysia crispatae 1

       Or *Elysia ornata* 1

Seaweeds (see text)

As long as the aquarium supplies a lush growth of the appropriate seaweed, these remarkable sea slugs should do well. However, they are quite delicate and demanding. See the model design on page 142 in chapter 9, "Biotope Tanks," for more information on *Elysia*.

The main thrust of this model design is to create a lawn of seaweed. Live rock, therefore, should be limited to a small amount for biofiltration purposes, placed so as to obscure the filter equipment. Set the tank up and make sure the seaweeds are growing well before you add the slug. The algae snails should help control growth that develops on the glass and should not harm the larger seaweeds intended for *Elysia*.

MODEL DESIGN 44 Atlantic-Caribbean Nanotank

Cultivated live rock from the Atlantic and the bright red peppermint shrimp make for a colorful desktop display.

Aquarium Capacity .5 gallons or less

Life Support . . . . .live rock, live sand, equipment supplied with tank

Lighting . . . . .compact fluorescent lamp, or light source supplied with tank

Background . . . . .black

Decoration . . . . .none

Special Requirements . . . . .reef water conditions

Fish

    none

Invertebrates

    Algae snails. 1

    Brittle star . . . . 1 small

    Lysmata wurdemanni . . . . 1 to 3

Once again, for a small tank such as this, one nice piece of live rock is better than a bunch of stacked-up little ones. Choose a specimen with plenty of colorful encrusting growth. The shrimp may feed on some of the small organisms on the rock, requiring you to replace the piece if significant damage is done. You will have to make this determination as the tank matures, since predicting accurately what the shrimp may find tasty is impossible.

Follow the setup procedures outlined for the other small tanks in this chapter.

MODEL DESIGN 45 Indo-Pacific Nanotank

Indo-Pacific live rock forms the basis for a tank featuring false corals and a zoanthid.

Aquarium Capacity . . . . 5 gallons or less

Life Support . . . . .live rock, live sand, equipment supplied with tank

Lighting . . . . .compact fluorescent lamp, or light source supplied with tank

Background . . . . .black

Decoration . . . . .none

Special Requirements . . . . .reef water conditions, a starter piece of live rock

Fish

    none

Invertebrates

    Algae snails. 1

    Rhodactis sp. 3 to 5 individual polyps

    Discosoma sp. 3 to 5 individual polyps

    Parazoanthus gracilis . . . . 1 small colony

You may not need any additional live rock if you select false coral and yellow polyps that have attached to a nice piece of rock. Make friends with your dealer and ask him or her to keep an eye out for something appropriate. He or she is sure to cooperate if you mention that you will be buying the nanotank for housing the specimens. The coelenterates all should do well with relatively subdued lighting, so the tank should be both inexpensive and a cinch to set up. Place a layer of live sand on the bottom, then add a chunk of live rock and the algae snail. Wait until the inevitable algae bloom subsides, remove the starter rock, and begin adding the display specimens. Space your additions about two weeks apart. Don't be surprised if the false corals multiply in this tank. If so, give extra ones to friends or explore the possibility of trading with your dealer.

For comparatively little expense, a small saltwater tank can be as breathtaking as a larger one. Remember not to overdo it. Be conservative with your additions of specimens. Quality is more important than quantity. Pick rocks, for example, with as much colorful life present as possible. Avoid using anything artificial, as it will look even more so in a confined space. With time, your microtank, or nanotank, will mature, taking on a natural look. Be patient, and your investment will be repaid many times over as you watch in fascination the goings-on in your "jewelry-box" aquarium.

Part IV

THE APPENDIXES

CATALOG OF SALTWATER FISH

I n the foregoing pages, I have covered over one hundred species of saltwater fish and their aquarium care. My list represents roughly one-fourth of the coral reef fish imported for the aquarium trade, but includes 90 percent of the species that are both commonly available and well suited to captive care by a home aquarist. The taxonomic outline should help you make sense of all this diversity. The cross-reference lists will assist you in choosing the perfect fish for any aquarium community you might be planning.

Classification of Saltwater Fish

Believe it or not, although nearly 25,000 fish species have been described, biologists disagree about what should be called a *fish*. Old schoolers include the jawless hagfishes and lampreys, as well as sharks, rays, and skates, with the bony fishes in one big vertebrate class. New thinking separates the bony fishes from the others and creates four groups at the taxonomic level of class. Thus, jawless fishes comprise the superclass Agnatha (jawless), with one class for hagfishes and another for lampreys. The other two classes are combined into the superclass Gnathostomata (jaw mouth). They are class Chondrichthyes, the cartilaginous sharks, rays, and skates; and class Actinopterygii (spine fin), the bony fishes. All coral reef fishes fall into one of the two classes with jaws. By far the majority of them are bony fishes.

Most of the saltwater fish covered in this book belong to the order Perciformes. Perciform fishes have enjoyed enormous evolutionary success, now numbering about 8000 species in both fresh and saltwater. With so many perciform species, it should come as no surprise that their lifestyles vary greatly. This has resulted in a profusion of fish families within the order, roughly 150 out of a total of 482 families. To clarify their relationships, biologists group families into suborders. The suborder designations are included here for the Perciformes, but not the other orders.

The following list omits families with no species mentioned in the book. The arrangement begins with orders and families considered to be more primitive and progresses to those considered more advanced. This does not mean that the former are less successful, only that their body plans show relatively little modification from fossil forms. Advanced families, on the other hand, exhibit the greatest degree of alteration from the body designs of their ancestors.

Class Chondrichthyes (cartilaginous fishes)

    Order Orectolobiformes

        Family Hemiscylliidae (bamboo sharks)

Class Actinopterygii (bony fishes)

    Order Anguilliformes

        Family Muraenidae (moray eels)

    Order Lophiiformes

        Family Antennariidae (frogfishes and anglerfishes)

    Order Beryciformes

        Family Monocentridae (pinecone fishes)

        Family Holocentridae (squirrel- and soldierfishes)

    Order Gasterosteiformes

        Family Syngnathidae (seahorses)

    Order Scorpaeniformes

        Family Scorpaenidae (lionfishes)

    Order Perciformes

   Suborder Percoidei

        Family Serranidae (groupers, anthias)

        Family Pseudochromidae (dottybacks)

        Family Grammatidae (fairy basslets, grammas)

        Family Plesiopidae (roundheads, longfins)

        Family Opisthognathidae (jawfishes)

        Family Cirrhitidae (hawkfishes)

        Family Apogonidae (cardinalfishes)

        Family Lutjanidae (snappers)

        Family Chaetodontidae (butterflyfishes)

        Family Pomacanthidae (angelfishes)

   Suborder Labroidei

        Family Pomacentridae (damselfishes)

        Family Labridae (wrasses)

Suborder Trachinoidei

    Family Pholidichthyidae (convict blennies)

 Suborder Blennioidei

    Family Blenniidae (blennies)

Suborder Callionymoidei

    Family Callionymidae (dragonets)

Suborder Gobioidei

    Family Gobiidae (gobies)

    Family Microdesmidae (dartfishes)

Suborder Acanthuroidei

    Family Siganidae (rabbitfishes)

    Family Acanthuridae (tangs)

Order Tetraodontiformes

    Family Balistidae (triggerfishes)

    Family Monacanthidae (filefishes)

    Family Tetraodontidae (puffers)

    Family Diodontidae (porcupine- and burrfishes)

...plus sixty-three additional families

Cross-Reference Lists

Scientific names often change as new research sheds light on the relationships among species. Current scientific names can be found via Internet sites such as FishBase. (See "Resources," Appendix E.) When looking up information about a specific fish, it is always best to use the genus and species names. Even outdated ones are less ambiguous than common names.

Common names for saltwater fish vary from place to place, even between two dealers in the same town. Anyone can make up a common name, but the ones given below turn up most frequently in the aquarium literature. Despite the wide variability in common names, many have become standardized by usage. The starting point for any biotope tank should be a specific geographic location. The locality information provided in Table 3 should help you choose fish from a single region. Table 4 ranks the species covered in this book by an index of their suitability for captivity developed by biologist and underwater photographer Scott Michael. On this scale, species with higher numbers are more likely to thrive in a home tank, while those with lower numbers will require more careful attention if they are to survive for a reasonable period of time.

Compatibility among different saltwater species may be difficult to predict with accuracy. The information presented in Table 5 should be taken as a general guide only. Individual specimens may not conform.

Sometimes, a normally docile fish will become the terror of the tank, and the occasional skulking predator will turn out to be a big sissy. In Table 5, if the fish is listed as incompatible with "aggressive species" it may be at risk from some large invertebrates as well as from other fishes. If a fish is listed as incompatible with "aggressive fishes," you may assume it can hold its own with potential invertebrate aggressors. Incompatibilities are also noted if the fish is likely to feed on certain invertebrate tank mates. Thus, several butterflyfishes are listed as incompatible with conspecifics, because they may fight, but also with sessile invertebrates, which the fish will regard as food.

Table 1: Alphabetic Cross-Reference by Scientific Name

Genus	Species	Common Name(s)
Acanthurus	achilles	tang, Achilles
Acanthurus	caeruleus	tang, Atlantic blue
Acanthurus	japonicus	tang, powder brown
Acanthurus	leucosternon	tang, powder blue
Acanthurus	sohal	tang, Arabian
Amblycirrhitus	pinos	hawkfish, red spotted
Amblyeleotris	guttata	goby, orange-hyspotted prawn
Amblyeleotris	randalli	goby, Randall's prawn
Amblyeleotris	wheeleri	goby, Wheeler's prawn
Amblygobius	hectori	goby, Hector's
Amblygobius	phalaena	goby, banded
Amblygobius	rainfordi	goby, Rainford's
Amphiprion	clarkii	clownfish, Clark's
Amphiprion	frenatus	clownfish, tomato
Amphiprion	ocellaris	clownfish, common
Amphiprion	percula	clownfish, true percula
Amphiprion	melanopus	clownfish, cinnamon
Antennarius	maculatus	frogfish, clown
Apogon	cyanosoma	cardinalfish, orange-hystriped
Apogon	maculatus	cardinalfish, flame
Assessor	flavissimus	mini-hygrouper, golden
Assessor	macneilii	mini-hygrouper, MacNiel's
Balistapus	undulatus	triggerfish, undulated
Balistoides	conspicillum	triggerfish, clown

Genus	Species	Common Name(s)
Calloplesiops	altivelis	comet grouper
Canthigaster	jactator	toby, whitespotted
Canthigaster	valentini	toby, saddled
Centropyge	argi	angelfish, cherub dwarf
Centropyge	bicolor	angelfish, bicolor dwarf
Centropyge	bispinosus	angelfish, coral beauty
Centropyge	flavissima	angelfish, lemonpeel
Centropyge	heraldi	angelfish, false lemonpeel
Centropyge	loriculus	angelfish, flame
Centropyge	potteri	angelfish, Potter's
Cephalopholis	miniata	grouper, coral
Chaetodon	auriga	butterflyfish, threadfin
Chaetodon	ephippium	butterflyfish, saddled
Chaetodon	kleinii	butterflyfish, Klein's
Chaetodon	lunula	butterflyfish, raccoon
Chaetodon	miliaris	butterflyfish, lemon
Chaetodon	semilarvatus	butterflyfish, golden
Chaetodontoplus	mesoleucus	angelfish, Singapore
Chelmon	rostratus	butterflyfish, copperband
Chilomycterus	antillarum	boxfish, spiny
Chiloscyllium	plagiosum	shark, white-hyspotted bamboo
Chromis	cyanea	chromis, blue
Chromis	vanderbilti	chromis, Vanderbilt's
Chromis	viridis	chromis, green
Chrysiptera	cyanea	damselfish, blue
Chrysiptera	parasema	damselfish, yellowtail
Cirrhilabrus	jordani	wrasse, Jordan's fairy
Cirrhilabrus	rubriventralis	wrasse, social fairy
Cirrhitichthys	oxycephalus	hawkfish, pixy
Coerodon	fasciatus	wrasse, harlequin tuskfish

continued

Table 1: Alphabetic Cross-Reference by Scientific Name (*continued*)

Genus	Species	Common Name(s)
Coris	gaimard	wrasse, clown
Cryptocentrus	cinctus	goby, yellow prawn
Ctenochaetus	hawaiiensis	tang, Hawaiian bristletooth
Dascyllus	aruanus	humbug, striped
Dascyllus	melanurus	humbug, black-hytailed
Dascyllus	trimaculatus	humbug, threespot
Dendrochirus	biocellatus	lionfish, Fu Manchu
Dendrochirus	brachypterus	lionfish, fuzzy dwarf
Dendrochirus	zebra	lionfish, dwarf
Diodon	holocanthus	puffer, porcupine
Echidna	nebulosa	moray eel, snowflake
Ecsenius	bicolor	blenny, bicolor
Ecsenius	gravieri	blenny, Red Sea mimic
Enchelycore	pardalis	moray eel, Hawaiian dragon
Forcipiger	flavissimus	butterflyfish, yellow longnose
Forcipiger	longifostris	butterflyfish, big longnose
Gobiodon	citrinus	goby, citron coral
Gobiodon	histrio	goby, blue-hyspotted coral
Gobiodon	okinawae	goby, yellow coral
Gobiosoma	evelynae	goby, sharknose
Gobiosoma	oceanops	goby, neon
Gomphosus	varius	wrasse, Hawaiian bird
Gramma	loreto	royal gramma
Gramma	melacara	basslet, blackcap
Gymnomuraena	zebra	moray eel, zebra
Gymnothorax	meleagris	moray eel, comet
Halichoeres	chrysus	wrasse, golden
Heniochus	acuminatus	bannerfish, longfin
Heniochus	diphreutes	bannerfish, schooling
Hippocampus	erectus	seahorse, giant

Genus	Species	Common Name(s)
Holacanthus	ciliaris	angelfish, queen
Liopropoma	rubre	basslet, swissguard
Lutjanus	kasmira	snapper, blue-hylined
Meiacanthus	atrodorsalis	blenny, yellowtail fanged
Melichthys	vidua	triggerfish, pink-hytailed
Naso	lituratus	tang, orange-hyspined unicorn
Nemateleotris	decora	goby, decorated firefish
Nemateleotris	helfrichi	goby, Helfrich's firefish
Nemateleotris	magnifica	goby, firefish
Neocirrhites	armatus	hawkfish, flame
Novaculichthys	taeniorus	wrasse, dragon
Odonus	niger	triggerfish, black
Opisthognathus	aurifrons	jawfish, yellow-hyheaded
Oxycirrhites	typus	hawkfish, longnosed
Paracanthurus	hepatus	tang, regal
Paracheilinus	octotaenia	wrasse, eightline
Paracirrhites	arcatus	hawkfish, arceye
Paraluteres	prionurus	filefish, saddled
Pervagor	spilosoma	filefish, Hawaiian
Pholidichthys	leucotaenia	blenny, convict
Pomacanthus	annularis	angelfish, blue ring
Pomacanthus	arcuatus	angelfish, gray
Pomacanthus	asfur	angelfish, Arabian
Pomacanthus	imperator	angelfish, emperor
Pomacanthus	maculosus	angelfish, maculosus
Pomacanthus	paru	angelfish, French
Pomacanthus	semicirculatus	angelfish, Koran
Pomacentrus	alleni	damselfish, Allen's
Premnas	biaculeatus	clownfish, maroon
Pseudanthias	bicolor	anthias, bicolored

continued

Table 1: Alphabetic Cross-Reference by Scientific Name *(continued)*

Genus	Species	Common Name(s)
Pseudanthias	pleurotaenia	anthias, purple square
Pseudobalistes	fuscus	triggerfish, bluelined
Pseudocheilinus	hexataenia	wrasse, sixline neon
Pseudocheilinus	tetrataenia	wrasse, fouline neon
Pseudochromis	aldebarensis	dottyback, Arabian
Pseudochromis	diadema	dottyback, diadem
Pseudochromis	flavivertex	dottyback, sunrise
Pseudochromis	fridmani	dottyback, orchid
Pseudochromis	paccagnellae	dottyback, royal
Pseudochromis	porphyreus	dottyback, purple
Pseudochromis	springeri	dottyback, Springer's
Pterapogon	kauderni	cardinalfish, Banggai
Ptereleotris	microlepis	goby, blue gudgeon
Pterois	antennata	lionfish, spotfin
Pterois	radiata	lionfish, clarfin
Pterois	volitans	lionfish, common
Pterosynchiropus	splendidus	mandarin, common
Rhinecanthus	aculeatus	triggerfish, Picasso
Rhinecanthus	assassi	triggerfish, Arabian picasso
Serranocirrhitus	latus	anthias, sunburst
Serranus	tabacarius	bass, tobacco
Serranus	tigrinus	bass, harlequin
Siganus	vulpinus	foxface
Signigobius	biocellatus	goby, signal
Sphaeramia	nematoptera	cardinalfish, pajama
Stonogobiops	nematodes	goby, threadfin prawn
Synchiropus	picturatus	mandarin, psychedelic
Taenianotus	triacanthus	scorpionfish, leaf
Thalassoma	bifasciatum	wrasse, bluehead
Thalassoma	duperryi	wrasse, orange saddle

Genus	Species	Common Name(s)
Thalassoma	*lunare*	wrasse, lyretail
Thalassoma	*lutescens*	wrasse, yellow
Valenciennea	*puellaris*	goby, pretty prawn
Xanthichthys	*auromarginatus*	triggerfish, bluechin
Xanthichthys	*mento*	triggerfish, crosshatch
Xanthichthys	*ringens*	triggerfish, Sargassum
Zebrasoma	*desjardini*	tang, Desjardin's sailfin
Zebrasoma	*flavescens*	tang, yellow
Zebrasoma	*veliferum*	tang, sailfin
Zebrasoma	*xanthurum*	tang, purple

Table 2: Fish Cross-Reference by Common Name

Common Name(s)	Genus	Species
angelfish, Arabian	*Pomacanthus*	*asfur*
angelfish, bicolor dwarf	*Centropyge*	*bicolor*
angelfish, blue ring	*Pomacanthus*	*annularis*
angelfish, cherub dwarf	*Centropyge*	*argi*
angelfish, coral beauty	*Centropyge*	*bispinosus*
angelfish, emperor	*Pomacanthus*	*imperator*
angelfish, false lemonpeel	*Centropyge*	*heraldi*
angelfish, flame	*Centropyge*	*loriculus*
angelfish, French	*Pomacanthus*	*paru*
angelfish, gray	*Pomacanthus*	*arcuatus*
angelfish, Koran	*Pomacanthus*	*semicirculatus*
angelfish, lemonpeel	*Centropyge*	*flavissima*
angelfish, maculosus	*Pomacanthus*	*maculosus*
angelfish, Potter's	*Centropyge*	*potteri*
angelfish, queen	*Holacanthus*	*ciliaris*
angelfish, Singapore	*Chaetodontoplus*	*mesoleucus*

continued

Table 2: Fish Cross-Reference by Common Name *(continued)*

Common Name(s)	Genus	Species
anthias, bicolored	*Pseudanthias*	*bicolor*
anthias, purple square	*Pseudanthias*	*pleurotaenia*
anthias, sunburst	*Serranocirrhitus*	*latus*
bannerfish, longfin	*Heniochus*	*acuminatus*
bannerfish, schooling	*Heniochus*	*diphreutes*
bass, harlequin	*Serranus*	*tigrinus*
bass, tobacco	*Serranus*	*tabacarius*
basslet, blackcap	*Gramma*	*melacara*
basslet, swissguard	*Liopropoma*	*rubre*
blenny, bicolor	*Ecsenius*	*bicolor*
blenny, convict	*Pholidichthys*	*leucotaenia*
blenny, Red Sea mimic	*Ecsenius*	*gravieri*
blenny, yellowtail fanged	*Meiacanthus*	*atrodorsalis*
boxfish, spiny	*Chilomycterus*	*antillarum*
butterflyfish, big longnose	*Forcipiger*	*longirostris*
butterflyfish, copperband	*Chelmon*	*rostratus*
butterflyfish, golden	*Chaetodon*	*semilarvatus*
butterflyfish, Klein's	*Chaetodon*	*kleinii*
butterflyfish, lemon	*Chaetodon*	*miliaris*
butterflyfish, raccoon	*Chaetodon*	*lunula*
butterflyfish, saddled	*Chaetodon*	*ephippium*
butterflyfish, threadfin	*Chaetodon*	*auriga*
butterflyfish, yellow longnose	*Forcipiger*	*flavissimus*
cardinalfish, Banggai	*Pterapogon*	*kauderni*
cardinalfish, flame	*Apogon*	*maculatus*
cardinalfish, orange-striped	*Apogon*	*cyanosoma*
cardinalfish, pajama	*Sphaeramia*	*nematoptera*
chromis, blue	*Chromis*	*cyanea*
chromis, green	*Chromis*	*viridis*
chromis, Vanderbilt's	*Chromis*	*vanderbilti*

Common Name(s)	Genus	Species
clownfish, cinnamon	*Amphiprion*	*melanopus*
clownfish, Clark's	*Amphiprion*	*clarkii*
clownfish, common	*Amphiprion*	*ocellaris*
clownfish, maroon	*Premnas*	*biaculeatus*
clownfish, tomato	*Amphiprion*	*frenatus*
clownfish, true percula	*Amphiprion*	*percula*
comet grouper	*Calloplesiops*	*altivelis*
damselfish, Allen's	*Pomacentrus*	*alleni*
damselfish, blue	*Chrysiptera*	*cyanea*
damselfish, yellowtail	*Chrysiptera*	*parasema*
dottyback, Arabian	*Pseudochromis*	*aldebarensis*
dottyback, diadem	*Pseudochromis*	*diadema*
dottyback, orchid	*Pseudochromis*	*fridmani*
dottyback, purple	*Pseudochromis*	*porphyreus*
dottyback, royal	*Pseudochromis*	*paccagnellae*
dottyback, Springer's	*Pseudochromis*	*springeri*
dottyback, sunrise	*Pseudochromis*	*flavivertex*
filefish, Hawaiian	*Pervagor*	*spilosoma*
filefish, saddled	*Paraluteres*	*prionurus*
foxface	*Siganus*	*vulpinus*
frogfish, clown	*Antennarius*	*maculatus*
goby, banded	*Amblygobius*	*phalaena*
goby, blue gudgeon	*Ptereleotris*	*heteroptera*
goby, blue-spotted coral	*Gobiodon*	*histrio*
goby, citron coral	*Gobiodon*	*citrinus*
goby, decorated firefish	*Nemateleotris*	*decora*
goby, firefish	*Nemateleotris*	*magnifica*
goby, Hector's	*Amblygobius*	*hectori*
goby, Helfrich's firefish	*Nemateleotris*	*helfrichi*
goby, neon	*Gobiosoma*	*oceanops*

continued

Table 2: Fish Cross-Reference by Common Name *(continued)*

Common Name(s)	Genus	Species
goby, orange-spotted prawn	*Amblyeleotris*	*guttata*
goby, pretty prawn	*Valenciennea*	*puellaris*
goby, Rainford's	*Amblygobius*	*rainfordi*
goby, Randall's prawn	*Amblyeleotris*	*randalli*
goby, sharknose	*Gobiosoma*	*evelynae*
goby, signal	*Signigobius*	*biocellatus*
goby, threadfin prawn	*Stonogobiops*	*nematodes*
goby, Wheeler's prawn	*Amblyeleotris*	*wheeleri*
goby, yellow coral	*Gobiodon*	*okinawae*
goby, yellow prawn	*Cryptocentrus*	*cinctus*
grouper, coral	*Cephalopholis*	*miniata*
hawkfish, arceye	*Paracirrhites*	*arcatus*
hawkfish, flame	*Neocirrhites*	*armatus*
hawkfish, longnosed	*Oxycirrhites*	*typus*
hawkfish, pixy	*Cirrhitichthys*	*oxycephalus*
hawkfish, red spotted	*Amblycirrhitus*	*pinos*
humbug, black-tailed	*Dascyllus*	*melanurus*
humbug, striped	*Dascyllus*	*aruanus*
humbug, threespot	*Dascyllus*	*trimaculatus*
jawfish, yellow-headed	*Opisthognathus*	*aurifrons*
lionfish, clarfin	*Pterois*	*radiata*
lionfish, common	*Pterois*	*volitans*
lionfish, dwarf	*Dendrochirus*	*zebra*
lionfish, Fu Manchu	*Dendrochirus*	*biocellatus*
lionfish, fuzzy dwarf	*Dendrochirus*	*brachypterus*
lionfish, spotfin	*Pterois*	*antennata*
mandarin, common	*Pterosynchiropus*	*splendidus*
mandarin, psychedelic	*Synchiropus*	*picturatus*
mini-grouper, golden	*Assessor*	*flavissimus*
mini-grouper, MacNiel's	*Assessor*	*macneilii*

Common Name(s)	Genus	Species
moray eel, comet	Gymnothorax	meleagris
moray eel, Hawaiian dragon	Enchelycore	pardalis
moray eel, snowflake	Echidna	nebulosa
moray eel, zebra	Gymnomuraena	zebra
puffer, porcupine	Diodon	holocanthus
royal gramma	Gramma	loreto
scorpionfish, leaf	Taenianotus	triacanthus
seahorse, giant	Hippocampus	erectus
shark, white-spotted bamboo	Chiloscyllium	plagiosum
snapper, blue-lined	Lutjanus	kasmira
tang, Achilles	Acanthurus	achilles
tang, Arabian	Acanthurus	sohal
tang, Atlantic blue	Acanthurus	caeruleus
tang, Desjardin's sailfin	Zebrasoma	desjardini
tang, Hawaiian bristletooth	Ctenochaetus	hawaiiensis
tang, orange-spined unicorn	Naso	lituratus
tang, powder blue	Acanthurus	loucosternon
tang, powder brown	Acanthurus	japonicus
tang, purple	Zebrasoma	xanthurum
tang, regal	Paracanthurus	hepatus
tang, sailfin	Zebrasoma	veliferum
tang, yellow	Zebrasoma	flavescens
toby, saddled	Canthigaster	valentini
toby, whitespotted	Canthigaster	jactator
triggerfish, Arabian picasso	Rhinecanthus	assassi
triggerfish, black	Odonus	niger
triggerfish, bluechin	Xanthichthys	auromarginatus
triggerfish, bluelined	Pseudobalistes	fuscus
triggerfish, clown	Balistoides	conspicillum
triggerfish, crosshatch	Xanthichthys	mento

continued

Table 2: Fish Cross-Reference by Common Name (*continued*)

Common Name(s)	Genus	Species
triggerfish, Picasso	*Rhinecanthus*	*aculeatus*
triggerfish, pink-tailed	*Melichthys*	*vidua*
triggerfish, Sargassum	*Xanthichthys*	*ringens*
triggerfish, undulated	*Balistapus*	*undulatus*
wrasse, bluehead	*Thalassoma*	*bifasciatum*
wrasse, clown	*Coris*	*gaimard*
wrasse, dragon	*Novaculichthys*	*taeniorus*
wrasse, eightline	*Paracheilinus*	*octotaenia*
wrasse, fourline neon	*Pseudocheilinus*	*tetrataenia*
wrasse, golden	*Halichoeres*	*chrysus*
wrasse, harlequin tuskfish	*Coerodon*	*fasciatus*
wrasse, Hawaiian bird	*Gomphosus*	*varius*
wrasse, Jordan's fairy	*Cirrhilabrus*	*jordani*
wrasse, lyretail	*Thalassoma*	*lunare*
wrasse, orange saddle	*Thalassoma*	*duperryi*
wrasse, sixline neon	*Pseudocheilinus*	*hexataenia*
wrasse, social fairy	*Cirrhilabrus*	*rubriventralis*
wrasse, yellow	*Thalassoma*	*lutescens*

Table 3: Fish Cross-Reference by Locality

Genus	Species	Common Name(s)	Range
Centropyge	*argi*	angelfish, cherub dwarf	Atlantic-Caribbean
Pomacanthus	*paru*	angelfish, French	Atlantic-Caribbean
Pomacanthus	*arcuatus*	angelfish, gray	Atlantic-Caribbean
Holacanthus	*ciliaris*	angelfish, queen	Atlantic-Caribbean
Serranus	*tigrinus*	bass, harlequin	Atlantic-Caribbean
Serranus	*tabacarius*	bass, tobacco	Atlantic-Caribbean
Gramma	*melacara*	basslet, blackcap	Atlantic-Caribbean
Liopropoma	*rubre*	basslet, swissguard	Atlantic-Caribbean

Genus	Species	Common Name(s)	Range
Chilomycterus	antillarum	boxfish, spiny	Atlantic-Caribbean
Apogon	maculatus	cardinalfish, flame	Atlantic-Caribbean
Chromis	cyanea	chromis, blue	Atlantic-Caribbean
Gobiosoma	oceanops	goby, neon	Atlantic-Caribbean
Gobiosoma	evelynae	goby, sharknose	Atlantic-Caribbean
Amblycirrhitus	pinos	hawkfish, red spotted	Atlantic-Caribbean
Opisthognathus	aurifrons	jawfish, yellow-headed	Atlantic-Caribbean
Gramma	loreto	royal gramma	Atlantic-Caribbean
Hippocampus	erectus	seahorse, giant	Atlantic-Caribbean
Acanthurus	caeruleus	tang, Atlantic blue	Atlantic-Caribbean
Thalassoma	bifasciatum	wrasse, bluehead	Atlantic-Caribbean
Amblygobius	hectori	goby, Hector's	Central to Western Pacific
Amblygobius	rainfordi	goby, Rainford's	Central to Western Pacific
Zebrasoma	desjardini	tang, Desjardin's sailfin	Central to Western Pacific
Zebrasoma	veliferum	tang, sailfin	Central to Western Pacific
Pseudocheilinus	tetrataenia	wrasse, fouline neon	Central to Western Pacific
Centropyge	potteri	angelfish, Potter's	Hawaii
Ctenochaetus	hawaiiensis	tang, Hawaiian bristletooth	Hawaii
Canthigaster	jactator	toby, whitespotted	Hawaii
Cirrhilabrus	jordani	wrasse, Jordan's fairy	Hawaii
Centropyge	loriculus	angelfish, flame	Hawaii to South Pacific
Chaetodon	kleinii	butterflyfish, Klein's	Hawaii, Indo-Pacific
Chaetodon	miliaris	butterflyfish, lemon	Hawaii, Indo-Pacific
Chaetodon	lunula	butterflyfish, raccoon	Hawaii, Indo-Pacific
Chaetodon	auriga	butterflyfish, threadfin	Hawaii, Indo-Pacific
Chromis	vanderbilti	chromis, Vanderbilt's	Hawaii, Indo-Pacific
Pervagor	spilosoma	filefish, Hawaiian	Hawaii, Indo-Pacific
Enchelycore	pardalis	moray eel, Hawaiian dragon	Hawaii, Indo-Pacific
Echidna	nebulosa	moray eel, snowflake	Hawaii, Indo-Pacific
Gymnomuraena	zebra	moray eel, zebra	Hawaii, Indo-Pacific

continued

Table 3: Fish Cross-Reference by Locality (*continued*)

Genus	Species	Common Name(s)	Range
Acanthurus	achilles	tang, Achilles	Hawaii, Indo-Pacific
Naso	lituratus	tang, orange-spined unicorn	Hawaii, Indo-Pacific
Zebrasoma	flavescens	tang, yellow	Hawaii, Indo-Pacific
Rhinecanthus	aculeatus	triggerfish, Picasso	Hawaii, Indo-Pacific
Gomphosus	varius	wrasse, Hawaiian bird	Hawaii, Indo-Pacific
Thalassoma	duperryi	wrasse, orange saddle	Hawaii, Indo-Pacific
Pomacentrus	alleni	damselfish, Allen's	Indian Ocean
Acanthurus	leucosternon	tang, powder blue	Indian Ocean
Premnas	biaculeatus	clownfish, maroon	Indian Ocean to West Pacific
Pseudochromis	aldebarensis	dottyback, Arabian	Indian Ocean, Red Sea
Cirrhilabrus	rubriventralis	wrasse, social fairy	Indian Ocean, Red Sea
Centropyge	bicolor	angelfish, bicolor dwarf	Indo-Pacific
Pomacanthus	annularis	angelfish, blue ring	Indo-Pacific
Centropyge	bispinosus	angelfish, coral beauty	Indo-Pacific
Pomacanthus	imperator	angelfish, emperor	Indo-Pacific
Pomacanthus	semicirculatus	angelfish, Koran	Indo-Pacific
Centropyge	flavissima	angelfish, lemonpeel	Indo-Pacific
Pseudanthias	bicolor	anthias, bicolored	Indo-Pacific
Heniochus	acuminatus	bannerfish, longfin	Indo-Pacific
Heniochus	diphreutes	bannerfish, schooling	Indo-Pacific
Ecsenius	bicolor	blenny, bicolor	Indo-Pacific
Pholidichthys	leucotaenia	blenny, convict	Indo-Pacific
Meiacanthus	atrodorsalis	blenny, yellowtail fanged	Indo-Pacific
Forcipiger	longifostris	butterflyfish, big longnose	Indo-Pacific
Chelmon	rostratus	butterflyfish, copperband	Indo-Pacific
Chaetodon	ephippium	butterflyfish, saddled	Indo-Pacific
Forcipiger	flavissimus	butterflyfish, yellow longnose	Indo-Pacific
Pterapogon	kauderni	cardinalfish, Banggai	Indo-Pacific
Apogon	cyanosoma	cardinalfish, orange-striped	Indo-Pacific
Sphaeramia	nematoptera	cardinalfish, pajama	Indo-Pacific

Genus	Species	Common Name(s)	Range
Chromis	viridis	chromis, green	Indo-Pacific
Amphiprion	melanopus	clownfish, cinnamon	Indo-Pacific
Amphiprion	clarkii	clownfish, Clark's	Indo-Pacific
Amphiprion	ocellaris	clownfish, common	Indo-Pacific
Amphiprion	frenatus	clownfish, tomato	Indo-Pacific
Amphiprion	percula	clownfish, true percula	Indo-Pacific
Calloplesiops	altivelis	comet grouper	Indo-Pacific
Paraluteres	prionurus	filefish, saddled	Indo-Pacific
Siganus	vulpinus	foxface	Indo-Pacific
Antennarius	maculatus	frogfish, clown	Indo-Pacific
Amblygobius	phalaena	goby, banded	Indo-Pacific
Ptereleotris	microlepis	goby, blue gudgeon	Indo-Pacific
Gobiodon	histrio	goby, blue-spotted coral	Indo-Pacific
Gobiodon	citrinus	goby, citron coral	Indo-Pacific
Nemateleotris	decora	goby, decorated firefish	Indo-Pacific
Nemateleotris	magnifica	goby, firefish	Indo-Pacific
Nemateleotris	helfrichi	goby, Helfrich's firefish	Indo-Pacific
Valenciennea	puellaris	goby, orange-spotted sleeper	Indo-Pacific
Stonogobiops	nematodes	goby, threadfin prawn	Indo-Pacific
Gobiodon	okinawae	goby, yellow coral	Indo-Pacific
Cryptocentrus	cinctus	goby, yellow prawn	Indo-Pacific
Cephalopholis	miniata	grouper, coral	Indo-Pacific
Paracirrhites	arcatus	hawkfish, arceye	Indo-Pacific
Oxycirrhites	typus	hawkfish, longnosed	Indo-Pacific
Cirrhitichthys	oxycephalus	hawkfish, pixy	Indo-Pacific
Dascyllus	aruanus	humbug, striped	Indo-Pacific
Dascyllus	trimaculatus	humbug, threespot	Indo-Pacific
Pterois	radiata	lionfish, clarfin	Indo-Pacific
Pterois	volitans	lionfish, common	Indo-Pacific
Dendrochirus	zebra	lionfish, dwarf	Indo-Pacific

continued

Table 3: Fish Cross-Reference by Locality *(continued)*

Genus	Species	Common Name(s)	Range
Dendrochirus	biocellatus	lionfish, Fu Manchu	Indo-Pacific
Dendrochirus	brachypterus	lionfish, fuzzy dwarf	Indo-Pacific
Pterois	antennata	lionfish, spotfin	Indo-Pacific
Gymnothorax	meleagris	moray eel, comet	Indo-Pacific
Taenianotus	triacanthus	scorpionfish, leaf	Indo-Pacific
Chiloscyllium	plagiosum	shark, white-spotted bamboo	Indo-Pacific
Paracanthurus	hepatus	tang, regal	Indo-Pacific
Canthigaster	valentini	toby, saddled	Indo-Pacific
Odonus	niger	triggerfish, black	Indo-Pacific
Xanthichthys	auromarginatus	triggerfish, bluechin	Indo-Pacific
Pseudobalistes	fuscus	triggerfish, bluelined	Indo-Pacific
Balistoides	conspicillum	triggerfish, clown	Indo-Pacific
Xanthichthys	mento	triggerfish, crosshatch	Indo-Pacific
Melichthys	vidua	triggerfish, pink-tailed	Indo-Pacific
Xanthichthys	ringens	triggerfish, Sargassum	Indo-Pacific
Balistapus	undulatus	triggerfish, undulated	Indo-Pacific
Coris	gaimard	wrasse, clown	Indo-Pacific
Novaculichthys	taeniorus	wrasse, dragon	Indo-Pacific
Paracheilinus	octotaenia	wrasse, eightline	Indo-Pacific
Halichoeres	chrysus	wrasse, golden	Indo-Pacific
Thalassoma	lunare	wrasse, lyretail	Indo-Pacific
Pseudocheilinus	hexataenia	wrasse, sixline neon	Indo-Pacific
Thalassoma	lutescens	wrasse, yellow	Indo-Pacific
Pomacanthus	asfur	angelfish, Arabian	Red Sea
Pomacanthus	maculosus	angelfish, maculosus	Red Sea
Ecsenius	gravieri	blenny, Red Sea mimic	Red Sea
Chaetodon	semilarvatus	butterflyfish, golden	Red Sea
Pseudochromis	fridmani	dottyback, orchid	Red Sea

Genus	Species	Common Name(s)	Range
Pseudochromis	springeri	dottyback, Springer's	Red Sea
Pseudochromis	flavivertex	dottyback, sunrise	Red Sea
Acanthurus	sohal	tang, Arabian	Red Sea
Zebrasoma	xanthurum	tang, purple	Red Sea
Rhinecanthus	assassi	triggerfish, Arabian Picasso	Red Sea
Centropyge	heraldi	angelfish, false lemonpeel	South and Western Pacific
Pseudanthias	pleurotaenia	anthias, purple square	South and Western Pacific
Serranocirrhitus	latus	anthias, sunburst	South and Western Pacific
Pseudochromis	porphyreus	dottyback, purple	South and Western Pacific
Neocirrhites	armatus	hawkfish, flame	South and Western Pacific
Amblyeleotris	wheeleri	goby, Wheeler's prawn	Western Pacific
Chaetodontoplus	mesoleucus	angelfish, Singapore	Western Pacific
Chrysiptera	cyanea	damselfish, blue	Western Pacific
Chrysiptera	parasema	damselfish, yellowtail	Western Pacific
Pseudochromis	diadema	dottyback, diadem	Western Pacific
Pseudochromis	paccagnellae	dottyback, royal	Western Pacific
Amblyeleotris	guttata	goby, orange-spotted prawn	Western Pacific
Amblyeleotris	randalli	goby, Randall's prawn	Western Pacific
Signigobius	biocellatus	goby, signal	Western Pacific
Dascyllus	melanurus	humbug, black-tailed	Western Pacific
Pterosynchiropus	splendidus	mandarin, common	Western Pacific
Synchiropus	picturatus	mandarin, psychedelic	Western Pacific
Assessor	flavissimus	mini-grouper, golden	Western Pacific
Assessor	macneilii	mini-grouper, MacNiel's	Western Pacific
Lutjanus	kasmira	snapper, blue-lined	Western Pacific
Acanthurus	japonicus	tang, powder brown	Western Pacific
Coerodon	fasciatus	wrasse, harlequin tuskfish	Western Pacific, Indian Ocean
Diodon	holocanthus	puffer, porcupine	Worldwide

Table 4: Fish Cross-Reference by Michael Suitability Index[1]

Genus	Species	Common Name(s)	Suitability Index
Pomacanthus	maculosus	angelfish, maculosus	5
Heniochus	acuminatus	bannerfish, longfin	5
Heniochus	diphreutes	bannerfish, schooling	5
Serranus	tigrinus	bass, harlequin	5
Serranus	tabacarius	bass, tobacco	5
Pholidichthys	leucotaenia	blenny, convict	5
Chaetodon	kleinii	butterflyfish, Klein's	5
Pterapogon	kauderni	cardinalfish, Banggai	5
Apogon	maculatus	cardinalfish, flame	5
Apogon	cyanosoma	cardinalfish, orange-striped	5
Sphaeramia	nematoptera	cardinalfish, pajama	5
Chromis	cyanea	chromis, blue	5
Chromis	vanderbilti	chromis, Vanderbilt's	5
Amphiprion	melanopus	clownfish, cinnamon	5
Amphiprion	clarkii	clownfish, Clark's	5
Amphiprion	ocellaris	clownfish, common	5
Premnas	biaculeatus	clownfish, maroon	5
Amphiprion	frenatus	clownfish, tomato	5
Amphiprion	percula	clownfish, true percula	5
Calloplesiops	altivelis	comet grouper	5
Pomacentrus	alleni	damselfish, Allen's	5
Chrysiptera	cyanea	damselfish, blue	5
Chrysiptera	parasema	damselfish, yellowtail	5
Pseudochromis	aldebarensis	dottyback, Arabian	5

[1] Based on the "Aquarium Suitability Index" in Michael (1999).
Scott Michael defines the categories as follows:
2 = most specimens do not acclimate to home aquariums
3 = most specimens acclimate to home aquariums with special attention
4 = most specimens adapt to home aquarium life with reasonable care
5 = most specimens generally hardy in home aquariums; unadaptable specimens are rare

WARNING Some readily available saltwater fish are venomous. This renders them unsuitable for aquariums around small children or others who might be at risk. Information on venomous species appears in the text where appropriate.

Genus	Species	Common Name(s)	Suitability Index
Pseudochromis	diadema	dottyback, diadem	5
Pseudochromis	fridmani	dottyback, orchid	5
Pseudochromis	porphyreus	dottyback, purple	5
Pseudochromis	paccagnellae	dottyback, royal	5
Pseudochromis	springeri	dottyback, Springer's	5
Pseudochromis	flavivertex	dottyback, sunrise	5
Nemateleotris	decora	goby, decorated firefish	5
Nemateleotris	magnifica	goby, firefish	5
Nemateleotris	helfrichi	goby, Helfrich's firefish	5
Cephalopholis	miniata	grouper, coral	5
Paracirrhites	arcatus	hawkfish, arceye	5
Oxycirrhites	typus	hawkfish, longnosed	5
Cirrhitichthys	oxycephalus	hawkfish, pixy	5
Amblycirrhitus	pinos	hawkfish, red spotted	5
Dascyllus	melanurus	humbug, black-tailed	5
Dascyllus	aruanus	humbug, striped	5
Dascyllus	trimaculatus	humbug, threespot	5
Pterois	radiata	lionfish, clearfin	5
Pterois	volitans	lionfish, common	5
Pterois	antennata	lionfish, spotfin	5
Assessor	flavissimus	mini-grouper, golden	5
Assessor	macneilii	mini-grouper, MacNiel's	5
Gymnothorax	meleagris	moray eel, comet	5
Echidna	nebulosa	moray eel, snowflake	5
Gramma	loreto	royal gramma	5
Chiloscyllium	plagiosum	shark, white-spotted bamboo	5
Lutjanus	kasmira	snapper, blue-lined	5
Zebrasoma	xanthurum	tang, purple	5
Zebrasoma	flavescens	tang, yellow	5
Rhinecanthus	assassi	triggerfish, Arabian Picasso	5

continued

Table 4: Fish Cross-Reference by Michael Suitability Index[1] *(continued)*

Genus	Species	Common Name(s)	Suitability Index
Odonus	*niger*	triggerfish, black	5
Xanthichthys	*auromarginatus*	triggerfish, bluechin	5
Pseudobalistes	*fuscus*	triggerfish, bluelined	5
Balistoides	*conspicillum*	triggerfish, clown	5
Xanthichthys	*mento*	triggerfish, crosshatch	5
Rhinecanthus	*aculeatus*	triggerfish, Picasso	5
Melichthys	*vidua*	triggerfish, pink-tailed	5
Xanthichthys	*ringens*	triggerfish, Sargassum	5
Balistapus	*undulatus*	triggerfish, undulated	5
Paracheilinus	*octotaenia*	wrasse, eightline	5
Pseudocheilinus	*tetrataenia*	wrasse, fouline neon	5
Gomphosus	*varius*	wrasse, Hawaiian bird	5
Thalassoma	*lunare*	wrasse, lyretail	5
Pseudocheilinus	*hexataenia*	wrasse, sixline neon	5
Centropyge	*argi*	angelfish, cherub dwarf	4
Centropyge	*bispinosus*	angelfish, coral beauty	4
Centropyge	*loriculus*	angelfish, flame	4
Pomacanthus	*paru*	angelfish, French	4
Pomacanthus	*arcuatus*	angelfish, gray	4
Pomacanthus	*semicirculatus*	angelfish, Koran	4
Centropyge	*potteri*	angelfish, Potter's	4
Holacanthus	*ciliaris*	angelfish, queen	4
Gramma	*melacara*	basslet, blackcap	4
Liopropoma	*rubre*	basslet, swissguard	4
Ecsenius	*bicolor*	blenny, bicolor	4
Ecsenius	*gravieri*	blenny, Red Sea mimic	4
Chaetodon	*miliaris*	butterflyfish, lemon	4
Chaetodon	*lunula*	butterflyfish, raccoon	4
Chaetodon	*auriga*	butterflyfish, threadfin	4
Forcipiger	*flavissimus*	butterflyfish, yellow longnose	4

Genus	Species	Common Name(s)	Suitability Index
Chromis	viridis	chromis, green	4
Pervagor	spilosoma	filefish, Hawaiian	4
Paraluteres	prionurus	filefish, saddled	4
Siganus	vulpinus	foxface	4
Antennarius	maculatus	frogfish, clown	4
Amblygobius	phalaena	goby, banded	4
Gobiodon	histrio	goby, blue-spotted coral	4
Gobiodon	citrinus	goby, citron coral	4
Amblygobius	hectori	goby, Hector's	4
Gobiosoma	oceanops	goby, neon	4
Amblyeleotris	guttata	goby, orange-spotted prawn	4
Amblygobius	rainfordi	goby, Rainford's	4
Amblyeleotris	randalli	goby, Randall's prawn	4
Gobiosoma	evelynae	goby, sharknose	4
Stonogobiops	nematodes	goby, threadfin prawn	4
Amblyeleotris	wheeleri	goby, Wheeler's prawn	4
Gobiodon	okinawae	goby, yellow coral	4
Cryptocentrus	cinctus	goby, yellow prawn	4
Neocirrhites	armatus	hawkfish, flame	4
Opisthognathus	aurifrons	jawfish, yellow-headed	4
Dendrochirus	zebra	lionfish, dwarf	4
Dendrochirus	brachypterus	lionfish, fuzzy dwarf	4
Enchelycore	pardalis	moray eel, Hawaiian dragon	4
Diodon	holocanthus	puffer, porcupine	4
Taenianotus	triacanthus	scorpionfish, leaf	4
Acanthurus	sohal	tang, Arabian	4
Acanthurus	caeruleus	tang, Atlantic blue	4
Zebrasoma	desjardini	tang, Desjardin's sailfin	4
Ctenochaetus	hawaiiensis	tang, Hawaiian bristletooth	4
Paracanthurus	hepatus	tang, regal	4

continued

Table 4: Fish Cross-Reference by Michael Suitability Index[1] (continued)

Genus	Species	Common Name(s)	Suitability Index
Zebrasoma	veliferum	tang, sailfin	4
Thalassoma	bifasciatum	wrasse, bluehead	4
Coris	gaimard	wrasse, clown	4
Novaculichthys	taeniorus	wrasse, dragon	4
Halichoeres	chrysus	wrasse, golden	4
Coerodon	fasciatus	wrasse, harlequin tuskfish	4
Cirrhilabrus	jordani	wrasse, Jordan's fairy	4
Thalassoma	duperryi	wrasse, orange saddle	4
Cirrhilabrus	rubriventralis	wrasse, social fairy	4
Thalassoma	lutescens	wrasse, yellow	4
Pomacanthus	asfur	angelfish, Arabian	3
Centropyge	bicolor	angelfish, bicolor dwarf	3
Pomacanthus	annularis	angelfish, blue ring	3
Pomacanthus	imperator	angelfish, emperor	3
Centropyge	heraldi	angelfish, false lemonpeel	3
Centropyge	flavissima	angelfish, lemonpeel	3
Chaetodontoplus	mesoleucus	angelfish, Singapore	3
Pseudanthias	bicolor	anthias, bicolored	3
Pseudanthias	pleurotaenia	anthias, purple square	3
Serranocirrhitus	latus	anthias, sunburst	3
Meiacanthus	atrodorsalis	blenny, yellowtail fanged	3
Forcipiger	longirostris	butterflyfish, big longnose	3
Chaetodon	semilarvatus	butterflyfish, golden	3
Chaetodon	ephippium	butterflyfish, saddled	3
Ptereleotris	heteroptera	goby, blue gudgeon	3
Dendrochirus	biocellatus	lionfish, Fu Manchu	3
Gymnomuraena	zebra	moray eel, zebra	3
Hippocampus	erectus	seahorse, giant	3
Acanthurus	achilles	tang, Achilles	3
Naso	lituratus	tang, orange-spined unicorn	3

Genus	Species	Common Name(s)	Suitability Index
Acanthurus	leucosternon	tang, powder blue	3
Acanthurus	japonicus	tang, powder brown	3
Canthigaster	valentini	toby, saddled	3
Canthigaster	jactator	toby, whitespotted	3
Chilomycterus	antillarum	boxfish, spiny	2
Chelmon	rostratus	butterflyfish, copperband	2
Valenciennea	puellaris	goby, pretty prawn	2
Signigobius	biocellatus	goby, signal	2
Pterosynchiropus	splendidus	mandarin, common	2
Synchiropus	picturatus	mandarin, psychedelic	2

Table 5: Fish Incompatibilities

Genus	Species	Common Name(s)	Incompatible With
Acanthurus	achilles	tang, Achilles	conspecifics
Acanthurus	caeruleus	tang, Atlantic blue	conspecifics
Acanthurus	leucosternon	tang, powder blue	conspecifics
Amphiprion	clarkii	clownfish, Clark's	different clownfish species
Amphiprion	frenatus	clownfish, tomato	different clownfish species
Amphiprion	ocellaris	clownfish, common	different clownfish species
Amphiprion	percula	clownfish, true percula	different clownfish species
Amphiprion	melanopus	clownfish, cinnamon	different clownfish species
Siganus	vulpinus	foxface	conspecifics unless mated
Naso	lituratus	tang, orange-spined unicorn	conspecifics
Paracanthurus	hepatus	tang, regal	aggressive tangs
Zebrasoma	flavescens	tang, yellow	aggressive fishes
Zebrasoma	veliferum	tang, sailfin	conspecifics, other tangs
Acanthurus	japonicus	tang, powder brown	other tangs
Acanthurus	sohal	tang, Arabian	unaggressive fishes
Ctenochaetus	hawaiiensis	tang, Hawaiian bristletooth	aggressive tangs

continued

Table 5: Fish Incompatibilities *(continued)*

Genus	Species	Common Name(s)	Incompatible With
Zebrasoma	*desjardini*	tang, Desjardin's sailfin	conspecifics
Zebrasoma	*xanthurum*	tang, purple	unaggressive fishes
Coerodon	*fasciatus*	wrasse, harlequin tuskfish	small fish, crustaceans, snails
Novaculichthys	*taeniorus*	wrasse, dragon	small fish, crustaceans, snails
Cirrhilabrus	*jordani*	wrasse, Jordan's fairy	small crustaceans
Cirrhilabrus	*rubriventralis*	wrasse, social fairy	small crustaceans
Paracheilinus	*octotaenia*	wrasse, eightline	predators
Pseudocheilinus	*hexataenia*	wrasse, sixline neon	predators
Pseudocheilinus	*tetrataenia*	wrasse, fourline neon	predators
Coris	*gaimard*	wrasse, clown	small fish, crustaceans, snails
Gomphosus	*varius*	wrasse, Hawaiian bird	small fish, crustaceans, snails
Halichoeres	*chrysus*	wrasse, golden	small crustaceans
Thalassoma	*bifasciatum*	wrasse, bluehead	small fish, crustaceans, snails
Thalassoma	*duperryi*	wrasse, orange saddle	small fish, crustaceans, snails
Thalassoma	*lunare*	wrasse, lyretail	small fish, crustaceans, snails
Thalassoma	*lutescens*	wrasse, yellow	small fish, crustaceans, snails
Pseudanthias	*bicolor*	anthias, bicolored	aggressive fishes, other anthias
Pseudanthias	*pleurotaenia*	anthias, purple square	aggressive fishes, other anthias
Serranocirrhitus	*latus*	anthias, sunburst	aggressive fishes, conspecifics unless mated
Pseudochromis	*aldebarensis*	dottyback, Arabian	conspecifics unless mated, predators
Pseudochromis	*diadema*	dottyback, diadem	conspecifics unless mated, predators
Pseudochromis	*flavivertex*	dottyback, sunrise	conspecifics unless mated, predators
Pseudochromis	*fridmani*	dottyback, orchid	predators
Pseudochromis	*paccagnellae*	dottyback, royal	conspecifics unless mated, predators

Genus	Species	Common Name(s)	Incompatible With
Pseudochromis	porphyreus	dottyback, purple	conspecifics unless mated, predators
Pseudochromis	springeri	dottyback, Springer's	conspecifics unless mated, predators
Gramma	loreto	royal gramma	predators, dottybacks
Gramma	melacara	basslet, blackcap	predators, dottybacks
Assessor	flavissimus	mini-grouper, golden	predators, dottybacks, possibly conspecifics
Assessor	macneilii	mini-grouper, MacNiel's	predators, dottybacks, possibly conspecifics
Calloplesiops	altivelis	comet grouper	conspecifics, aggressive fishes
Cirrhitichthys	oxycephalus	hawkfish, pixy	small fish, crustaceans
Neocirrhites	armatus	hawkfish, flame	small fish, crustaceans
Oxycirrhites	typus	hawkfish, longnosed	small fish, crustaceans
Paracirrhites	arcatus	hawkfish, arceye	small fish, crustaceans
Amblyeleotris	guttata	goby, orange-spotted prawn	predators, aggressive species
Amblyeleotris	randalli	goby, Randall's prawn	predators, aggressive species
Amblyeleotris	wheeleri	goby, Wheeler's prawn	predators, aggressive species
Amblygobius	hectori	goby, Hector's	predators, aggressive species
Amblygobius	phalaena	goby, banded	predators, aggressive species
Amblygobius	rainfordi	goby, Rainford's	predators, aggressive species
Cryptocentrus	cinctus	goby, yellow prawn	predators, aggressive species
Gobiodon	citrinus	goby, citron coral	predators, aggressive species
Gobiodon	histrio	goby, blue-spotted coral	predators, aggressive species
Gobiodon	okinawae	goby, yellow coral	predators, aggressive species
Gobiosoma	evelynae	goby, sharknose	predators, aggressive species
Gobiosoma	oceanops	goby, neon	predators, aggressive species
Signigobius	biocellatus	goby, signal	predators, aggressive species
Stonogobiops	nematodes	goby, threadfin prawn	predators, aggressive species
Valenciennea	puellaris	goby, pretty prawn	predators, aggressive species

continued

Table 5: Fish Incompatibilities *(continued)*

Genus	Species	Common Name(s)	Incompatible With
Nemateleotris	decora	goby, decorated firefish	conspecifics, aggressive species
Nemateleotris	helfrichi	goby, Helfrich's firefish	conspecifics, aggressive species
Nemateleotris	magnifica	goby, firefish	conspecifics, aggressive species
Ptereleotris	microlepis	goby, blue gudgeon	aggressive species
Pholidichthys	leucotaenia	blenny, convict	aggressive species
Synchiropus	picturatus	mandarin, psychedelic	conspecific males, aggressive fishes
Pterosynchiropus	splendidus	mandarin, common	conspecific males, aggressive fishes
Opisthognathus	aurifrons	jawfish, yellow-headed	predators, aggressive species
Pterois	volitans	lionfish, common	small fish, crustaceans
Dendrochirus	zebra	lionfish, dwarf	small fish, crustaceans, conspecifics
Dendrochirus	brachypterus	lionfish, fuzzy dwarf	small fish, crustaceans, conspecifics
Dendrochirus	biocellatus	lionfish, Fu Manchu	small fish, crustaceans, conspecifics
Pterois	radiata	lionfish, clearfin	small fish, crustaceans
Chiloscyllium	plagiosum	shark, white-spotted bamboo	any potential prey
Enchelycore	pardalis	moray eel, Hawaiian dragon	any potential prey
Echidna	nebulosa	moray eel, snowflake	any potential prey
Gymnomuraena	zebra	moray eel, zebra	any potential prey
Gymnothorax	meleagris	moray eel, comet	any potential prey
Antennarius	maculatus	frogfish, clown	any potential prey
Hippocampus	erectus	seahorse, giant	other fishes, predatory invertebrates
Taenianotus	triacanthus	scorpionfish, leaf	any potential prey
Pterois	antennata	lionfish, spotfin	small fish, crustaceans

Genus	Species	Common Name(s)	Incompatible With
Serranus	tigrinus	bass, harlequin	small fish, crustaceans, conspecifics
Serranus	tabacarius	bass, tobacco	small fish, crustaceans, conspecifics
Cephalopholis	miniata	grouper, coral	any potential prey, conspecifics
Liopropoma	rubre	basslet, swissguard	conspecifics, aggressive fishes
Amblycirrhitus	pinos	hawkfish, red spotted	conspecifics, aggressive fishes
Apogon	cyanosoma	cardinalfish, orange-striped	aggressive species, predators
Apogon	maculatus	cardinalfish, flame	conspecifics, aggressive fishes
Sphaeramia	nematoptera	cardinalfish, pajama	aggressive species, predators
Pterapogon	kauderni	cardinalfish, Banggai	aggressive species, predators
Lutjanus	kasmira	snapper, blue-lined	conspecifics, prey items
Chaetodon	auriga	butterflyfish, threadfin	conspecifics, sessile invertebrates
Chaetodon	ephippium	butterflyfish, saddled	conspecifics, sessile invertebrates
Chaetodon	kleinii	butterflyfish, Klein's	conspecifics, sessile invertebrates
Chaetodon	lunula	butterflyfish, raccoon	sessile invertebrates
Chaetodon	miliaris	butterflyfish, lemon	conspecifics, sessile invertebrates
Chaetodon	semilarvatus	butterflyfish, golden	sessile invertebrates
Chelmon	rostratus	butterflyfish, copperband	conspecifics, sessile invertebrates
Forcipiger	flavissimus	butterflyfish, yellow longnose	conspecifics, sessile invertebrates, crustaceans
Forcipiger	longifostris	butterflyfish, big longnose	conspecifics, sessile invertebrates, crustaceans
Heniochus	diphreutes	bannerfish, schooling	sessile invertebrates

continued

Table 5: Fish Incompatibilities *(continued)*

Genus	Species	Common Name(s)	Incompatible With
Heniochus	*acuminatus*	bannerfish, longfin	sessile invertebrates
Centropyge	*argi*	angelfish, cherub dwarf	conspecifics unless mated, other dwarf angels
Centropyge	*bicolor*	angelfish, bicolor dwarf	conspecifics unless mated, other dwarf angels
Centropyge	*bispinosus*	angelfish, coral beauty	conspecifics unless mated, other dwarf angels
Centropyge	*flavissima*	angelfish, lemonpeel	conspecifics unless mated, other dwarf angels
Centropyge	*heraldi*	angelfish, false lemonpeel	conspecifics unless mated, other dwarf angels
Centropyge	*loriculus*	angelfish, flame	conspecifics unless mated, other dwarf angels
Centropyge	*potteri*	angelfish, Potter's	conspecifics unless mated, other dwarf angels
Chaetodontoplus	*mesoleucus*	angelfish, Singapore	conspecifics unless mated, other dwarf angels
Holacanthus	*ciliaris*	angelfish, queen	conspecifics, similar looking species
Pomacanthus	*annularis*	angelfish, blue ring	conspecifics, similar looking fishes
Pomacanthus	*arcuatus*	angelfish, gray	conspecifics, similar looking fishes
Pomacanthus	*asfur*	angelfish, Arabian	conspecifics, similar looking fishes
Pomacanthus	*imperator*	angelfish, emperor	conspecifics, similar looking fishes
Pomacanthus	*maculosus*	angelfish, maculosus	conspecifics, similar looking fishes
Pomacanthus	*paru*	angelfish, French	conspecifics, similar looking fishes
Pomacanthus	*semicirculatus*	angelfish, Koran	conspecifics, similar looking fishes
Chromis	*cyanea*	chromis, blue	predators, aggressive species

Genus	Species	Common Name(s)	Incompatible With
Chromis	viridis	chromis, green	predators, aggressive species
Chromis	vanderbilti	chromis, Vanderbilt's	predators, aggressive species
Chrysiptera	cyanea	damselfish, blue	predators, conspecifics unless mated
Chrysiptera	parasema	damselfish, yellowtail	predators, conspecifics unless mated
Dascyllus	aruanus	humbug, striped	predators, conspecifics unless mated
Dascyllus	melanurus	humbug, black-tailed	predators, conspecifics unless mated
Dascyllus	trimaculatus	humbug, threespot	predators, conspecifics unless mated
Pomacentrus	alleni	damselfish, Allen's	predators, conspecifics unless mated
Premnas	biaculeatus	clownfish, maroon	conspecifics unless mated, other clownfish
Ecsenius	bicolor	blenny, bicolor	conspecifics, predators
Ecsenius	gravierl	blenny, Red Sea mimic	conspecifics, predators
Meiacanthus	atrodorsalis	blenny, yellowtail fanged	conspecifics, predators
Balistapus	undulatus	triggerfish, undulated	most other fishes and invertebrates
Odonus	niger	triggerfish, black	conspecifics, unaggressive fishes, invertebrates
Pseudobalistes	fuscus	triggerfish, bluelined	conspecifics, unaggressive fishes, invertebrates
Balistoides	conspicillum	triggerfish, clown	conspecifics, unaggressive fishes, invertebrates
Melichthys	vidua	triggerfish, pink-tailed	conspecifics, unaggressive fishes, invertebrates
Rhinecanthus	aculeatus	triggerfish, Picasso	conspecifics, unaggressive fishes, invertebrates

continued

Table 5: Fish Incompatibilities *(continued)*

Genus	Species	Common Name(s)	Incompatible With
Rhinecanthus	*assassi*	triggerfish, Arabian Picasso	conspecifics, unaggressive fishes, invertebrates
Xanthichthys	*auromarginatus*	triggerfish, bluechin	conspecifics, unaggressive fishes, invertebrates
Xanthichthys	*mento*	triggerfish, crosshatch	conspecifics, unaggressive fishes, invertebrates
Xanthichthys	*ringens*	triggerfish, Sargassum	conspecifics, unaggressive fishes, invertebrates
Paraluteres	*prionurus*	filefish, saddled	invertebrates, conspecifics
Pervagor	*spilosoma*	filefish, Hawaiian	invertebrates, conspecifics
Canthigaster	*jactator*	toby, whitespotted	invertebrates, conspecifics
Canthigaster	*valentini*	toby, saddled	invertebrates, conspecifics
Diodon	*holocanthus*	puffer, porcupine	small fish, crustaceans, snails
Chilomycterus	*antillarum*	boxfish, spiny	small fish, crustaceans, snails

An old saying in the aquarium business holds that fish do not read the rule books. These guidelines are intended to provide a margin of error when combining species. *Conspecific* means "fish of the same species." Fish may sometimes mistake a similar-appearing species for one of their own, resulting in aggression.

CATALOG OF INVERTEBRATES, SEAWEEDS, AND MARINE PLANTS

O ver 150 types of invertebrates are represented in the designs presented in chapters 9 and 10. Were we to consider individual species, the total would be much higher than this. Unfortunately, accurate identification of many of the invertebrates imported for the aquarium trade sometimes requires expert knowledge. Even experts may disagree as to the appropriate species name for a given specimen. Shimek (2004), Borneman (2001), and other invertebrate specialists have pointed out the futility of trying to identify corals, in particular, when information about the locality and habitat type from which they came is unavailable. If you are fortunate enough to be able to collect your own invertebrates, you may be able to identify at least most of them to the species level. Fortunately, recognizing the genus to which an individual should be assigned usually suffices for understanding its captive care.

Classification of Invertebrates

Far more diverse than vertebrates, invertebrates comprise about 95 percent of all animal species. With the exception of insects, most invertebrates live in saltwater, with coral reefs possessing the greatest diversity of species. Nevertheless, comparatively few find their way into your local aquarium shop. Aquarists direct their interest most frequently to species with bright or interesting color patterns, and those ranging in size from about an inch to around ten inches. Adaptability to captivity, another important criterion for aquarium purposes, can have little to do with collectors' preferences. Species that are impossible to keep, or nearly so, regularly appear in shipments.

Sorting out the bewildering variety of saltwater invertebrate types requires an understanding of basic invertebrate classification. The following taxonomic outline should help you make sense not only of the various specimens you see, but also of the relationships among them. Invertebrate taxonomy is every bit as contentious as fish taxonomy—indeed, more so. Thus, others will disagree with the fine points of my arrangement. The broad outline, however, should meet with the approval of most. I include several minor groups in addition to the six major aquarium phyla in order to delineate relationships. As with the fish classification in the previous chapter, the arrangement begins with phyla considered to be more primitive and progresses to those considered more advanced. This does not mean that the former are less successful, only that their body plans show relatively little modification from fossil forms. Advanced families, on the other hand, exhibit the greatest degree of alteration from the body designs of their ancestors.

Phylum Porifera (Sponges)

Sponges are animals with no definite tissues. Specialized cell types carry out body functions. Sponges feed by extracting food from massive amounts of water pumped through their porous bodies.

Class Demospongiae (sponges with proteinaceous skeletons; includes the majority of species deliberately collected for the aquarium)

Class Calcarea (sponges with calcified skeletal elements)

Class Hexactinellida (sponges with skeletal elements of silica)

Class Sclerospongia (coralline sponges)

Note: The three minor sponge groups may be introduced to the aquarium via live rock but are seldom collected.

Phylum Cnidaria (Coelenterata)

Coelenterate animals possess two body layers. They are radially symmetrical. Specialized stinging cells called nematocysts aid in defense and prey capture. They may be either free swimming (medusa form) or attached (polyp form), with some types alternating between these two body designs at different points in the life cycle.

Class Hydrozoa (hydroids usually alternate between medusa and polyp forms, often small)

Order Milleporina (fire corals)

Order Stylasterina (lace corals)

Class Schyphozoa (jellyfish, usually medusa form dominates; few aquarium species)

Class Anthozoa (solitary or colonial polyps, medusa stage rare or absent)

Subclass Octocorallia (eight-tentacled corals)

Order Helioporacea (blue corals)

Order Alcyonacea (soft corals)

Suborder Stolonifera (*Xenia* and relatives)

Suborder Alcyoniina (soft corals with flabby skeletons composed of loose elements)

Suborder Scleraxonia (gorgonians)

Suborder Holaxonia (gorgonians)

Note: The two suborders of gorgonians are separated on the basis of details of the skeletal structure. For aquarium purposes, the skeleton is more rigid than that of alcyonians and may be upright, netlike, or encrusting.

    Order Pennatulacea (sea pens, seldom good aquarium subjects, though imported)

  Subclass Hexacorallia (six-tentacled corals)

    Order Actiniaria (sea anemones, solitary polyps lacking a skeleton)

    Order Zoanthidia (sea mats, colonial polyps, often interconnected, lacking a skeleton)

    Order Corallimorpharia (false or mushroom corals, solitary or colonial disc-shaped polyps, not interconnected, lacking a skeleton)

    Order Scleractinia (stony corals, solitary or colonial polyps with a calcareous skeleton)

  Subclass Ceriantipatharia (tube anemones and black corals)

    Order Antipatharia (black corals, colonial)

    Order Ceriantharia (tube anemones, solitary)

Phylum Platyhelminthes (Flatworms)

Though endowed with only two body layers, flatworms are the most primitive animals exhibiting bilateral symmetry, that is, definite left and right sides. Many are parasites. Flatworms are seldom deliberately collected for the aquarium.

Class Cestoda (parasitic tapeworms)

Class Trematoda (parasitic flukes)

Class Turbellaria (free-living flatworms)

    Order Polycladia (large, colorful species typically seen in aquarium trade)

Phylum Nemertina (Ribbon Worms)

Closely allied to the flatworms, this group of predators is poorly studied.

Phylum Phoronida (Entoprocts, Phoronid Worms)

Similar to bryzoans but not thought to be closely related, this minor group is sometimes seen on live rock specimens. It differs from bryzoans in details of internal anatomy and feeding structures. In phoronids, the anus opens inside the circle of feeding tentacles.

Phylum Brachiopoda (Lamp Shells, Brachiopods)

Enormously abundant and diverse as fossils, modern brachiopods include relatively few species, about 350. They resemble bivalve mollusks but possess a specialized feeding structure, the lophophore, in common with the entoprocts. In mollusks, the two shells cover the left and right halves of the animal, while in the brachiopods the shells cover the top and bottom halves. Brachiopods either burrow or sit on the bottom. They are seldom seen in aquariums.

Phylum Ectoprocta (Bryozoa)

The bryozoans, though important components of live rock fauna, are seldom collected deliberately for the aquarium. Individual members of the colony are called zooids. In contrast with entoprocts, bryozoans have the anus opening outside the circle of feeding tentacles.

Class Stenolaemata (skeleton calcified with rounded opening for zooids)

Class Gymnolaemata (skeleton uncalcified, opening for zooids have "doors")

Phylum Mollusca (Mollusks)

With over 100,000 species, this is among the most successful of invertebrate groups. Relatively few are collected for the aquarium trade, however.

Class Polyplacophora (chitons, shell composed of eight calcified plates, feed by rasping algae from solid substrates)

Class Bivalvia (bivalves, mollusks with paired shells, all suspension feeders)

> Order Anisomyaria (scallops and oysters)

> Order Heterodonta (clams, including tridacnids)

Class Gastropoda (snails, single shell in spiral configuration or shell absent; most diverse mollusk group, includes herbivores, predators, and scavengers)

> Subclass Prosobranchia (primitive gastropods, spiral shells, body exhibits torsion resulting in proximity of anus and gills)

> Order Diotocardia (abalones, turban shells, limpets)

> Order Mesogastropoda (conchs, coweries, and others)

> Order Neogastropoda (whelks, tulip snails, cone snails)

> Subclass Opisthobranchia (shell reduced or absent, body exhibits detorsion, or secondary untwisting)

> Order Bullomorpha (bubble shells)

> Order Pyramidellomorpha (pyramid shells)

> Order Aplysiomorpha (sea hares)

> Order Nudibranchia (nudibranchs, sea slugs)

Class Cephalopoda (highly evolved mollusks with large, well-developed eyes, all predators)

> Subclass Nautiloidea (nautiloids, cephalopods with a shell)

> Subclass Coeloidea (cephalopods with reduced or no shell)

> Order Sepioida (squid and cuttlefish)

> Order Octopoda (octopus)

Phylum Annelida (Segmented Worms)

With some 12,000 species, the segmented worms offer few of interest to aquarists. Many of these are difficult to maintain in captivity owing to their food requirements. Classification of the saltwater polychaetes is limited to family designations, as relationships are unclear.

Class Polychaeta (many-segmented annelids, appendages and/or bristles on each segment)

Family Amphinomidae (mobile polychaetes, including bristleworms, often seen in aquariums)

Family Cirratulidae (hair worms, sedentary polychaetes with a crown of spaghetti-like feeding tentacles, often red in color)

Family Sabellidae (feather duster worms, sedentary polychaetes that build a soft tube from particulate matter combined with a secretion)

Family Sabellariidae (feather duster types that incorporate sand into their fragile tubes, often colonial)

Family Serpulidae (hard-tube dusters and Christmas tree worms, tube of calcium carbonate, attached, often with a "door"; frequently brightly colored)

Family Spirorbidae (produces a small, calcified spiral shell attached to a solid substrate)

Family Terebellidae (spaghetti worms, sedentary polychaetes, similar to cirratulids, usually larger and with fewer tentacles)

Class Oligochaeta (freshwater annelids, earthworms)

Class Hirudinea (leeches)

Minor Worm Phyla

Three minor worm phyla are thought to be closely related to annelids. Poorly studied, they are not often seen in aquariums except as hitchhikers on live rock. Phyla Echiurida (spoon worms) and Sipunculida (peanut worms) are the ones most often encountered.

Phylum Arthropoda (Arthropods)

The largest and most diverse animal group, the arthropod phylum has three major subdivisions. Possibly the most familiar subphylum is Uniramia, including millipedes, centipedes, and insects, all mostly terrestrial. The subphylum Chelicerata includes spiders, scorpions, mites, ticks, and the marine horseshoe crabs and sea spiders. The latter two groups are of little interest to aquarists, although horseshoe crabs are sometimes offered. The aquarium arthropods all belong to the subphylum Crustacea, the crustaceans. Of the eleven classes, only one includes commonly kept species, though members of the others turn up as food items.

Class Cephalocarida (shrimplike, rare, and of no interest to aquarists)

Class Branchiopoda (fairy shrimps, including *Artemia*, the brine shrimps)

Class Ramipedia (only one species known)

Class Tantulocarida (only four species known)

Class Mystacocarida (tiny, sand-dwelling species)

Class Branchiura (fish lice, often parasitic)

Class Copepoda (copepods, often appear in well-aged aquariums)

Class Cirripedia (barnacles, sometimes enter aquariums on other objects, suspension feeders)

Class Ostracoda (seed shrimps)

Class Malacostraca (more than 20,000 species of familiar crustaceans, such as shrimps and lobsters)

   Subclass Phyllocarida (small group of primitive species)

   Subclass Hoplocarida

     Order Stomatopoda (mantis shrimps)

   Subclass Eumalacostraca

    Superorder Percarida

    Order Mysidacea (mysid shrimps, often sold for aquarium food)

    Order Isopoda (isopods, some fish parasites)

    Order Amphipoda (amphipods, or gravel shrimps, similar to copepods)

    Superorder Eucarida

    Order Euphausiacea (krill, often sold for aquarium food)

    Order Decapoda (shrimps, lobsters, crabs)

      Suborder Dendrobrachiata or Natantia (shrimps and prawns)

      Suborder Pleocyemata or Reptantia (crabs, hermit crabs, and lobsters)

       Infraorder Stenopodidae (boxer shrimps, *Stenopus*)

       Infraorder Caridea (caridean shrimps, including the majority of aquarium species)

         Family Hippolytidae (*Lysmata*, *Saron*)

         Family Rhynchocinetidae (*Rhynchocinetes*)

         Family Palaemonidae (anemone shrimps, *Periclimenes*)

         Family Gnathophyllidae (harlequin shrimps, *Hymenoceros*)

       Infraorder Astacidea (lobsters, including the Maine variety)

 Infraorder Palinura (spiny lobsters)

       Infraorder Thalassinidea (mud shrimps and mud lobsters)

         Family Axiidae (reef lobsters, *Enoplometopus*)

       Infraorder Anomura (hermit crabs and others)

         Family Paguridae (*Pagurus* and relatives)

         Family Porcellanidae (porcelain crabs, anemone crabs)

       Infraorder Brachyura (true crabs)

         Family Dromiidae (sponge crabs)

         Family Calappidae (box crabs)

         Family Majidae (spider crabs, *Stenorhynchus*, *Podochela*, *Mithrax*)

Family Portunidae (swimming crabs, including edible blue crabs)

Family Xanthidae (stone crabs)

Family Grapsidae (spray crabs, *Percnon*, *Lybia*)

Note: There are more than forty additional crab families.

Phylum Echinodermata (Spiny Skins)

Radially symmetrical and unsegmented, the echinoderms have no brain, no eyes, and a unique water vascular system. Subphylum Crinozoa includes the delicate feather stars, or crinoids, that make very poor aquarium subjects. Subphylum Asterozoa includes sea stars and brittle stars, while subphylum Echinozoa includes sea urchins and sea cucumbers.

Class Asteroidea (sea stars)

Class Ophiuroidea (brittle and basket stars)

Order Phyrnophiurida (serpent stars, basket stars)

Family Asteroschematidae (serpent stars)

Family Gorgonocephalidae (basket stars)

Order Ophiurida (brittle stars)

Class Echinoidea (sea urchins)

Order Cidaroida

Family Cidaridae (pencil urchins, *Eucidaris*)

Order Diadematoida

Family Diadematidae (longspine urchins, *Diadema*)

Order Temnopleuroida

Family Lytechinidae (purple urchins, *Lytechinus*)

Order Echinoida

Family Echinometridae (rock urchins, *Echinometra*)

Class Holothuroidea (sea cucumbers)

Order Aspidochirotida (shield-shaped tentacles, *Actinopyga*)

Order Dendrochirotida (treelike tentacles, *Pseudocolochirus*, *Colochirus*)

Phylum Chordata (Chordates)

This phylum is perhaps of most interest because it includes humans and our closest relatives among the invertebrates. All chordates possess a cartilaginous rod, the notochord, at some point during their lives. In vertebrates, the notochord is a precursor to the vertebral column during embryonic development. Subphylum Urochordata, or Tunicata, includes the sea squirts, in which the notochord is apparent only in the larval stage. There are three classes of tunicates, of which only one is of aquarium interest.

Class Ascidacea (sea squirts; sessile, solitary, or colonial tunicates)

Class Thaliacea (mobile sea squirts, salps)

Class Appendicularia or Larvacea (free-swimming, tadpolelike tunicates)

Subphylum Cephalochordata includes the lancelets, small, fishlike creatures that live in sandy substrates, seldom seen in aquaria. The chordate phylum is unique in that it includes both invertebrate and vertebrate forms. Subphylum Euchordata, or Vertebrata, includes all vertebrate animals, including fish, amphibians, reptiles, birds, and mammals.

Cross-Reference Lists

Scientific names often change, especially with some of the more poorly studied invertebrate groups. For example, *Elysia crispata* was formerly known as *Tridachia crispata*. No single, easy way exists to keep up with all the changes. In the aquarium trade, older names are seldom quickly abandoned, though, so it is not essential always to have the most recently accepted name.

As is the case with fish, anyone can make up a common name. The ones I have listed are those most often used in the literature on aquariums. Always use the scientific name when possible.

Knowing the general locality from which a given type of invertebrate originates can help you choose specimens for a biotope aquarium. You can achieve an even narrower biotope target by seeking out individual species. Species typically have a more narrow range than the genus to which they belong. A major drawback to this approach stems from the great difficulty some species pose in regard to their identification. Corals, for example, may be impossible to name with accuracy unless you have much more information that is likely to be available for an aquarium specimen. Generally speaking, for invertebrates you will need to seek out specialized references devoted to a particular group in order to investigate the taxonomy in depth.

The invertebrate suitability index presented in Table 4 is my own, modeled after Scott Michael's index for fishes. As such, it reflects my experience and should not be considered an infalliable guide.

The information on compatibility is provided with the same caveats expressed earlier for the fish lists: precise predictions are difficult and the information here is merely a rough guide. The ability for different types of sessile invertebrates to sting each other, for example, has not been thoroughly studied. In any case, trying to include all possible combinations would produce a very large table indeed. Use common sense, and arrange all specimens so plenty of room separates neighbors.

Table 1: Alphabetic Listing of Invertebrates by Scientific Name

Genus	Species	Common Name(s)
Acropora	sp.	none
Actinodendron	sp.	tree anemone
Actinopyga	agassizi	Florida cucumber
Alcyonium	sp.	colt soft coral
Alpheus	armatus	curlicue anemone pistol shrimp
Amplexidiscus	fenestrafer	elephant ear polyp
Anthelia	sp.	waving hand
Asthenosoma	varium	fire urchin
Astraea	tecta	star shell
Astrophyton	muricatum	basket star
Bartholomea	annulata	curlicue anemone
Blastomussa	sp.	none
Brierium	abestinum	sea fingers
Bulla	sp.	bubble shell
Calliactis	sp.	hermit crab anemone
Cassiopea	sp.	upside-down jellyfish
Catalaphyllia	jardinei	elegance coral
Caulastrea	sp.	trumpet coral
Cerianthus	sp.	tube anemone
Cerithium	sp.	cerith shell
Cespitularia	sp.	blue "Xenia"
Choriaster	granulatus	doughboy star
Cladiella	sp.	cauliflower soft coral
Clibanarius	tricolor	blue leg hermit crab
Clibanarius	vittatus	striped hermit crab
Colochirus	robustus	yellow sea cucumber
Condylactis	gigantea	pink-tipped anemone
Cryptodendrum	adhaesivum	pizza anemone

continued

Table 1: Alphabetic Listing of Invertebrates by Scientific Name (*continued*)

Genus	Species	Common Name(s)
Culcita	*novaeguineae*	cushion star
Cynarina	*lacrymalis*	button coral
Cypraea	*moneta*	money cowerie
Dardanus	*pedunculatus*	anemone hermit crab
Dendronephthya	*sp.*	tree soft coral
Diadema	*antillarum*	longspine urchin
Discosoma	*sp.*	mushroom polyp
Discosoma	*neglecta*	Atlantic-Caribbean mushroom polyp
Dromia	*sp.*	sponge crab
Echinometra	*lacunter*	shortspine urchin
Elysia	*crispata*	lettuce slug
Elysia	*ornata*	lettuce slug
Enoplometopus	*sp.*	red lobster
Entacmaea	*quadricolor*	bulb anemone
Erythropodium	*sp.*	encrusting gorgonian
Eucidaris	*tribuloides*	slate pencil urchin
Eunicea	*sp.*	knobby sea rod
Euphyllia	*ancora*	anchor coral
Euphyllia	*divisa*	frogspawn coral
Euphyllia	*glabrescens*	torch coral
Fasciolaria	*tulipa*	tulip snail
Favia	*sp.*	moon coral
Fromia	*sp.*	marble star
Fungia	*sp.*	plate coral
Galaxea	*sp.*	star coral
Goniopora	*sp.*	sunflower coral
Gorgonia	*ventalina*	sea fan
Haliotis	*sp.*	abalone
Haminoea	*sp.*	bubble shell
Heliofungia	*sp.*	giant plate coral

Genus	Species	Common Name(s)
Heliopora	coerulea	blue coral
Herpolitha	limax	tongue coral
Heteractis	aurora	beaded anemone
Heteractis	crispa	sebae anemone
Heteractis	magnifica	"ritteri" anemone
Heteractis	malu	white sand anemone
Heterocentrotus	mammillatus	slate pencil urchin
Hippolysmata	wurdemanni	peppermint shrimp
Hippopus	hippopus	hoof giant clam
Hydnophora	sp.	horn coral
Hymenocera	picta	harlequin shrimp
Lambis	sp.	spider conch
Lebrunia	danae	antler anemone
Leptogorgia	miniata	Red Sea whip
Lima	scabra	flame scallop
Linckia	laevigata	blue star
Litophyton	sp.	tree soft coral
Lobophyllia	sp.	open brain coral
Lobophytum	sp.	leather soft coral
Lybia	dubia	boxing crab
Lysmata	amboiensis	scarlet cleaner shrimp
Lysmata	debelius	fire shrimp
Lytechinus	variatus	carrier urchin
Macrodactyla	doreensis	long tentacle anemone
Millepora	sp.	fire coral
Mithrax	sculptus	emerald crab
Montipora	sp.	none
Muricea	sp.	spiny sea rod
Nassarius	sp.	sand shell
Nautilus	sp.	chambered nautilus

continued

Table 1: Alphabetic Listing of Invertebrates by Scientific Name *(continued)*

Genus	Species	Common Name(s)
Nemenzophyllia	*turbida*	ridge coral
Neopetrolisthes	sp.	anemone crab
Nephthea	sp.	tree soft coral
Nerita	sp.	nerite shell
Octopus	*joubani*	dwarf octopus
Oreaster	*reticulata*	Bahama star
Ophiactis	sp.	spiny brittle star
Ophiocoma	sp.	black-spined brittle star
Ophioderma	*brevispinum*	serpent star
Paguristes	*cadenati*	scarlet hermit crab
Palythoa	*caribaeorum*	brown sea mat
Palythoa	*grandis*	giant sea mat
Parazoanthus	*swiftii*	yellow sponge sea mat
Percnon	*gibbesi*	Sally Lightfoot
Periclimenes	*pedersoni*	Pederson's cleaner shrimp
Periclimenes	*yucatanensis*	anemone shrimp
Petrochirus	*diogenes*	giant hermit crab
Petrolisthes	sp.	porcelain crab
Phymanthus	*crucifer*	flower anemone
Physogyra	*lichtensteini*	small bubble coral
Platygyra	sp.	closed brain coral
Plerogyra	*sinuosa*	large bubble coral
Pocillopora	sp.	none
Podocheila	*reisi*	decorator arrow crab
Porites	sp.	none
Protopalythoa	sp.	Pacific green sea mat
Protoreaster	sp.	chocolate chip star
Protula	*magnifica*	hard-tube duster
Pseudocolochrius	sp.	sea apple
Pseudocorynactis	sp.	dotted mushroom polyp

Genus	Species	Common Name(s)
Pseudopterogorgia	sp.	sea plume
Pylopagurus	operculatus	trap door hermit crab
Rhodactis	sp.	blue mushroom polyp
Rhodactis	sanctithomae	warty Atlantic-Caribbean mushroom polyp
Rhynchocinetes	sp.	camel shrimp
Ricordea	florida	Florida false coral
Sabella	sp.	dwarf feather duster
Sabellastarte	magnifica	giant feather duster
Saron	marmoratus	Saron shrimp
Sarcophyton	sp.	leather mushroom soft coral
Sepia	sp.	cuttlefish
Seriatopora	sp.	none
Sinularia	sp.	cabbage soft coral
Sinularia	sp.	finger leather coral
Spirobranchus	giganteus	Christmas tree worm
Stenopus	hispidus	coral shrimp
Stenopus	scutellatus	golden coral shrimp
Stenorhynchus	seticornis	arrow crab
Stichodactyla	gigantea	giant carpet anemone
Stichodactyla	haddoni	Haddon's carpet anemone
Stichodactyla	helianthus	sun anemone
Stichodactyla	mertensi	Mertens' carpet anemone
Strombus	gigas	queen conch
Studeriotes	longiramosa	Christmas tree soft coral
Stylaster	sp.	pink lace coral
Stylophora	sp.	none
Swiftia	exerta	orange finger gorgonian
Tectus	sp.	pyramid top shell
Thor	amboiensis	sexy shrimp

continued

Table 1: Alphabetic Listing of Invertebrates by Scientific Name (*continued*)

Genus	Species	Common Name(s)
Trachyphyllia	sp.	open brain coral
Tridacna	crocea	crocea giant clam
Tridacna	derasa	smooth giant clam
Tridacna	gigas	giant clam
Tridacna	maxima	maxima giant clam
Tridacna	squamosa	fluted giant clam
Trochus	sp.	top shell
Tubastrea	aurea	orange polyp coral
Tubipora	musica	organ pipe coral
Turbinaria	sp.	pagoda coral
Turbo	sp.	turbo snail
Xenia	sp.	pulse corals
Zoanthus	sp.	Atlantic-Caribbean green sea mat

Table 2: Alphabetic Cross-Reference by Common Name

Common Name(s)	Genus	Species
abalone	Haliotis	sp.
anchor coral	Euphyllia	ancora
anemone crab	Neopetrolisthes	sp.
anemone hermit crab	Dardanus	pedunculatus
anemone shrimp	Periclimenes	yucatanensis
antler anemone	Lebrunia	danae
arrow crab	Stenorhynchus	seticornis
Bahama star	Oreaster	reticulata
basket star	Astrophyton	muricatum
beaded anemone	Heteractis	aurora
black-spined brittle star	Ophiocoma	sp.
blue "Xenia"	Cespitularia	sp.

Common Name(s)	Genus	Species
blue coral	*Heliopora*	*coerulea*
blue leg hermit crab	*Clibanarius*	*tricolor*
blue mushroom polyp	*Rhodactis*	*sp.*
blue star	*Linckia*	*laevigata*
boxing crab	*Lybia*	*dubia*
brown sea mat	*Palythoa*	*caribaeorum*
bubble shell	*Bulla*	*sp.*
bubble shell	*Haminoea*	*sp.*
bulb anemone	*Entacmaea*	*quadricolor*
button coral	*Cynarina*	*lacrymalis*
cabbage soft coral	*Sinularia*	*sp.*
camel shrimp	*Rhynchocinetes*	*sp.*
Atlantic-Caribbean green sea mat	*Zoanthus*	*sp.*
Atlantic-Caribbean mushroom polyp	*Discosoma*	*neglecta*
carrier urchin	*Lytechinus*	*variatus*
cauliflower soft coral	*Cladiella*	*sp.*
cerith shell	*Cerithium*	*sp.*
chambered nautilus	*Nautilus*	*sp.*
chocolate chip star	*Protoreaster*	*sp.*
Christmas tree soft coral	*Studeriotes*	*longiramosa*
Christmas tree worm	*Spirobranchus*	*giganteus*
closed brain coral	*Platygyra*	*sp.*
colt soft coral	*Alcyonium*	*sp.*
coral shrimp	*Stenopus*	*hispidus*
crocea giant clam	*Tridacna*	*crocea*
curlicue anemone	*Bartholomea*	*annulata*
curlicue anemone pistol shrimp	*Alpheus*	*armatus*
cushion star	*Culcita*	*novaeguineae*
cuttlefish	*Sepia*	*sp.*
decorator arrow crab	*Podocheila*	*reisi*

continued

Common Name(s)	Genus	Species
dotted mushroom polyp	*Pseudocorynactis*	sp.
doughboy star	*Choriaster*	*granulatus*
dwarf feather duster	*Sabella*	sp.
dwarf octopus	*Octopus*	*joubani*
elegance coral	*Catalaphyllia*	*jardinei*
elephant ear polyp	*Amplexidiscus*	*fenestrafer*
emerald crab	*Mithrax*	*sculptus*
encrusting gorgonian	*Erythropodium*	sp.
finger leather coral	*Sinularia*	sp.
fire coral	*Millepora*	sp.
fire shrimp	*Lysmata*	*debelius*
fire urchin	*Asthenosoma*	*varium*
flame scallop	*Lima*	*scabra*
Florida cucumber	*Actinopyga*	*agassizi*
Florida false coral	*Ricordea*	*florida*
flower anemone	*Phymanthus*	*crucifer*
fluted giant clam	*Tridacna*	*squamosa*
frogspawn coral	*Euphyllia*	*divisa*
giant carpet anemone	*Stichodactyla*	*gigantea*
giant clam	*Tridacna*	*gigas*
giant feather duster	*Sabellastarte*	*magnifica*
giant hermit crab	*Petrochirus*	*diogenes*
giant plate coral	*Heliofungia*	sp.
giant sea mat	*Palythoa*	*grandis*
golden coral shrimp	*Stenopus*	*scutellatus*
green star polyps	*Pachyclavularia*	sp.
Haddon's carpet anemone	*Stichodactyla*	*haddoni*
hard-tube duster	*Protula*	*magnifica*
harlequin shrimp	*Hymenocera*	*picta*
hermit crab anemone	*Calliactis*	sp.

Common Name(s)	Genus	Species
hoof giant clam	Hippopus	hippopus
horn coral	Hydnophora	sp.
knobby sea rod	Eunicea	sp.
large bubble coral	Plerogyra	sinuosa
leather mushroom soft coral	Sarcophyton	sp.
leather soft coral	Lobophytum	sp.
lettuce slug	Elysia	crispata
lettuce slug	Elysia	ornata
long tentacle anemone	Macrodactyla	doreensis
longspine urchin	Diadema	antillarum
marble star	Fromia	sp.
maxima giant clam	Tridacna	maxima
Mertens' carpet anemone	Stichodactyla	mertensi
money cowerie	Cypraea	moneta
moon coral	Favia	sp
mushroom polyp	Discosoma	sp.
nerite shell	Nerita	sp.
none	Acropora	sp.
none	Blastomussa	sp.
none	Montipora	sp.
none	Pocillopora	sp.
none	Porites	sp.
none	Seriatopora	sp.
none	Stylophora	sp.
open brain coral	Lobophyllia	sp.
open brain coral	Trachyphyllia	sp.
orange finger gorgonian	Swiftia	exerta
orange polyp coral	Tubastrea	aurea
organ pipe coral	Tubipora	musica
Pacific green sea mat	Protopalythoa	sp.

continued

Table 2: Alphabetic Cross-Reference by Common Name (*continued*)

Common Name(s)	Genus	Species
pagoda coral	*Turbinaria*	sp.
Pederson's cleaner shrimp	*Periclimenes*	*pedersoni*
peppermint shrimp	*Hippolysmata*	*wurdemanni*
pink lace coral	*Stylaster*	sp.
pink-tipped anemone	*Condylactis*	*gigantea*
pizza anemone	*Cryptodendrum*	*adhaesivum*
plate coral	*Fungia*	sp.
porcelain crab	*Petrolisthes*	sp.
pulse corals	*Xenia*	sp.
pyramid top shell	*Tectus*	sp.
queen conch	*Strombus*	*gigas*
red lobster	*Enoplometopus*	sp.
Red Sea whip	*Leptogorgia*	*miniata*
ridge coral	*Nemenzophyllia*	*turbida*
"ritteri" anemone	*Heteractis*	*magnifica*
Sally Lightfoot	*Percnon*	*gibbesi*
sand shell	*Nassarius*	sp.
Saron shrimp	*Saron*	*marmoratus*
scarlet cleaner shrimp	*Lysmata*	*amboiensis*
scarlet hermit crab	*Paguristes*	*cadenati*
sea apple	*Pseudocolochrius*	sp.
sea fan	*Gorgonia*	*ventalina*
sea fingers	*Brierium*	*abestinum*
sea plume	*Pseudopterogorgia*	sp.
sebae anemone	*Heteractis*	*crispa*
serpent star	*Ophioderma*	*brevispinum*
sexy shrimp	*Thor*	*amboiensis*
shortspine urchin	*Echinometra*	*lacunter*
slate pencil urchin	*Eucidaris*	*tribuloides*
slate pencil urchin	*Heterocentrotus*	*mammillatus*

Common Name(s)	Genus	Species
small bubble coral	Physogyra	lichtensteini
smooth giant clam	Tridacna	derasa
spider conch	Lambis	sp.
spiny brittle star	Ophiactis	sp.
spiny sea rod	Muricea	sp.
sponge crab	Dromia	sp.
star coral	Galaxea	sp.
star shell	Astraea	tecta
striped hermit crab	Clibanarius	vittatus
sun anemone	Stichodactyla	helianthus
sunflower coral	Goniopora	sp.
tongue coral	Herpolitha	limax
top shell	Trochus	sp.
torch coral	Euphyllia	glabrescens
trap door hermit crab	Pylopagurus	operculatus
tree anemone	Actinodendron	sp.
tree soft coral	Dendronephthya	sp.
tree soft coral	Litophyton	sp.
tree soft coral	Nephthea	sp.
trumpet coral	Caulastrea	sp.
tube anemone	Cerianthus	sp.
tulip snail	Fasciolaria	tulipa
turbo snail	Turbo	sp.
upside-down jellyfish	Cassiopea	sp.
warty Atlantic-Caribbean mushroom polyp	Rhodactis	sanctithomae
waving hand	Anthelia	sp.
white sand anemone	Heteractis	malu
yellow sea cucumber	Colochirus	robustus
yellow sponge sea mat	Parazoanthus	swiftii

Table 3: Invertebrate Cross-Reference by Locality

Genus	Species	Common Name(s)	Range
Nassarius	sp.	sand shell	Atlantic-Caribbean
Actinopyga	*agassizi*	Florida cucumber	Atlantic-Caribbean
Alpheus	*armatus*	curlicue anemone pistol shrimp	Atlantic-Caribbean
Astraea	*tecta*	star shell	Atlantic-Caribbean
Astrophyton	*muricatum*	basket star	Atlantic-Caribbean
Bartholomea	*annulata*	curlicue anemone	Atlantic-Caribbean
Brierium	*abestinum*	sea fingers	Atlantic-Caribbean
Calliactis	sp.	hermit crab anemone	Atlantic-Caribbean
Cassiopea	sp.	upside-down jellyfish	Atlantic-Caribbean
Cerithium	sp.	cerith shell	Atlantic-Caribbean
Clibanarius	*tricolor*	blue leg hermit crab	Atlantic-Caribbean
Clibanarius	*vittatus*	striped hermit crab	Atlantic-Caribbean
Condylactis	*gigantea*	pink-tipped anemone	Atlantic-Caribbean
Culcita	*novaeguineae*	cushion star	Atlantic-Caribbean
Dardanus	*pedunculatus*	anemone hermit crab	Atlantic-Caribbean
Discosoma	*neglecta*	Atlantic-Caribbean mushroom polyp	Atlantic-Caribbean
Echinometra	*lacunter*	shortspine urchin	Atlantic-Caribbean
Elysia	*crispata*	lettuce slug	Atlantic-Caribbean
Elysia	*ornata*	lettuce slug	Atlantic-Caribbean
Erythropodium	sp.	encrusting gorgonian	Atlantic-Caribbean
Eucidaris	*tribuloides*	slate pencil urchin	Atlantic-Caribbean
Eunicea	sp.	knobby sea rod	Atlantic-Caribbean
Fasciolaria	*tulipa*	tulip snail	Atlantic-Caribbean
Gorgonia	*ventalina*	sea fan	Atlantic-Caribbean
Haminoea	sp.	bubble shell	Atlantic-Caribbean
Hippolysmata	*wurdemanni*	peppermint shrimp	Atlantic-Caribbean
Lebrunia	*danae*	antler anemone	Atlantic-Caribbean
Leptogorgia	*miniata*	Red Sea whip	Atlantic-Caribbean
Lima	*scabra*	flame scallop	Atlantic-Caribbean
Lytechinus	*variatus*	carrier urchin	Atlantic-Caribbean

Genus	Species	Common Name(s)	Range
Mithrax	sculptus	emerald crab	Atlantic-Caribbean
Muricea	sp.	spiny sea rod	Atlantic-Caribbean
Nerita	sp.	nerite shell	Atlantic-Caribbean
Octopus	joubani	dwarf octopus	Atlantic-Caribbean
Ophioderma	brevispinum	serpent star	Atlantic-Caribbean
Oreaster	reticulata	Bahama star	Atlantic-Caribbean
Paguristes	cadenati	scarlet hermit crab	Atlantic-Caribbean
Palythoa	caribaeorum	brown sea mat	Atlantic-Caribbean
Palythoa	grandis	giant sea mat	Atlantic-Caribbean
Parazoanthus	swiftii	yellow sponge sea mat	Atlantic-Caribbean
Percnon	gibbesi	Sally Lightfoot	Atlantic-Caribbean
Periclimenes	pedersoni	Pederson's cleaner shrimp	Atlantic-Caribbean
Periclimenes	yucatanensis	anemone shrimp	Atlantic-Caribbean
Petrochirus	diogenes	giant hermit crab	Atlantic-Caribbean
Phymanthus	crucifer	flower anemone	Atlantic-Caribbean
Pseudocorynactis	sp.	dotted mushroom polyp	Atlantic-Caribbean
Pseudopterogorgia	sp.	sea plume	Atlantic-Caribbean
Pylopagurus	operculatus	trap door hermit crab	Atlantic-Caribbean
Rhodactis	sanctithomae	warty Atlantic-Caribbean mushroom polyp	Atlantic-Caribbean
Ricordea	florida	Florida false coral	Atlantic-Caribbean
Sabellastarte	magnifica	giant feather duster	Atlantic-Caribbean
Stenopus	scutellatus	golden coral shrimp	Atlantic-Caribbean
Stenorhynchus	seticornis	arrow crab	Atlantic-Caribbean
Stichodactyla	helianthus	sun anemone	Atlantic-Caribbean
Strombus	gigas	queen conch	Atlantic-Caribbean
Swiftia	exerta	orange finger gorgonian	Atlantic-Caribbean
Zoanthus	sp.	Atlantic-Caribbean green sea mat	Atlantic-Caribbean
Podocheila	reisi	decorator arrow crab	Gulf of Mexico
Actinodendron	sp.	tree anemone	Indo-Pacific
Alcyonium	sp.	colt soft coral	Indo-Pacific

continued

Table 3: Invertebrate Cross-Reference by Locality *(continued)*

Genus	Species	Common Name(s)	Range
Amplexidiscus	*fenestrafer*	elephant ear polyp	Indo-Pacific
Anthelia	sp.	waving hand	Indo-Pacific
Asthenosoma	*varium*	fire urchin	Indo-Pacific
Blastomussa	sp.	none	Indo-Pacific
Catalaphyllia	*jardinei*	elegance coral	Indo-Pacific
Caulastrea	sp.	trumpet coral	Indo-Pacific
Cespitularia	sp.	blue "Xenia"	Indo-Pacific
Choriaster	*granulatus*	doughboy star	Indo-Pacific
Cladiella	sp.	cauliflower soft coral	Indo-Pacific
Colochirus	*robustus*	yellow sea cucumber	Indo-Pacific
Cryptodendrum	*adhaesivum*	pizza anemone	Indo-Pacific
Cynarina	*lacrymalis*	button coral	Indo-Pacific
Cypraea	*moneta*	money cowerie	Indo-Pacific
Dendronephthya	sp.	tree soft coral	Indo-Pacific
Enoplometopus	sp.	red lobster	Indo-Pacific
Entacmaea	*quadricolor*	bulb anemone	Indo-Pacific
Euphyllia	*ancora*	anchor coral	Indo-Pacific
Euphyllia	*divisa*	frogspawn coral	Indo-Pacific
Euphyllia	*glabrescens*	torch coral	Indo-Pacific
Fromia	sp.	marble star	Indo-Pacific
Galaxea	sp.	star coral	Indo-Pacific
Goniopora	sp.	sunflower coral	Indo-Pacific
Haliotis	sp.	abalone	Indo-Pacific
Heliofungia	sp.	giant plate coral	Indo-Pacific
Heliopora	*coerulea*	blue coral	Indo-Pacific
Herpolitha	*limax*	tongue coral	Indo-Pacific
Heteractis	*aurora*	beaded anemone	Indo-Pacific
Heteractis	*crispa*	sebae anemone	Indo-Pacific
Heteractis	*magnifica*	"ritteri" anemone	Indo-Pacific
Heteractis	*malu*	white sand anemone	Indo-Pacific

Genus	Species	Common Name(s)	Range
Heterocentrotus	*mammillatus*	slate pencil urchin	Indo-Pacific
Hippopus	*hippopus*	hoof giant clam	Indo-Pacific
Hydnophora	sp.	horn coral	Indo-Pacific
Hymenocera	*picta*	harlequin shrimp	Indo-Pacific
Lambis	sp.	spider conch	Indo-Pacific
Linckia	*laevigata*	blue star	Indo-Pacific
Litophyton	sp.	tree soft coral	Indo-Pacific
Lobophyllia	sp.	open brain coral	Indo-Pacific
Lobophytum	sp.	leather soft coral	Indo-Pacific
Lybia	*dubia*	boxing crab	Indo-Pacific
Lysmata	*amboiensis*	scarlet cleaner shrimp	Indo-Pacific
Lysmata	*debelius*	fire shrimp	Indo-Pacific
Macrodactyla	*doreensis*	long tentacle anemone	Indo-Pacific
Nautilus	sp.	chambered nautilus	Indo-Pacific
Nemenzophyllia	*turbida*	ridge coral	Indo-Pacific
Neopetrolisthes	sp.	anemone crab	Indo-Pacific
Nephthea	sp.	tree soft coral	Indo-Pacific
Pachyclavularia	sp.	green star polyps	Indo-Pacific
Physogyra	*lichtenstoini*	small bubble coral	Indo-Pacific
Platygyra	sp.	closed brain coral	Indo-Pacific
Plerogyra	*sinuosa*	large bubble coral	Indo-Pacific
Pocillopora	sp.	none	Indo-Pacific
Protopalythoa	sp.	Pacific green sea mat	Indo-Pacific
Protoreaster	sp.	chocolate chip star	Indo-Pacific
Protula	*magnifica*	hard-tube duster	Indo-Pacific
Pseudocolochrius	sp.	sea apple	Indo-Pacific
Rhodactis	sp.	blue mushroom polyp	Indo-Pacific
Sarcophyton	sp.	leather mushroom soft coral	Indo-Pacific
Saron	*marmoratus*	Saron shrimp	Indo-Pacific
Seriatopora	sp.	none	Indo-Pacific

continued

Table 3: Invertebrate Cross-Reference by Locality (*continued*)

Genus	Species	Common Name(s)	Range
Sinularia	sp.	cabbage soft coral	Indo-Pacific
Sinularia	sp.	finger leather coral	Indo-Pacific
Stichodactyla	gigantea	giant carpet anemone	Indo-Pacific
Stichodactyla	haddoni	Haddon's carpet anemone	Indo-Pacific
Stichodactyla	mertensi	Mertens' carpet anemone	Indo-Pacific
Studeriotes	longiramosa	Christmas tree soft coral	Indo-Pacific
Stylaster	sp.	pink lace coral	Indo-Pacific
Stylophora	sp.	none	Indo-Pacific
Tectus	sp.	pyramid top shell	Indo-Pacific
Trachyphyllia	sp.	open brain coral	Indo-Pacific
Tridacna	crocea	crocea giant clam	Indo-Pacific
Tridacna	derasa	smooth giant clam	Indo-Pacific
Tridacna	gigas	giant clam	Indo-Pacific
Tridacna	maxima	maxima giant clam	Indo-Pacific
Tridacna	squamosa	fluted giant clam	Indo-Pacific
Trochus	sp.	top shell	Indo-Pacific
Tubastrea	aurea	orange polyp coral	Indo-Pacific
Tubipora	musica	organ pipe coral	Indo-Pacific
Turbinaria	sp.	pagoda coral	Indo-Pacific
Turbo	sp.	turbo snail	Indo-Pacific
Xenia	sp.	pulse corals	Indo-Pacific
Acropora	sp.	none	Worldwide
Bulla	sp.	bubble shell	Worldwide
Cerianthus	sp.	tube anemone	Worldwide
Diadema	antillarum	longspine urchin	Worldwide
Discosoma	sp.	mushroom polyp	Worldwide
Dromia	sp.	sponge crab	Worldwide
Favia	sp.	moon coral	Worldwide
Fungia	sp.	plate coral	Worldwide
Millepora	sp.	fire coral	Worldwide

Genus	Species	Common Name(s)	Range
Montipora	sp.	none	Worldwide
Ophiactis	sp.	spiny brittle star	Worldwide
Ophiocoma	sp.	black-spined brittle star	Worldwide
Petrolisthes	sp.	porcelain crab	Worldwide
Porites	sp.	none	Worldwide
Rhynchocinetes	sp.	camel shrimp	Worldwide
Sabella	sp.	dwarf feather duster	Worldwide
Sepia	sp.	cuttlefish	Worldwide
Spirobranchus	giganteus	Christmas tree worm	Worldwide
Stenopus	hispidus	coral shrimp	Worldwide
Thor	amboiensis	sexy shrimp	Worldwide

Table 4: Invertebrates by Suitability Index

Genus	Species	Common Name(s)	Suitability Index	Caution
Dendronephthya	sp.	tree soft coral	1	
Fromia	sp.	marble star	1	
Linckia	laevigata	blue star	1	
Nephthea	sp.	tree soft coral	1	
Protula	magnifica	hard-tube duster	1	
Pseudocolochrius	sp.	sea apple	1	toxic
Swiftia	exerta	orange finger gorgonian	1–2	
Sabellastarte	magnifica	giant feather duster	1–2	
Spirobranchus	giganteus	Christmas tree worm	1–2	
Stylaster	sp.	pink lace coral	1	
Astrophyton	muricatum	basket star	2	
Cassiopea	sp.	upside-down jellyfish	2	
Cryptodendrum	adhaesivum	pizza anemone	2	
Elysia	crispata	lettuce slug	2	

continued

Table 4: Invertebrates by Suitability Index *(continued)*

Genus	Species	Common Name(s)	Suitability Index	Caution
Elysia	ornata	lettuce slug	2	
Goniopora	sp.	sunflower coral	2	
Gorgonia	ventalina	sea fan	2	
Heteractis	aurora	beaded anemone	2	
Heteractis	crispa	sebae anemone	2	
Heteractis	magnifica	"ritteri" anemone	2	
Heteractis	malu	white sand anemone	2	
Leptogorgia	miniata	Red Sea whip	2	
Lima	scabra	flame scallop	2	
Macrodactyla	doreensis	long tentacle anemone	2	
Nautilus	sp.	chambered nautilus	2	
Neopetrolisthes	sp.	anemone crab	2	
Octopus	joubani	dwarf octopus	2	
Protoreaster	sp.	chocolate chip star	2	
Sepia	sp.	cuttlefish	2	
Stichodactyla	gigantea	giant carpet anemone	2	
Stichodactyla	haddoni	Haddon's carpet anemone	2	
Stichodactyla	mertensi	Mertens' carpet anemone	2	
Studeriotes	longiramosa	Christmas tree soft coral	2	
Tubastrea	aurea	orange polyp coral	2	
Acropora	sp.	none	3	
Cerianthus	sp.	tube anemone	3	catches fish
Choriaster	granulatus	doughboy star	3	
Condylactis	gigantea	pink-tipped anemone	3	
Culcita	novaeguineae	cushion star	3	
Entacmaea	quadricolor	bulb anemone	3	
Fungia	sp.	plate coral	3	
Heliofungia	sp.	giant plate coral	3	
Hymenocera	picta	harlequin shrimp	3	
Lybia	dubia	boxing crab	3	

Genus	Species	Common Name(s)	Suitability Index	Caution
Oreaster	reticulata	Bahama star	3	
Periclimenes	pedersoni	Pederson's cleaner shrimp	3	
Periclimenes	yucatanensis	anemone shrimp	3	
Pocillopora	sp.	none	3	
Sabella	sp.	dwarf feather duster	3	
Stichodactyla	helianthus	sun anemone	3	
Thor	amboiensis	sexy shrimp	3	
Pseudopterogorgia	sp.	sea plume	3–4	
Actinodendron	sp.	tree anemone	4	stings
Actinopyga	agassizi	Florida cucumber	4	toxic
Alcyonium	sp.	colt soft coral	4	
Alpheus	armatus	curlicue anemone pistol shrimp	4	
Amplexidiscus	fenestrafer	elephant ear polyp	4	catches fish
Anthelia	sp.	waving hand	4	
Asthenosoma	varium	fire urchin	4	venomous
Bartholomea	annulata	curlicue anemone	4	
Blastomussa	sp.	none	4	
Brierium	abestinum	sea fingers	4	
Bulla	sp.	bubble shell	4	
Calliactis	sp.	hermit crab anemone	4	
Catalaphyllia	jardinei	elegance coral	4	
Caulastrea	sp.	trumpet coral	4	
Cespitularia	sp.	blue "Xenia"	4	
Cladiella	sp.	cauliflower soft coral	4	
Colochirus	robustus	yellow sea cucumber	4	
Cynarina	lacrymalis	button coral	4	
Cypraea	moneta	money cowerie	4	
Diadema	antillarum	longspine urchin	4	sharp spines
Discosoma	neglecta	Caribbean mushroom polyp	4	
Discosoma	sp.	mushroom polyp	4	

continued

Table 4: Invertebrates by Suitability Index (continued)

Genus	Species	Common Name(s)	Suitability Index	Caution
Echinometra	lacunter	shortspine urchin	4	
Erythropodium	sp.	encrusting gorgonian	4	
Eunicea	sp.	knobby sea rod	4	
Euphyllia	ancora	anchor coral	4	
Euphyllia	divisa	frogspawn coral	4	
Euphyllia	glabrescens	torch coral	4	
Favia	sp.	moon coral	4	
Galaxea	sp.	star coral	4	
Haliotis	sp.	abalone	4	
Haminoea	sp.	bubble shell	4	
Heliopora	coerulea	blue coral	4	
Herpolitha	limax	tongue coral	4	
Heterocentrotus	mammillatus	slate pencil urchin	4	
Hippopus	hippopus	hoof giant clam	4	
Hydnophora	sp.	horn coral	4	
Lambis	sp.	spider conch	4	
Lebrunia	danae	antler anemone	4	
Litophyton	sp.	tree soft coral	4	
Lobophyllia	sp.	open brain coral	4	
Lobophytum	sp.	leather soft coral	4	
Lytechinus	variatus	carrier urchin	4	
Millepora	sp.	fire coral	4	
Mithrax	sculptus	emerald crab	4	
Montipora	sp.	none	4	
Muricea	sp.	spiny sea rod	4	
Nemenzophyllia	turbida	ridge coral	4	
Ophiactis	sp.	spiny brittle star	4	
Ophiocoma	sp.	black-spined brittle star	4	
Ophioderma	brevispinum	serpent star	4	
Pachyclavularia	sp.	green star polyps	4	

Genus	Species	Common Name(s)	Suitability Index	Caution
Palythoa	caribaeorum	brown sea mat	4	toxic
Palythoa	grandis	giant sea mat	4	toxic
Parazoanthus	swiftii	yellow sponge sea mat	4	
Petrolisthes	sp.	porcelain crab	4	
Phymanthus	crucifer	flower anemone	4	
Physogyra	lichtensteini	small bubble coral	4	
Platygyra	sp.	closed brain coral	4	
Plerogyra	sinuosa	large bubble coral	4	
Podocheila	reisi	decorator arrow crab	4	
Porites	sp.	none	4	
Protopalythoa	sp.	Pacific green sea mat	4	toxic
Pseudocorynactis	sp.	dotted mushroom polyp	4	
Pylopagurus	operculatus	trap door hermit crab	4	
Rhodactis	sanctithomae	warty Caribbean mushroom polyp	4	
Rhodactis	sp.	blue mushroom polyp	4	
Rhynchocinetes	sp.	camel shrimp	4	
Ricordea	florida	Florida false coral	4	
Sarcophyton	sp.	leather mushroom soft coral	4	
Seriatopora	sp.	none	4	
Sinularia	sp.	cabbage soft coral	4	
Sinularia	sp.	finger leather coral	4	
Strombus	gigas	queen conch	4	
Stylophora	sp.	none	4	
Trachyphyllia	sp.	open brain coral	4	
Tridacna	crocea	crocea giant clam	4	
Tridacna	derasa	smooth giant clam	4	
Tridacna	gigas	giant clam	4	
Tridacna	maxima	maxima giant clam	4	
Tridacna	squamosa	fluted giant clam	4	
Trochus	sp.	top shell	4	

continued

Table 4: Invertebrates by Suitability Index *(continued)*

Genus	Species	Common Name(s)	Suitability Index	Caution
Tubipora	musica	organ pipe coral	4	
Turbinaria	sp.	pagoda coral	4	
Xenia	sp.	pulse corals	4	
Zoanthus	sp.	Caribbean green sea mat	4	toxic?
Lysmata	amboiensis	scarlet cleaner shrimp	4–5	
Lysmata	debelius	fire shrimp	4–5	
Saron	marmoratus	Saron shrimp	4–5	
Stenopus	hispidus	coral shrimp	4–5	
Stenopus	scutellatus	golden coral shrimp	4–5	
Stenorhynchus	seticornis	arrow crab	4–5	
Tectus	sp.	pyramid top shell	4–5	
Turbo	sp.	turbo snail	4–5	
Astraea	tecta	star shell	5	
Cerithium	sp.	cerith shell	5	
Clibanarius	tricolor	blue leg hermit crab	5	
Clibanarius	vittatus	striped hermit crab	5	
Dardanus	pedunculatus	anemone hermit crab	5	
Dromia	sp.	sponge crab	5	
Enoplometopus	sp.	red lobster	5	
Eucidaris	tribuloides	slate pencil urchin	5	
Fasciolaria	tulipa	tulip snail	5	
Hippolysmata	wurdemanni	peppermint shrimp	5	
Nassarius	sp.	sand shell	5	
Nerita	sp.	nerite shell	5	
Paguristes	cadenati	scarlet hermit crab	5	
Percnon	gibbesi	Sally Lightfoot	5	
Petrochirus	diogenes	giant hermit crab	5	

Designations of suitability are necessarily subjective and open to discussion. These rankings take into account the limitations of home aquarists, such as the ability to consistently produce and provide a plankton substitute. *Reef tank conditions* means full salinity, correct water chemistry, lighting adequate for the species' needs, and appropriate water movement. Within a given category, wide variation in adaptability can exist. Even though most stony corals are rated the same, some are more challenging than others.

5 = Tolerant, survives moderate or temporary deviations from optimal conditions

4 = Grows well under reef tank conditions and may reproduce

3 = Demanding, but thrives when needs are met

2 = Requires extraordinary effort to maintain, seldom reaches natural life expectancy

1 = Impossible with current level of understanding, seldom survives more than a few weeks or months in captivity

Table 5: Invertebrate Incompatibilities

Genus	Species	Common Name(s)	Phylum	May Be Harmed By	May Harm
Actinopyga	*agassizi*	Florida cucumber	Echinodermata	has few enemies	harmless, possibly toxic
Acropora	sp.	none	Coelenterata	predators, toxic or aggressive soft corals	moderately aggressive, may encroach other sessile species
Actinodendron	sp.	tree anemone	Coelenterata	few enemies	small fishes, some crustaceans, stings
Alcyonium	sp.	colt soft coral	Coelenterata	predators	aggressive, likely to encroach other sessile species
Alpheus	*armatus*	curlicue anemone pistol shrimp	Arthropoda	predators	conspecifics unless mated
Amplexidiscus	*fenestrafer*	elephant ear polyp	Coelenterata	predators	will eat small fishes

continued

Table 5: Invertebrate Incompatibilities (*continued*)

Genus	Species	Common Name(s)	Phylum	May Be Harmed By	May Harm
Anthelia	sp.	waving hand	Coelenterata	predators, toxic or aggressive soft corals	moderately aggressive and may encroach other sessile species
Asthenosoma	*varium*	fire urchin	Echinodermata	has few enemies	seaweeds, some sessile invertebrates, stings
Astraea	*tecta*	star shell	Mollusca	hermit crabs, wrasses	harmless
Astrophyton	*muricatum*	basket star	Echinodermata	predatory fishes	harmless
Bartholomea	*annulata*	curlicue anemone	Coelenterata	few enemies	small fishes, some crustaceans, stings
Blastomussa	sp.	none	Coelenterata	predators, aggressive corals	few other species
Brierium	*abestinum*	sea fingers	Coelenterata	invasive algae, predators	highly toxic, many other sessile invertebrates negatively affected
Bulla	sp.	bubble shell	Mollusca	hermit crabs, wrasses	harmless
Calliactis	sp.	hermit crab anemone	Coelenterata	only does well attached to host	small fish, crustaceans
Cassiopea	sp.	upside-down jellyfish	Coelenterata	has few enemies	other sessile invertebrates, stings
Catalaphyllia	*jardinei*	elegance coral	Coelenterata	soft corals, invasive algae	nearby stony corals and other sessile invertebrates
Caulastrea	sp.	trumpet coral	Coelenterata	invasive algae	few other species
Cerianthus	sp.	tube anemone	Coelenterata	has few enemies	may catch fish, sting nearby invertebrates

Genus	Species	Common Name(s)	Phylum	May Be Harmed By	May Harm
Cerithium	sp.	cerith shell	Mollusca	hermit crabs, wrasses	harmless
Cespitularia	sp.	blue "Xenia"	Coelenterata	may be stung	can overgrow some sessile invertebrates
Choriaster	granulatus	doughboy star	Echinodermata	has few enemies	mollusks, some sessile invertebrates
Cladiella	sp.	cauliflower soft coral	Coelenterata	toxic or aggressive corals, invasive algae	may overgrow some sessile invertebrates
Clibanarius	tricolor	blue leg hermit crab	Arthropoda	wrasses, triggerfishes, etc.	small snails, some sessile invertebrates
Clibanarius	vittatus	striped hermit crab	Arthropoda	large predators	snails, worms, some sessile invertebrates
Colochirus	robustus	yellow sea cucumber	Echinodermata	predatory fishes	probably toxic
Condylactis	gigantea	pink-tipped anemone	Coelenterata	predators	may catch small fish
Cryptodendrum	adhaesivum	pizza anemone	Coelenterata	has few enemies	catches fish, possibly shrimps
Culcita	novaeguineae	cushion star	Echinodermata	has few enemies	mollusks, some sessile invertebrates
Cynarina	lacrymalis	button coral	Coelenterata	toxic or aggressive corals, invasive algae	few other species
Cypraea	moneta	money cowerie	Mollusca	hermit crabs, wrasses	harmless
Dardanus	pedunculatus	anemone hermit crab	Arthropoda	has few enemies	snails, worms, some sessile invertebrates
Dendronephthya	sp.	tree soft coral	Coelenterata	other soft corals, predators	toxic

continued

Table 5: Invertebrate Incompatibilities *(continued)*

Genus	Species	Common Name(s)	Phylum	May Be Harmed By	May Harm
Diadema	*antillarum*	longspine urchin	Echinodermata	triggerfishes	seaweeds, some sessile invertebrates
Discosoma	*neglecta*	Caribbean mushroom polyp	Coelenterata	stung by some soft corals	aggressive, likely to encroach other sessile species
Discosoma	sp.	mushroom polyp	Coelenterata	stung by some soft corals	aggressive, likely to encroach other sessile species
Dromia	sp.	sponge crab	Arthropoda	large predators	sponges, small shrimps or fishes
Echinometra	*lacunter*	shortspine urchin	Echinodermata	triggerfish	seaweeds, some sessile invertebrates
Elysia	*crispata*	lettuce slug	Mollusca	predatory fishes	some seaweeds
Elysia	*ornata*	lettuce slug	Mollusca	predatory fishes	some seaweeds
Enoplometopus	sp.	red lobster	Arthropoda	large predators	harmless in large tank
Entacmaea	*quadricolor*	bulb anemone	Coelenterata	clownfishes too large, some predators	may catch fish
Erythropodium	sp.	encrusting gorgonian	Coelenterata	few enemies	aggressive, likely to encroach other sessile species
Eucidaris	*tribuloides*	slate pencil urchin	Echinodermata	triggerfishes	seaweeds, some sessile invertebrates
Eunicea	sp.	knobby sea rod	Coelenterata	few enemies	toxic
Euphyllia	*ancora*	anchor coral	Coelenterata	soft corals, invasive algae	many other sessile invertebrates negatively affected

Genus	Species	Common Name(s)	Phylum	May Be Harmed By	May Harm
Euphyllia	*divisa*	frogspawn coral	Coelenterata	soft corals, invasive algae	many other sessile invertebrates negatively affected
Euphyllia	*glabrescens*	torch coral	Coelenterata	soft corals, invasive algae	many other sessile invertebrates negatively affected
Fasciolaria	*tulipa*	tulip snail	Mollusca	large predators, hermit crabs	other mollusks
Favia	sp.	moon coral	Coelenterata	predators	nearby stony corals and other sessile invertebrates
Fromia	sp.	marble star	Echinodermata	predatory fishes	harmless, possibly toxic
Fungia	sp.	plate coral	Coelenterata	predators, removal from water	virtually any other stony coral
Galaxea	sp.	star coral	Coelenterata	predators, toxic or aggressive soft corals	other corals by means of long sweeper tentacles
Goniopora	sp.	sunflower coral	Coelenterata	predators	may chemically harm other coral types
Gorgonia	*ventalina*	sea fan	Coelenterata	invasive algae	may chemically harm other coral types
Haliotis	sp.	abalone	Mollusca	has few enemies	harmless
Haminoea	sp.	bubble shell	Mollusca	wrasses, butterflyfishes	harmless
Heliofungia	sp.	giant plate coral	Coelenterata	predators, removal from water	small fish, other corals

continued

Table 5: Invertebrate Incompatibilities (continued)

Genus	Species	Common Name(s)	Phylum	May Be Harmed By	May Harm
Heliopora	*coerulea*	blue coral	Coelenterata	toxic or aggressive corals, invasive algae	few other species
Herpolitha	*limax*	tongue coral	Coelenterata	predators, removal from water	some stony corals, other sessile invertebrates
Heteractis	*aurora*	beaded anemone	Coelenterata	predators, toxic or aggressive soft corals	catches fish
Heteractis	*crispa*	sebae anemone	Coelenterata	predators, toxic or aggressive soft corals	catches fish
Heteractis	*magnifica*	"ritteri" anemone	Coelenterata	predators, toxic or aggressive soft corals	stings most other coelenterates
Heteractis	*malu*	white sand anemone	Coelenterata	predators, toxic or aggressive soft corals	catches fish, stings
Heterocentrotus	*mammillatus*	slate pencil urchin	Echinodermata	triggerfishes	seaweeds, some sessile invertebrates
Hippopus	*hippopus*	hoof giant clam	Mollusca	most carnivorous fish	harmless
Hydnophora	sp.	horn coral	Coelenterata	invasive algae	nearby stony corals and other sessile invertebrates
Hymenocera	*picta*	harlequin shrimp	Arthropoda	predators	specimen starfish
Lambis	sp.	spider conch	Mollusca	hermit crabs, wrasses	
Lebrunia	*danae*	antler anemone	Coelenterata	few enemies	catches fish, stings
Leptogorgia	*miniata*	Red Sea whip	Coelenterata	invasive algae	few other species

Genus	Species	Common Name(s)	Phylum	May Be Harmed By	May Harm
Lima	*scabra*	flame scallop	Mollusca	sea stars, wrasses, butterflyfishes	harmless
Linckia	*laevigata*	blue star	Echinodermata	predatory fishes	harmless, possibly toxic
Litophyton	sp.	tree soft coral	Coelenterata	toxic or aggressive corals, invasive algae	highly toxic, many other sessile invertebrates negatively affected
Lobophyllia	sp.	open brain coral	Coelenterata	some aggressive corals, invasive algae	nearby stony corals and other sessile invertebrates
Lobophytum	sp.	leather soft coral	Coelenterata	predators	toxic, may overgrow sessile invertebrates
Lybia	*dubia*	boxing crab	Arthropoda	predatory fishes, hermit crabs	harmless
Lysmata	*amboiensis*	scarlet cleaner shrimp	Arthropoda	some fishes	may damage sessile invertebrates
Lysmata	*debelius*	fire shrimp	Arthropoda	some fishes	may damage sessile invertebrates
Lysmata	*wurdemanni*	peppermint shrimp	Arthropoda	predatory fishes	may damage sessile invertebrates
Lytechinus	*variatus*	carrier urchin	Echinodermata	triggerfishes	seaweeds, some sessile invertebrates
Macrodactyla	*doreensis*	long tentacle anemone	Coelenterata	predators, corals in same tank	may catch fish
Millepora	sp.	fire coral	Coelenterata	few enemies	potently stings
Mithrax	*sculptus*	emerald crab	Arthropoda	predatory fishes	may damage sessile invertebrates

continued

Table 5: Invertebrate Incompatibilities *(continued)*

Genus	Species	Common Name(s)	Phylum	May Be Harmed By	May Harm
Montipora	sp.	none	Coelenterata	many other stony and soft corals	few other species
Muricea	sp.	spiny sea rod	Coelenterata	invasive algae	toxic, may negatively affect other sessile invertebrates
Nassarius	sp.	sand shell	Mollusca	hermit crabs, wrasses	harmless
Nautilus	sp.	chambered nautilus	Mollusca	large predators	fish, crustaceans
Nemenzophyllia	turbida	ridge coral	Coelenterata	predators	few other species
Neopetrolisthes	sp.	anemone crab	Arthropoda	anemonefishes	harmless
Nephthea	sp.	tree soft coral	Coelenterata	predators	highly toxic, many other sessile invertebrates negatively affected
Nerita	sp.	nerite shell	Mollusca	hermit crabs, wrasses	harmless
Octopus	joubani	dwarf octopus	Mollusca	morays	fish, crustaceans
Ophiactis	sp.	spiny brittle star	Echinodermata	predatory fishes, large crustaceans	may steal food from anemones
Ophiocoma	sp.	black-spined brittle star	Echinodermata	predatory fishes	harmless
Ophioderma	brevispinum	serpent star	Echinodermata	predatory fishes	harmless
Oreaster	reticulata	Bahama star	Echinodermata	has few enemies	mollusks, some sessile invertebrates
Pachyclavularia	sp.	green star polyps	Coelenterata	invasive algae, Aiptasia, aggressive corals	may overgrow other species
Paguristes	cadenati	scarlet hermit crab	Arthropoda	wrasses	small snails, some sessile invertebrates

Genus	Species	Common Name(s)	Phylum	May Be Harmed By	May Harm
Palythoa	*caribaeorum*	brown sea mat	Coelenterata	few enemies	toxic, may overgrow sessile invertebrates
Palythoa	*grandis*	giant sea mat	Coelenterata	few enemies	toxic
Parazoanthus	sp.	yellow polyp colony	Coelenterata	invasive algae	probably toxic
Percnon	*gibbesi*	Sally Lightfoot	Arthropoda	predatory fishes, when small	harmful to many species when large
Periclimenes	*pedersoni*	Pederson's cleaner shrimp	Arthropoda	predatory fishes	generally harmless with host in reef tank
Periclimenes	*yucatanensis*	anemone shrimp	Arthropoda	predatory fishes	generally harmless with host in reef tank
Petrochirus	*diogenes*	giant hermit crab	Arthropoda	has few enemies	all delicate invertebrates and small fishes
Petrolisthes	sp.	porcelain crab	Arthropoda	predatory fishes, hermit crabs	harmless
Phymanthus	*crucifer*	flower anemone	Coelenterata	may be stung by other anemones, corals	small fish
Physogyra	*lichtensteini*	small bubble coral	Coelenterata	predators, some soft corals	may harm stony corals, other sessile invertebrates
Platygyra	sp.	closed brain coral	Coelenterata	invasive algae	nearby stony corals and other sessile invertebrates
Plerogyra	*sinuosa*	large bubble coral	Coelenterata	predators, some soft corals	nearby stony corals and other sessile invertebrates

continued

Table 5: Invertebrate Incompatibilities *(continued)*

Genus	Species	Common Name(s)	Phylum	May Be Harmed By	May Harm
Pocillopora	sp.	none	Coelenterata	repeated physical contact, predators, toxic or aggressive soft corals	short sweeper tentacles may affect species within reach
Podocheila	reisi	decorator arrow crab	Arthropoda	predators	sessile invertebrates
Porites	sp.	none	Coelenterata	most other corals and soft corals, predators	rarely damages other species
Protopalythoa	sp.	Pacific green sea mat	Coelenterata	few enemies	toxic, may overgrow sessile invertebrates
Protoreaster	sp.	chocolate chip star	Echinodermata	has few enemies	mollusks, some sessile invertebrates
Protula	magnifica	hard-tube duster	Annelida	predatory fishes, hermit crabs	harmless
Pseudocolochrius	sp.	sea apple	Echinodermata	fish that might harass it	entire tank if stressed or dies
Pseudocorynactis	sp.	dotted mushroom polyp	Coelenterata	butterflyfishes and shrimps may eat them	harmless
Pseudopterogorgia	sp.	sea plume	Coelenterata	invasive algae	toxic, may harm other corals
Pylopagurus	operculatus	trap door hermit crab	Arthropoda	wrasses	snails, worms, some sessile invertebrates
Rhodactis	sanctithomae	warty Caribbean mushroom polyp	Coelenterata	butterflyfishes and shrimps may eat them	may overgrow some sessile invertebrates
Rhodactis	sp.	blue mushroom polyp	Coelenterata	predators	may overgrow other coelenterates
Rhynchocinetes	sp.	camel shrimp	Arthropoda	predatory fishes	small polyps, anemones

Genus	Species	Common Name(s)	Phylum	May Be Harmed By	May Harm
Ricordea	*florida*	Florida false coral	Coelenterata	predators	may negatively affect other sessile species nearby
Sabella	sp.	dwarf feather duster	Annelida	predatory fishes, hermit crabs	harmless
Sabellastarte	*magnifica*	giant feather duster	Annelida	predatory fishes, hermit crabs	harmless
Sarcophyton	sp.	leather mushroom soft coral	Coelenterata	parasites, predators, invasive algae	highly toxic, many other sessile invertebrates negatively affected
Saron	*marmoratus*	Saron shrimp	Arthropoda	large predators	small polyps, anemones
Sepia	sp.	cuttlefish	Mollusca	morays	fish, crustaceans
Seriatopora	sp.	none	Coelenterata	predators, toxic or aggressive soft corals	not particularly aggressive
Sinularia	sp.	cabbage soft coral	Coelenterata	parasites, predators, invasive algae	highly toxic, likely to encroach other sessile species
Sinularia	sp.	finger leather coral	Coelenterata	parasites, predators, invasive algae	highly toxic, likely to encroach other sessile species
Spirobranchus	*giganteus*	Christmas tree worm	Annelida	predatory fishes, hermit crabs	harmless
Stenopus	*hispidus*	coral shrimp	Arthropoda	large predators	smaller crustaceans, worms, snails
Stenopus	*scutellatus*	golden coral shrimp	Arthropoda	large predators	smaller crustaceans, worms, snails

continued

Table 5: Invertebrate Incompatibilities *(continued)*

Genus	Species	Common Name(s)	Phylum	May Be Harmed By	May Harm
Stenorhynchus	seticornis	arrow crab	Arthropoda	large predators	smaller crustaceans, worms, snails
Stichodactyla	gigantea	giant carpet anemone	Coelenterata	other coelenterates in tank	stings other invertebrates, catches fish
Stichodactyla	haddoni	Haddon's carpet anemone	Coelenterata	other coelenterates in tank	stings other invertebrates, catches fish
Stichodactyla	helianthus	sun anemone	Coelenterata	other coelenterates in tank	stings other invertebrates, catches fish
Stichodactyla	mertensi	Mertens' carpet anemone	Coelenterata	other coelenterates in tank	stings other invertebrates, catches fish
Strombus	gigas	queen conch	Mollusca	hermit crabs, large predators	seaweeds
Studeriotes	longiramosa	Christmas tree soft coral	Coelenterata	invasive algae	few other species
Stylaster	sp.	pink lace coral	Coelenterata	invasive algae	harmless
Stylophora	sp.	none	Coelenterata	most other corals and soft corals, predators	short sweeper tentacles may affect species within reach
Swiftia	exerta	orange finger gorgonian	Coelenterata	bright illumination, algae growth	harmless
Tectus	sp.	pyramid top shell	Mollusca	hermit crabs, wrasses	harmless
Thor	amboiensis	sexy shrimp	Arthropoda	predatory fishes	generally harmless with host in reef tank
Trachyphyllia	sp.	open brain coral	Coelenterata	tangs, many soft corals	small fish
Tridacna	crocea	crocea giant clam	Mollusca	most carnivorous fish	harmless
Tridacna	derasa	smooth giant clam	Mollusca	most carnivorous fish	harmless

Genus	Species	Common Name(s)	Phylum	May Be Harmed By	May Harm
Tridacna	gigas	giant clam	Mollusca	most carnivorous fish	harmless
Tridacna	maxima	maxima giant clam	Mollusca	most carnivorous fish	harmless
Tridacna	squamosa	fluted giant clam	Mollusca	most carnivorous fish	harmless
Trochus	sp.	top shell	Mollusca	hermit crabs, wrasses	harmless
Tubastrea	aurea	orange polyp coral	Coelenterata	predators, algae growth	other corals by means of chemical secretiosn
Tubipora	musica	organ pipe coral	Coelenterata	invasive algae, toxic or aggressive corals	few other species
Turbinaria	sp.	pagoda coral	Coelenterata	aggressive or toxic corals, predators	few other species
Turbo	sp.	turbo snail	Mollusca	hermit crabs, wrasses	harmless
Xenia	sp.	pulse corals	Coelenterata	may be stung by anemones, corals	may overgrow other sessile invertebrates
Zoanthus	sp.	Caribbean green sea mat	Coelenterata	may be stung by other sea mats, eaten by some shrimps	harmless, possibly toxic

Combining predators and prey should be an obvious incompatibility. Most carnivorous fish will feed on crustaceans if they can catch and subdue them. Tridacnid clams are also readily subject to predation. Among the sessile invertebrates, the biggest problem is so-called nettling, which I define as any negative interaction between two sessile species. Usually, at least one of the parties to the interaction is a coelenterate. Nettling may be accomplished via direct contact with the body, through contact with specialized sweeper tentacles produced by some species, or through chemical interactions. For example, many soft corals exude chemicals harmful to other coral species, and the two cannot be maintained in the same aquarium. Consult your dealer or references to learn specific kinds of interactions you might expect with a given specimen.

Over Twenty Seaweeds and Saltwater Plants

Seaweeds and saltwater plants can add a new dimension to saltwater aquarium keeping. Of the two flowering plants, a mangrove is easier to grow than turtle grass, but either will flourish in the proper environment. Turtle grass needs a deep layer of sediment in which to root, along with extremely bright illumination.

Seaweeds are, in general, easy to keep with abundant light and proper water chemistry. Some may grow so profusely as to become pests and should be avoided. *Valonia*, in particular, can be a problem. Species of *Caulerpa* adapt readily to cultivation. These are the best selections for beginning saltwater gardeners and will need regular pruning to keep them in bounds. More challenging, calcareous algae such as *Penicillus* and *Udotea* can bring a touch of green to a brightly illuminated tank with ample calcium.

Table 6: Common Seaweeds and Marine Plants

Genus	Species	Common Name(s)	Comments	Group
Rhizopora	*mangle*	mangrove, red		Anthophyta
Thalassia	sp.	turtle grass		Anthophyta
Acetabularia	*crenulata*	mermaid's wine glass		Chlorophyta
Avrainvillea	*nigricans*	soft fan seaweed	upright, like *Udotea* but uncalcified	Chlorophyta
Bryopsis	sp.	bryopsis	similar to *Caulerpa* but much smaller, sometimes becomes a pest	Chlorophyta
Caulerpa	*cupressoides*	*Caulerpa*, spiky		Chlorophyta
Caulerpa	*mexicana*	*Caulerpa*, fernleaf		Chlorophyta
Caulerpa	*prolifera*	*Caulerpa*, common		Chlorophyta
Caulerpa	*racemosa*	*Caulerpa*, grape		Chlorophyta
Caulerpa	*sertularioides*	*Caulerpa*, feather		Chlorophyta
Caulerpa	*verticillata*	*Caulerpa*, dwarf		Chlorophyta
Cymopolia	*barbata*	string-of-pearls		Chlorophyta
Dasycladus	*vermicularis*	none	upright, light green "cigars"	Chlorophyta
Dictyosphaeria	*cavernosa*	golf ball seaweed	may become a pest	Chlorophyta
Enteromorpha	sp.	sea grass	tubelike, attached to rocks in shallow water	Chlorophyta
Halimeda	*incrassata*	*Halimeda*, erect	upright, body of calcified articulated plates anchored in bottom by fibrous holdfast	Chlorophyta
Halimeda	*opuntia*	*Halimeda*, common		Chlorophyta
Halimeda	*tuna*	*Halimeda*, giant		Chlorophyta

Genus	Species	Common Name(s)	Comments	Group
Penicillus	capitatus	shaving brush, large	upright, appearance suggested by common name	Chlorophyta
Penicillus	dumetosus	shaving brush, small		Chlorophyta
Rhipocephalus	phoenix	paint brush		Chlorophyta
Udotea	flabelliforme	fan seaweed		Chlorophyta
Ulva	sp.	sea lettuce	sheetlike, attached to rocks in shallow water	Chlorophyta
Valonia	ventricosa	bubble algae	may become a pest	Chlorophyta
Dictyota	dichotoma	none	yellow to greenish brown sheets, repeatedly dividing to form branches	Phaeophyta

TANK SPECIFICATIONS

Standard Aquarium Tank Sizes, Floor Loads, and Lighting Requirements

(ß=ßreeder, H=High, L=Long, X=Extra High)

Tank Capacity	L (in)	D (in)	H (in)	Floor Load (lbs/ft^2)	Surface Area (m^2)	Lumens Needed for 5000 lux
30 X	24	12	24	120	0.19	926
110 X	48	18	30	147	0.56	2778
20 H	24	12	16	80	0.19	926
20 L	30	12	12	64	0.23	1158
25	24	12	20	100	0.19	926
29	30	12	18	93	0.23	1158
30	36	12	16	80	0.28	1389
30 B	36	18	12	53	0.42	2084
33 L	48	13	12	66	0.40	2006
37	30	12	22	118	0.23	1158
38	36	12	20	101	0.28	1389
40 B	36	18	16	71	0.42	2084
40 L	48	13	16	80	0.40	2006
45	36	12	24	120	0.28	1389

continued

Standard Aquarium Tank Sizes, Floor Loads, and Lighting Requirements (continued)

Tank Capacity	L (in)	D (in)	H (in)	Floor Load (lbs/ft^2)	Surface Area (m^2)	Lumens Needed for 5000 lux
50	36	18	18	89	0.42	2084
55	48	13	20	110	0.40	2006
65	36	18	24	116	0.42	2084
75	48	18	20	100	0.56	2778
90	48	18	24	120	0.56	2778
120	48	24	24	120	0.74	3704
77	60	13	24	154	0.50	2508
125	72	18	22	111	0.83	4167
150	72	18	28	133	0.83	4167
180	72	24	24	120	1.11	5556
210	72	24	29	140	1.11	5556
35H X	23	20	24	128	0.30	1479
60H X	27	24	28	130	0.42	2084

MEASUREMENTS AND CONVERSIONS

Water

1 gallon of water weighs 8 pounds (lb), or 3.6 kilograms (kg)

1 cubic foot of water contains 7.5 gallons (gal), or 28.5 liters (L)

Liquid Measure

1 gal = 3.8 L = 4 quarts (qt) = 8 pints (pt) = 128 fluid ounces (fl oz) = 231 cubic inches (in^3)

1 L = 1000 milliliters (ml) = 1000 cubic centimeters (cc) = 1 kg = 2.2 lb

1 tablespoon = 3 teaspoons = 0.5 fl oz = 15 ml = 300 drops

1 cup (C) = 8 fl oz = 236.8 ml

Surface Area

1 square meter (m^2) = 1555 square inches (in^2) = 10.76 square feet (ft^2)

1 ft^2 = 0.0929 m^2 = 144 in^2

Light Intensity

1 foot-candle (fc) = 1 lumen

1 lux = 1 lumen per square meter = 1 foot-candle per 10.76 square feet

Temperature Conversions

°Centigrade = (°Fahrenheit − 32) ÷ 1.8

°Fahrenheit = (°Centigrade × 1.8) + 32

Alkalinity Conversions

50 ppm $CaCO_3$ = 2.92 gr/gal $CaCO_3$ = 2.8 dKH = 1 Meq/L

ppm = parts per million

gr/gal = grains per gallon

dKH = degrees of German hardness

Meq/L = milliequivalents per liter

very soft = < 75 ppm $CaCO_3$

soft = 75–150 ppm $CaCO_3$

moderately hard = 150–225 ppm $CaCO_3$

hard = 225–350 ppm $CaCO_3$

very hard = > 350 ppm $CaCO_3$

INDEX

M

mail-order suppliers, fish acquisition issues, 15
maintenance service, using, 42–43
mangroves, aquarium design uses, 59–60
mangrove swamps, coral reef zone, 129
mantis shrimps, invertebrate pests, 76
medications, environmental cause of disease, 94
Meiacanthus atrodorsalis (flanged blenny), 161
metal halide lighting
    aquarium design guidelines, 27, 57
    built-in aquariums, 81
    free-standing aquariums, 84
microinvertebrates, aquarium design element, 66
minimalist look, low-maintenance design, 111–112

N

nanotanks, design considerations, 176
natural habitats, aquarium design inspiration, 63
natural sand, substrate use, 61
nauplii (larval brine shrimp), 32
Nemateleotris decora (dartfish), 161
Nemateleotris helfrichi (dartfish), 162
Nemateleotris magnifica (dartfish), 161
Neocirrhites armatus (hawkfish), 118
Neopetrolisthes (anemone crabs), 157

Nephthea, 156
Nerita sp. (nerite snails), 71
nitrates, water-testing element, 36–38
nitrogen compounds, biological filtration, 22, 36–38
nocturnal fish, low-maintenance design, 123–124
Novaculichthys taeniorus (dragon wrasse), 151

O

octopus
    biotope tank design model, 167–168
    venomous invertebrates, 77
Octopus joubani (dwarf octopus), 167
Ophioderma appressum (serpent stars), 138
Ophioderma rubicundum (serpent stars), 138
Opisthognathus aurifrons (yellow-head jawfish), 11, 153
overcrowding, environmental cause of disease, 94
overfeeding, environmental cause of disease, 94
Oxycirrhites (longnosed hawkfish), 118
Oxycirrhites typus (hawkfish), 150

P

Pachyclavularia (green star polyp), 63
Paguristes cadenati (scarlet hermit), 71
Paguristes digueti (red leg hermit), 71

painted backgrounds, application methods, 98
Palace for a Queen, biotope tank design model, 172–173
Palythoa sp. (sea mats), 166
Paracanthurus hepatus (regal tangs), 114
Paracanthurus hepatus (regal tang), 150
Paracheilinus octotaenia (wrasse), 153
parasites
    invertebrate troubleshooting, 93
    troubleshooting, 89–91
parasitic snails, invertebrate infestations, 93
patch reefs, described, 128
Periclimenes pedersoni (shrimp), 144, 179
Periclimenes yucatanensis (shrimp), 144, 170
Pervagor spilosoma (filefish), 158
Pholidichthys leucotaenia (convict blenny), 159
Pholidichthys leucotaenia (convict eel), 125
phosphate, test kits, 21–22
photographs, aquarium background, 59
photoplankton, 33
photosynthesizers, feeding strategies, 29–30
photosynthetics, invertebrate grouping, 73–74
pH testing
    guidelines, 38
    saltwater, 19–20
    water movement determinations, 25
Physogyra (corals), 161
plastic corals, substrate use, 61
plastic trash cans, auxiliary aquarium use, 104